The Billy Butlin Story
'A Showman to the End'

The Billy Butlin Story
'A Showman to the End'

Sir Billy Butlin
with Peter Dacre

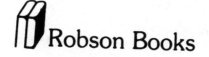 Robson Books

ACKNOWLEDGEMENTS We wish to thank the following for kind permission to reproduce articles and reports: Sir John Junor, Editor, *Sunday Express*; Mr David English, Editor, *Daily Mail*; Mr Christopher Ward, Editor, *Daily Express*; Mr William Anderson, Editor, *The Sunday Post*; and Mr Art Buchwald, columnist, *New York Herald Tribune*.

This paperback edition first published in Great Britain in 1993 by Robson Books, 64 Brewery Road, London N7 9NT

Reprinted 2002

British Library Cataloguing Data
A catalogue record for this title is available from the British Library

ISBN 0 86051 864 7

Printed and bound by Creative Print and Design (Wales), Ebbw Vale

Contents

Foreword

THE rich have always been the targets of envious abuse. Some may have deserved it, although it is worth remembering that there are many things for which we can be grateful to rich philanthropists.

Billy Butlin started poor and became rich by his own intelligence and enterprise, but he then proceeded to give away his wealth with typically realistic and perceptive compassion. Few men have done so much real good in secret and out of sheer kindness of heart.

Untold thousands must be better off thanks to Billy Butlin's wise generosity and I am sure that many more will be inspired and encouraged by this story of a kind and gentle man.

Editor's Note

THIS is not one book but two. First of all it is the autobiography of Billy Butlin, Showman Extraordinary, Holiday Camp 'King' and generous philanthropist.   Billy Butlin, who died on 12 June 1980, was all of these things. But he was also something else. He was the antithesis of his public image as the man behind the Redcoat razzmatazz, the frenetic, all-go, never-a-dull-moment atmosphere of his camps. For Billy Butlin was a genuinely shy and modest man.

. In helping him to write his life story I repeatedly ran into the brick wall of this shyness and modesty. 'Oh, I don't think we want to say that. It makes me sound like a Smart Alec.' Or: 'It makes me look as though I'm boasting.'

As a result, his autobiography, which he completed just before the start of his last serious illness, effectively tells his most amazing story. But it gives little insight into Billy Butlin the man, the enigma who was a quiet-spoken, unassuming, warm-hearted character with a dry wit—and yet also a shrewd, farsighted businessman, capable of being ruthless.

So with the agreement of his widow, Lady (Sheila) Butlin, who has written a most moving account of his last months, I have added comments and recollections from her, his family, close friends and associates which give an extra dimension.

In the three years I worked with Bill on his book I naturally came to know him well. I believe that these new and revealing facets of his personality give a more rounded picture of Billy Butlin.

They certainly do more justice to a great man than he would have done left to himself.

PETER DACRE

Preface by Lady Butlin

BILL'S last illness began just before Christmas, 1979. But for about two months previously he had seemed to sense that something was going to happen to him and that his days were numbered.

He finished his book in a flurry of activity and then began attending all the Christmas functions held by organizations he belonged to and had worked for. In all the thirty years we had been together I had never known him attend so many in such a short period. It was just as if he was saying 'Goodbye'. But the effort of it all, the shuttling back and forth between Jersey and London, took its toll. One morning I went into his bathroom while he was shaving. Seeing his reflection in the mirror I realized how ill and tired he was.

'For God's sake, Bill,' I said, 'have you looked at yourself? You look terrible.' 'Sheil, I'll be all right,' he said.

In a few weeks' time we were due to spend a holiday in Miami, but there and then I decided to cancel it. I went downstairs, picked up the phone and did it. Then I returned to the bathroom. Bill was still shaving.

'I've cancelled Miami,' I said. 'We're going to sit back here and take it easy. I'm not going to have a hotel room turned into a hospital again.' I put my arms around him and hugged him, getting soap all over my face. 'Please, Bill, steady up a bit. You can't go on doing all these things.'

He wiped his face and asked: 'You've cancelled Miami?'

11

'Yes,' I replied firmly.

'In that case I can have another trip to London,' he said, splashing himself with aftershave.

You could never win with Bill Butlin.

Two weeks before Christmas he insisted on going to London, for what proved to be the last time. I was intensely worried there might be a repetition of what had happened in London three years earlier when he had fallen seriously ill before going to Monte Carlo— Bill refers to this in his Introduction, but he gives no idea of the drama involved, nor of his stubborn refusal to admit he was desperately ill.

I first knew about it when his specialist, Dr Joe Mountrose, who had accompanied him to an evening function, telephoned me in Jersey.

'Bill is ill,' he said. 'You'd better come over. If he's not in his room at the hotel, it will mean I've had him moved to hospital.'

I caught the first available plane to London but, because of a strike at Heathrow, it was diverted to Southampton—I had to complete the rest of the journey by car. I dashed into Selfridge's Hotel, where he always stayed; to my horror his room was empty, the bed made up.

I don't know why—probably it was a case of grasping at straws—but having got over the initial shock, I suddenly thought: 'I wonder if he's gone to the Butlin office?' I ran out of the hotel, dodging people on the crowded pavement and hared across Oxford Street, oblivious of the traffic.

Sure enough, there he was, at his office desk. He looked terrible. His face was like wax, his eyes were sunk into the back of his head and a large balloon of perspiration hung from his chin. 'I'm working,' he said.

I didn't reply, but took his black hold-all and swept everything on his desk, including an ashtray, into it. 'The only thing you're doing is going to bed,' I told him.

When he stood up, the back of his chair was soaked in perspiration. I got his coat and draped it over his shoulders, while he continually protested: 'I've work to do, Sheil.'

12

Eventually I got him, still protesting, as far as the pavement outside Butlin's. He turned to me. 'Go away,' he said, 'I don't know you.' Several women in a nearby bus queue watched the scene with obvious concern. 'Leave the poor old fellow alone,' they shouted. 'He says he doesn't know you.'

Finally, with the help of Dick, the office commissionaire, we put him into a taxi that had pulled up to drop off a passenger, and took him back to the hotel. There, another battle began. 'I'm going to Monte Carlo,' he kept insisting.

I knew how important the visit was for him, because he was due to make a report to the Variety Club's International Board on the Jersey 'Tent'. So, with Dr Mountrose's permission, I told Bill: 'If you stay in this bed for forty-eight hours, and don't move, I promise you can go.'

And go he did—in a wheelchair.

While Bill was ill, there was a waiters' strike in the Monte Carlo hotel we stayed at. On one occasion, Lord Mountbatten came to visit Bill and complained that he could not get a cup of tea in the hotel. 'I'll make you a cup of tea,' I said.

Before the start of the strike, to avoid Bill being disturbed by waiters bringing tea to the room, I had arranged for an electric water heater to be installed and, with an ample supply of tea bags, I made my own tea. Because of the short length of flex, I had to make it on the floor and so whenever Lord Louis came, there I was sitting on the floor brewing tea. He certainly appreciated his 'cuppa'.

During the strike, room service was very poor or non-existent, and when Bill suddenly said he felt like a piece of gateau I thought, 'He'll be asleep by the time it arrives.' So I went down to the restaurant, which was still operating, and asked for a piece of gateau to take to my sick husband. 'No,' they said, 'you cannot take food out of the restaurant.'

I was walking away—looking dejected, I suppose—when I met a group of Variety International members. When I told them my problem, they marched into the restaurant, commandeered the sweet trolley and, ignoring the waiter, cut several pieces of gateau. 'Give these to Bill with our love,' they said.

But to revert to Bill's last trip to London in December 1979: much to my relief he kept well and, after I had joined him, we flew to Guernsey for the local Variety Club Tent's Christmas Ball.

In a touching gesture the 'Tent' presented Bill with a red jacket, a replica of those worn by Butlin Redcoats, except that this one had the insignia of the International Variety Club on the breast pocket. Bill was clearly moved. He danced, wearing the jacket, and seemed his old lively and humorous self. Looking back, it was fitting that on his last public appearance he should wear the symbol of his famous Redcoats, who still today epitomize the Butlin camps in the public's mind.

We were prevented from returning to Jersey for two days by a fierce storm and when we finally got home Bill looked tired and complained of stomach pains. They got steadily worse and he was taken into hospital in St Helier for an examination. As the ambulance men carried him down the stairs on a stretcher he called repeatedly, 'Jack, Jack.' He wanted to say goodbye to his daugher Jacquie. He loved both our children, but he had always had a father's soft spot for his daughter.

Once, on returning from London, he had telephoned from St Helier airport to discover that I had taken Jacquie on medical advice to London for an examination. He immediately decided to fly back and join us, but the next plane was already full. However, little obstacles like that did not deter Bill. No doubt if all else had failed he would have chartered a private plane, but as a number of passengers were already waiting at the airport for the London plane, he went round them offering £20 to anyone who would give up a place. One man agreed; but as usual, Bill had no money on him. There was still an hour before the plane left, so he rushed home, borrowed the money from the housekeeper and arrived back just in time to pay the man and get on the plane.

This incident, so typical of Bill, flashed through my mind as Jack came to kiss her father before he was put into the ambulance. Next day, after Bill had had his examination, the specialist asked to see me at the hospital, but when I arrived I was told he would not be available for another hour. Bill was

14

still dopey from the anaesthetic and, as I could not bear that distinctive hospital smell, I went for a walk in the town—even though it was snowing. It was the last weekend before Christmas and the streets were thronged with people in festive mood carrying gaily-wrapped parcels. I could not help wondering sadly what Christmas was all about. It was certainly not going to be a very happy one for us.

I am the Queen of the 'What ifs?', always thinking 'What if this?' or 'What if that?' And on that winter's afternoon I was thinking of so many 'What ifs?', even to the ultimate.

'What if Bill dies?'

As I walked along, huddled into my coat, I came to a Salvation Army band playing 'Silent Night'. I stood there listening, the tears pouring down my cheeks, mingling with the snowflakes.

Back at the hospital, the specialist told me the examination had revealed 'something' in Bill's stomach and they had decided to operate.

The operation lasted for five and a half hours and it was eight days before Bill regained consciousness. On the sixth day he had yet another heart attack. When he finally came round he was very disorientated so, to help his mind to begin working properly again, I had a number of photographs blown up large. Each had a particular association for Bill. They included shots of myself and the children, one of him wearing his chain of office on one of the two occasions when he was President of the Printers' Charitable Corporation and one of Prince Charles.

I had an easel put into his room and the nurse on duty placed one picture at a time on it. She talked to him about the photograph and asked him what it meant to him. Gradually Bill's memory was stirred. Looking at the one of him wearing his chain, he told the nurse about it, adding 'I succeeded Prince Charles as President and he placed that chain around my neck.' There was no doubt in all our minds that this exercise helped Bill to recover his memory more speedily.

As soon as he began to get better he kept insisting: 'Sheil, you must take me home. I'll die if I stay here.' This was no reflection on the hospital, for Bill's treatment was first class.

15

But he hated being in any hospital. After his first heart attack in Monte Carlo he had told me, 'If you ever think I'm going to die, you must see that it happens in my own bed in my own home.' And, when he was in the Intensive Care Unit at Westminster Hospital, London, after suffering a heart attack in the office of Sir David McNee, the Metropolitan Police Commissioner, he had kept pulling off his oxygen mask and saying to me, 'Get me out of here.' He was a very stubborn man, but I had told him, 'You're not going anywhere. You're too ill.'

But this time I agreed to take him back to his own bed. The first night I sat up with him, because I had not had time to arrange for a nurse. It was a long, exhausting night, for if I made the slightest move to leave my chair he stirred and called my name.

From then on he was cared for by two nurses. One of them, Clarrie, had a great sense of humour and Bill, who himself had an impish wit, enjoyed teasing her. Whenever she entered his room to begin her period of duty he called out, 'Don't come any nearer to me. You're fired.'

As he gradually improved he was able to get out of bed and walk a little with the assistance of a frame. But he had made up his mind to walk unaided, and with great determination he achieved his aim in a month or so. First he managed to get from his room to mine on the other side of the house with the help of his nurse, and finally he progressed to little walks alone in the garden. He seemed to be getting on so well that one day I took him to lunch with friends. It was a happy, just-like-old-times occasion, and afterwards he said, 'Let's go for a drive round the island.'

We both enjoyed the trip and I thought, 'I'll settle for this: a potter in the garden and an outing every month.' But that was not to be. Suddenly, almost from that day, he began to fade. Between periods of lucidity he started living in the past. Sometimes he was back in the fairground days, asking for the takings. At other times he was reliving the problems of the camps and instructing me to set up a meeting of his senior staff.

As he became weaker he realized he was dying. One day he

16

cried out, 'Sheil, I'm not afraid to die, but what hurts me is leaving you. We've been so happy.' Then he asked, 'Will you continue with the charity work?'

'I don't know, Bill. I suppose I will for your sake,' I replied. I knew how much his charity work meant to him.

'Well,' he said, 'whatever you do, enjoy it. If you don't, walk away from it.' It was the philosophy that had guided Bill throughout his life.

The following morning I noticed a change in him. He looked serene, as though he had thrown off all his worries. I sensed the end was near, and I told his nurses that one of them must always be by his bedside holding his hand. 'You must let him know he is not alone,' I insisted.

He died at 3.30 in the afternoon of Thursday, 12 June 1980. I had spent the day talking quietly to him, and at one moment I put my face next to his. Though he was terribly weak he pulled himself up from his pillow to kiss me. It was his last act.

On several occasions Bill and I had talked about dying, and he had said, 'The only thing that worries me is that I may be pronounced dead when I am not really. So get the doctor to give me a lethal drug, to make quite sure.' Of course, I realized it would be pointless asking the doctor to do this, but on thinking about how I could fulfil Bill's wish, I decided that the process of embalming him would be the answer to his fear. And so he was embalmed, wearing a new blue suit, one of four he had had for years and never worn, and—in the tradition of showmen—brown shoes. The symbolic meaning of this ritual is now shrouded in mystery, but for generations fairground showmen have been buried in brown boots.

His lead-lined coffin with a glass top lay in a funeral parlour in St Helier, and many islanders and holidaymakers filed past to pay their respects. The day before the funeral he was brought home and during the night a mystifying event occurred. We were awakened by a loud crash in the room where he lay. Rushing in, we found that a large painting of Bill holding a child's hand in a Dublin hospital had fallen from the wall. A simple accident? Well, what would you think if you had found the picture hook still attached to the wall and the cord which

17

had supported the picture unbroken? And in the next room, a huge piece of Waterford glass had cracked.

There is no logical explanation for these mishaps, but I believe Bill brought them about to let me know there is something after death. It was as though he was saying, 'You can't see me, Sheil, but look what I can do.'

A far more incredible experience, however, happened to me six weeks after Bill had died. I still felt exhausted and drained, and I was lying in bed half asleep and telling myself I must get up. I was not thinking about Bill. Suddenly, my room was filled with the fragrance of the cologne he had used and I heard his footstep in the corridor. His voice called, 'I'm going, Sheil.' Automatically I replied, 'OK, darling.' Momentarily, I thought he was still alive and calling to tell me he was leaving to catch the early plane to London—until the dreaded truth dawned on me. Then an amazing thing happened. The footsteps entered the room and I distinctly saw him standing by the bed, wearing a macintosh and his favourite trilby. He was smiling and looked so happy.

'Sheil, are you all right, because I'm going now?' he said. 'Give me a kiss before I go.'

I kissed him and he felt cold, but the smile on his face was warm.

Some may scoff at this story, and indeed Bill and I had often joked, 'No one has come back from the dead.' But he had always insisted, 'If I go first I will come back.' And he did, I swear on my life he did.

The *Jersey Weekly Post*'s accurate comment on his funeral was that he certainly would have enjoyed it: it was undoubtedly the biggest and most spectacular the island had ever seen. The church of St John was full to overflowing and the mourners, some of whom had been waiting in the unseasonal wind and rain for two hours, were so numerous they had to be accommodated in the Parish Hall. The service was relayed there and also to the many other people who waited outside the church.

I was greatly touched by the messages of condolence from Prince Philip, Prince Charles and the Archbishop of Canterbury. And also by the fact that the family of Lord Mountbatten, who was a close and long-time friend of Bill—Lord Louis's terrible death had had a profound effect on Bill and his health had begun to decline from the time he heard of it—was represented by his secretary, John Barratt.

I was honoured, too, by the number of distinguished people from Jersey and Guernsey who were present, and by the many people who flew over from London: members of the Variety Club as well as show business friends like Eric Morecambe, Richard O'Sullivan, Ted Rogers, Norman Rossiter, Hughie Green—Bill had known his father in the First World War—and Vera Lynn, who sang one of Bill's favourite songs, 'We'll Meet Again'. Alan Whicker, who lives near us in Jersey, read the Lesson.

Some wonderful things were said about my darling Bill that day. The Reverend Peter Manton, Rector of St John's, declared that part of Britain had gone with him and that life would never be quite the same again. He made the point that despite his fame and success Bill was a humble man, and he told how coachloads of tourists regularly stopped outside the Butlin house, but the sightseers never recognized Bill working in the garden wearing an old trilby held together with string.

Eric Morley referred to Bill's quiet sense of humour and told the story of how Sir Fred Pontin once said to him, 'You've taught me everything I know about holiday camps.' And Bill had replied quietly, 'Maybe, but not everything *I* know.'

I believe it to be true, as Hughie Green said, that through his camps and his generosity, Bill brought great happiness to millions of British people.

He was buried in St John's cemetery and in the first few days after the funeral more than a thousand people visited his grave. The tomb, to hold ten, has a headstone engraved with carvings depicting important aspects of his life: an amusement park, a camp scene with chalets and swimming pool, and the jolly fisherman who appeared on the famous poster bearing the legend 'Skegness is so bracing'.

Now Bill has gone and millions will undoubtedly remember him with gratitude and affection. But few of them knew what he was really like. The Reverend Manton was right in saying he was a humble man. But, as his old friend and colleague Basil Brown said in his address to a packed congregation attending Bill's Memorial Service at St Martin's-in-the-Field, London, he was also 'a combination of two characters—the super showman, the brash opportunist, at times ruthless in the pursuit of his objective, and just one layer under the tough exterior the quiet, nature-loving, humble, self-effacing loyal friend, who ever sought to do good by stealth.'

There was, in fact, a world of difference between Billy Butlin, the man who ran a business empire and Billy Butlin, the private man. He was shy and totally unostentatious. At home with his family he was not a bit like a tycoon. He had no side to him at all. Even during the days when I worked in the office, if he joined me for a cup of tea he would happily pour if I was busy on the phone. I doubt you would find many tycoons doing that.

Despite his wealth he lived a simple life. He hardly ever carried any money and consequently he always had to sign the bill in restaurants. Many a time the hotel porter had to pay his taxi fare. On other occasions, cabbies would say: 'That's all right, Bill, have it on me.' For they knew that he was a generous patron of the London Taxi Drivers' Fund for Underprivileged Children. I was greatly honoured when, after his death, the Fund invited me to succeed him as patron.

But though he had this idiosyncrasy about not carrying money—due mainly to absent-mindedness—he gave huge amounts of it away. I estimate he donated more than £5,000,000 to a great number of charities and he quietly helped many thousands who were in difficulties. He had a long list of former employees to whom he paid pensions.

A year before he died he faced up to the inevitable by choosing the site of his grave. We went to the cemetery together and almost immediately he picked a spot a mere twenty yards from the road. 'This is it,' he said.

'But, Bill,' I replied, 'you'll be so near a busy road.'

He grinned. 'When you're dead you don't hear the noise.'

I looked at the low stone wall which was all that separated the cemetery from the road. 'There'll be sightseers and coaches all the time,' I protested.

He looked at me and grinned again. 'I don't mind that, Sheil. I want people to stop and say: "There's Billy Butlin." I want them to see me.'

That was my Bill, an ordinary guy—but a showman to the end.

LADY BUTLIN

Introduction

ONE day, early in May 1977, a bulky envelope arrived on my desk. It contained clippings of more than a hundred newspaper reports about me forwarded by an agency which collects such items for subscribers. They were all about the same subject: a serious illness I had suffered a few weeks earlier while attending an International Convention in Monte Carlo of that great charitable organization, the Variety Club. They ranged from the front page of the London *Daily Mirror* with the headline 'Sir Billy Fights for Life' to smaller stories in Canadian, South African and American newspapers. I was surprised at all this publicity as I had retired ten years earlier and I had forgotten the amount of news I used to make.

My illness had started with a bad cough. At the age of 77, I suppose I should have retired to my bed, but foolishly I determined to attend the Convention. On the first day I managed to attend a meeting of the Executive Council of the Club and make a brief report, but I do not remember anything of the meeting or much of the next three days. I had developed double pneumonia and then suffered a heart attack. For more than a week I lay in bed attended constantly by my wife Sheila, who hardly left the room. I was also cheered by my old friend Lord Mountbatten, who was on an official visit to the Riviera and came to see me every day, once bringing Cary Grant with him. Often he sat with me for two hours or more.

At the end of that touch-and-go week I was flown to my

retirement home in Jersey by chartered plane, and there I slowly recovered.

When I was well enough to read the newspaper reports, it became clear to me that while news of my impending demise had been exaggerated by some newspapers, I would have had 'a good Press' if I had died. Unfortunately, not all the stories were accurate. Some versions of my life were nearly true—and some were far from true. 'What,' I asked myself, 'will my youngest children, Billy and Jacquie, think of their father if their knowledge of me is limited to such newspaper stories which are likely to be reproduced all over again?' So, for them, I decided to put down the real story of my life. If the reaction of the newspapers to my illness is any guide, perhaps others will find it interesting.

In my study, surrounded by mementoes and memories, or wandering around the garden I love, I began to recall a long and eventful life. How ironic it was, I thought, that more than thirty years earlier I had been turned down for a life insurance policy on medical grounds. I was told, 'Your life expectancy is not very good.'

However, later in 1977, my life expectancy was certainly not very good. For in August I had a severe heart attack in the office of the Metropolitan Police Commissioner, Mr (now Sir) David McNee, while we were discussing the Police Dependents' Fund which I had founded with Lord Stonham in 1966. If I had been taken ill anywhere else I might not have survived, but Sir David was able to summon immediate assistance and have me rushed with a police escort to Westminster Hospital, where I was put into the intensive care unit. Sir David also arranged for police officers to locate my own heart specialist, Dr Joseph Mountrose, who was in Surrey, and have him brought speedily to the hospital. I will never be able to thank Dr Mountrose or Sir David and his men, enough.

Now, after a long haul back to health, I am quite fit again. I have finished the story of my life as far as it goes. Remembering it in such detail has not been easy. But as the door of my memory gradually opened and an event, a photograph, a name

24

pushed it open still further, I have enjoyed the experience.

I would like to thank everyone, family, friends and former colleagues, who has helped in writing this book. I hope reading about my life gives you as much pleasure as I have had living it—and remembering it.

Jersey, Channel Islands, December 1979   BILLY BUTLIN

PART **1**

Early Days

1

'One day I'll build a camp . . .'

ONCE or twice a week during the summer of 1934, a maroon, fabric-topped Austin Seven, driven by a stocky man in his mid-thirties, roundish-faced and smooth-haired, trundled along the narrow winding road between Skegness and Mablethorpe on the flat Lincolnshire coast.

The man at the wheel was me, and though I did not know it then, I was travelling a road that was not only to change my life dramatically, but was to start a social revolution in Britain. For I was about to take the first positive step towards realizing an idea of mine that had been simmering for years: to open a holiday centre for the great mass of middle-income families for whom no one seemed to be catering, where they could have a good holiday irrespective of the unreliable British weather.

In the summer of 1934, however, it was still all in my mind. Until then I had been solely a fairground man, a travelling showman. I had begun with one hoop-la stall in 1921 and now, thirteen years later, I had eight seaside amusement parks and operated most of the attractions at several big Christmas fairs, which included one at Glasgow's Kelvin Hall and another attached to Bertram Mills's famous circus at London's Olympia. I also had seven amusement centres in various parts of London.

With their liking for the colourful phrase, journalists had described me in various extravagant terms, ranging from 'the amusement park king' to 'the man who makes whoopee'. It is

29

no exaggeration, however, to say that by the time I'd reached 34, I was regarded as one of the most successful showmen in Europe. I still looked very young for my age, though, and consequently, when people came to see me with business propositions and I turned them down, they often said: 'Can I see your father? I'd likę to discuss it with him.' So, when I was 35, I decided to grow a small, clipped moustache to make me look older.

Young looking or not, I was earning about £25,000 a year at a time when taxes were low; and over the years I had ploughed back most of my earnings into the business. More recently, however, I had concentrated on accumulating enough capital to launch my holiday camp idea. It had been born in the early Twenties, when, as a young and struggling travelling showman, I had taken a short holiday on Barry Island in South Wales.

I had stayed at a small boarding house. It was my first experience of such places and I was astounded at the way the guests were treated. We had to leave the premises after breakfast and were not encouraged to return until lunch-time. After lunch we were again made not welcome until dinner in the evening. When the weather was fine the 'routine' became acceptable, but when it rained life became a misery. And it rained incessantly all the time I was on Barry Island. I felt sorry for myself, but I felt even sorrier for the families with young children as they trudged around wet and bedraggled, or forlornly filled in time in amusement arcades until they could return to their boarding houses. Since those days, most boarding houses have improved. Perhaps it has been due to the competition!

But, watching those unhappy holiday-makers of the 1920s, I thought, 'What they need is a place where there are things for them to do when it rains.' I remembered my years in Canada, and the summer camp on the shores of Lake Ontario run by Eaton's, the big Toronto department store, for its employees. I had gone there as a very junior employee and I had greatly enjoyed the swimming, canoeing and fishing. But most of all I recalled the atmosphere: it was happy and friendly, largely due to the fact that everyone paid the same for their holiday and there was no snobbery.

In the rain on Barry Island I decided, 'One day I'll build a camp like that here in Britain, with the same happy atmosphere. But it will have more indoor facilities to allow for the British weather.'

The idea of holiday camps was not new in Britain. I believe the first one was opened at Caister on the Norfolk coast in 1902, followed by another one on the Isle of Man. By the Thirties they were beginning to spread throughout the country, but they were still primitive affairs, with hardy holiday-makers living in huts or tents. Those who went to them were mainly young men, for you needed to be a tough, outdoor type to put up with the rigorous conditions.

My idea was to build a permanent camp with all the necessary indoor and outdoor facilities. These camps would, I envisaged, combine the best qualities of those I had known in Canada; most of these were quite luxurious, and often a little more expensive than ordinary hotels. But in the early Twenties there was no likelihood that I could find the money for such a project.

Now, more than a decade later, my conception of the idea had developed and I visualized a completely self-contained holiday village catering for families and young children. It would have chalets set in landscaped gardens and plenty of indoor and outdoor sports and entertainment facilities.

And, at long last, I was in a position to put my ideas into practice. I had part of the cash required and my credit with Barclays Bank and my suppliers was good. There was one big snag, however. If my ideas were wrong, if I had misjudged what the British people wanted for their holidays, I would end up many thousands of pounds in debt. For I sensed that this was not a venture where I could start small and feel my way. To achieve the right atmosphere with the right facilities I would need to cater for large numbers. I would have to go all out from the start.

All this was in my mind as I drove on towards Mablethorpe. I had already decided that Skegness itself would be an ideal

31

place for the camp. I was established there with a fairground and I liked the town. It was growing fast and was conveniently situated for the heavily-populated Midlands and the North. All I needed now was a site.

And then one morning I saw it. I had driven past many times without noticing it, but now it suddenly struck me. There it was—a huge field of sugar beet, flat and sheltered from the fresh North Sea breeze by a line of sand dunes. It was just down the road from the small village of Ingoldmells and about three miles from Skegness. I stopped the car and walked around. I was convinced this was the spot. A few weeks later I bought about forty acres for £3,000. The dream was about to become a reality. And that reality was to surpass my most optimistic expectations. My judgement was proved right, for Butlin-style holiday camps were successful from the start.

In 1937 Butlin's became a public company and in the following year I opened my second camp at Clacton. Eventually the company owned nine holiday camps, a string of amusement parks and various hotels and restaurants, including the one at the top of London's Post Office Tower. In 1972 Butlins was sold to the Rank Organization for £43,000,000.

What led to that road from Skegness to Mablethorpe and what led from it is what this book is all about.

2

'I was always looking out for something better'

EVERY road starts somewhere—and mine started in Cape Town, South Africa on 29 September 1899. I was born there after my parents had emigrated from Gloucestershire towards the end of the nineteenth century.

My father, I suspect, was what they used to call a 'remittance man', a black sheep who was paid to go abroad and never darken the family conscience again. For he and my mother came from widely different social classes. When they met she was little more than sixteen, the daughter of a small-town baker who had become a travelling showman. But my father's side of the family was generally well-connected—though this in no way helped me in my early struggles.

Indeed, it was not until many years later that curious about my background, I discovered that in the eighteenth century the Butlins were a Rugby family who ran a bank in the town. Butlin's Bank was established in 1791 and was absorbed by Lloyds Bank in 1868. The family had close connections with Rugby School, for several of the boys had been educated there. I also discovered that I was not the first Butlin to have been knighted, for my great-uncle, my grandfather's younger brother, who lived from 1845 to 1912, was the eminent surgeon, Sir Henry Trentham Butlin. He held several senior posts at St Bartholomew's Hospital in London, was President of the Royal College of Surgeons, President of the British Medical

Association and the inventor of a new type of surgical scissors.

He seems to have been a remarkable man who would almost certainly have been successful had he gone into business: he was apparently far-seeing, had large ideas, and from a business point of view was said to be one of the best occupants of the Presidential Chair at the Royal College. I have always thought I was a born showman from my mother's side. Possibly I was a born businessman from my father's side. It is interesting, too, that Sir Henry seems to have had a touch of the showman about him as well—he rode around in a coach painted a distinctive olive green, and drawn by an exceptionally smart pair of horses.

Wealthy families always had a sprinkling of clergymen in their ranks, and the Butlins were no exception. Sir Henry's father, my great-grandfather, was the Reverend William Wright Butlin and held various appointments in Cornwall. From 1847 to 1890 he was what was known as Perpetual Curate of Penponds, where he raised subscriptions and built the church. He ended his days in Camborne. His eldest son, my grandfather, William Heygate Butlin, was a priest in Gloucester and Bristol, a curate at Stroud, Principal of Dartmouth Grammar School and for twenty-seven years was vicar of the beautiful Priory Church of St Swithun, founded in 1129, in Leonard Stanley, Gloucester. He and my grandmother are buried near the north porch. And it was there at Leonard Stanley, when the travelling fair came to visit, that my father William—the name abounds in the Butlin family tree— met the travelling showman's daughter. By all accounts it was love at first sight.

My father was a typical country gentleman of his time. He was not trained for anything, and had never expected to work for his living. He was, however, an excellent tennis player and later won several championships in Cape Town; indeed, I only remember him as dressed in white. From all accounts he was always a dapper dresser, and was nicknamed 'The Baron'.

By contrast my mother, Bertha Hill, had started work as a young girl in her father's bakery business in Coaley, near

34

Stroud. As part of his stock-in-trade he baked gingerbread which he sold at the local fairs. He must have been attracted by the atmosphere of the fairgrounds, for he eventually gave up his bakery to travel the fairs in Gloucestershire and Somersetshire with a ride of wooden horses which was first turned by hand and then by a live horse plodding round in the centre.

In time his four sons, Clifford, Marshall, Ernest and Bernard, all became travelling showmen; it was to be through them that I would eventually become a travelling showman myself. However, this was all very much in the future when William and Bertha met and married.

In the social climate of the time neither side was happy about a marriage of such contrasts and so, with the quiet encouragement of both families, they left for South Africa. They settled in Mowbray, a suburb of Cape Town, in a small timber house and started a business in a shed at the back—selling and hiring out the new safety bicycle, the successor to the pennyfarthing and the first bike recognizably like today's machine. Father imported the parts from Britain and assembled them in the shed. For a time the business prospered, but it was badly hit by the Boer War.

When I was born I was christened William Heygate Edmund Colborne Butlin—but I have never used Heygate or Colborne. In *Who's Who* I am listed as William Edmund Butlin, but I have always preferred to be called Bill or Billy. Heygate and Colborne were the names of some of my father's well-to-do relations and I was undoubtedly named after them in the hope that they might look kindly on me in their wills. But the only one who did was an aunt named Miss Colborne, who, later—when I was a boy living in Bristol—invited me to tea every Thursday afternoon. I hated going there, mainly because she made me read aloud to her (though I had little schooling as a child, my mother taught me to read) and insisted on calling me William Colborne all the time. She died when I was about fourteen leaving me £10 to be inherited when I came of age. But as far as I can remember my mother would not let me accept it.

35

Despite its obviously romantic beginnings and the arrival of a baby brother, Binkie, my parents' marriage began to fail. Father was often away playing tennis and mother had to run the bicycle business alone, leaving me in the care of a coloured nanny who spoke only Afrikaans.

One of my special treats, which I still remember, was being taken by my nanny to the zoo on Table Mountain. This consisted of a series of caves, carved out of the mountainside, in which the animals lived behind bars. I believe it was those visits which sparked off my interest in wildlife. Many years later I would create small zoos in my camps and amusement parks, and in one I was to reproduce those South African caves.

Mother never talked to me much about those days, but she did once tell me that she was always urging my father to be more ambitious and consider his business more, instead of spending so much time playing tennis. She was obviously unhappy, and when I was about six she returned to England with Binkie and me, leaving father behind. She went to work for her brother Marshall, who by then had several roundabouts or 'rides'.

Leaving us with her sister Jessie, who ran the Swan public house in Coaley, she travelled the West Country in a caravan owned by another sister, Milly. But after about a year she returned to South Africa with us in the hope of mending her marriage. She failed and again we came back to England. We were obviously poor for we travelled steerage and—although I remember little of these journeys—I vividly recall that the ships were infested with rats. They gnawed through the decks in search of water and to stop them the crew put down tins of water for them.

When we returned to England the second time, my mother again travelled the fairs and once again I stayed with Aunt Jessie in Coaley. Here at about the age of eight, I first started school. I had spoken mainly Afrikaans until I was five, and all the schoolkids teased me mercilessly because of my poor English.

We had not long been settled in England when Binkie died of infantile paralysis and, after his death, my mother took me with her on her travels. In those days, of course, it was much easier to avoid attending school than it would be now. Mother had acquired her own small gipsy-type caravan which was pulled by an elderly nag called Blackbird. He was so frail that when we went uphill we had to get off and push. Like her father, years before, she had a stall selling gingerbread baked in all kinds of shapes—hearts adorned with gold-coloured confectionery, little men, crescents and houses.

When travelling showmen stopped for the night at dusk, it was customary to put the horses into any handy field, taking them out early in the morning before the owner of the field was aware they had been there. This was known as 'pouving', and it resulted in our poor old Blackbird meeting a sad end. One night, when we were travelling to the fair at Bridgewater, our caravan was the last to arrive at the stopping place. I asked 'Where are the horses?'

'Down the road, first gate on the right,' I was told. It was pitch black as I walked Blackbird along there, but I managed to find the gate and took him through. I did not see any of the other horses, but as it was dark that did not worry me. Unfortunately, I should have been told 'First gate on the *left*.' The gate I had opened led on to the railway line—and during the night Blackbird was killed by a train.

The accident was a double blow: to lose a faithful old friend in this way grieved us; and it meant we had to buy another horse we could ill afford. So we had to wait until the rest of the fair moved on to Bridgewater and then someone, with the camaraderie typical of travelling showmen, sent his horse back to pull us in.

Horses were then the main means of moving the fairground equipment. It was often hard work for man and beast. A lot of the West Country roads were rough and unmade, and when we came to a steep hill everyone's horses were pooled. I have seen as many as sixteen struggling to pull a loaded wagon to the top, or to drag it out of a sticky muddy field. They were a fine lot of horses, well loved and well kept.

One way and another the fairs we travelled to played a significant role in the lives of country people. At the start of the summer, in what was known as the 'May Round', the hiring fairs were held—a kind of agricultural Labour Exchange. Here farmers hired their workers for the year and men and women seeking work attended the fairs sporting some sign which indicated their occupation. A farmhand would put three stalks of wheat in his hat, a horse handler wore a wisp of horse's tail and a herdsman a strand of cow's tail. A dairymaid wore the well-known costume and bonnet of her trade.

The fairs also provided other social services—particularly the travelling dentists. In those days few small towns had a dentist and the only chance most people had of having a tooth pulled was by going to these fairground practitioners. Unhappily most were quacks with little or no training and they relied on trickery to lure their customers. They always travelled with a small band, usually a trio of loud brass instruments, and pitched their site alongside the platform where the band played. There was a 'spieler' who drew the crowd and a 'gee' who was the first to come forward and have his tooth pulled. The dentist went through the motions of extracting a tooth, and then triumphantly produced one that had been secreted in his hand, whereupon the 'gee' would loudly proclaim his satisfaction.

When an unsuspecting customer stepped forward he usually got a painful shock, for the dentist's methods were crude and primitive. He was forcibly held down by an assistant and the dentist who were highly expert in holding their victim's jaws so he could not yell. But even if he did, the band, playing lustily away, drowned his cries. 'Dentistry' was a lucrative racket; the quacks charged about a shilling a tooth and they were so plausible they drew a lot of teeth during the fair.

At least the bands provided entertainment for the watching crowds, for in the country areas music was in short supply. Indeed, the only music many people heard was at the fairs, and was mainly provided by the colourful, ornate steam organs on the big roundabouts which played perforated music rolls. People stood listening to them for hours. They always played light classical music because the popular songs of the day went out of fashion too quickly.

As well as gingerbread, Mother also sold confetti and 'teasers'. Those were the days when country fairs were the main meeting places for many young men and women, and there was much larking about with boyish bravado and girlish giggles. The boys bought bags of confetti at a halfpenny a time and threw it at any girl who took their fancy. The girls retaliated with teasers, cylindrical containers made of soft lead with an opening at the top like a toothpaste tube. You got two for a halfpenny, filled them with water and squirted them. Many a West Country marriage sprang from such pranks.

All in all, travelling the fairs was a wonderful life for a boy, with its kaleidoscope of ever-changing scenes and activities. Between fairs I sat on the driving seat of the caravan with my mother, as we trundled through the winding lanes, and absorbed the sounds and scents of the countryside.

It was a hard life, though, and in the winter we often could not afford coal for heating and cooking. Many a time we were helped out by my uncle, Jack Watts, a miner married to my mother's sister Millie, who brought us coal he had scrounged from the tips. (In those days Somerset was still a mining area.) But despite such hardships it was a way of life I enjoyed and one I took for granted. I never thought it would change.

It was, however, soon to do so radically. For my mother divorced my father—who had remained in South Africa—and married again. My stepfather was Charlie Rowbotham, a gas fitter with the Bristol Gas Company. After that, Mother left the fairgrounds and we lived in Bedminster, Bristol, where I went to Bedminster Down School for about nine months.

Around 1910, however, Charlie and my mother emigrated to Canada. As they did not know what might face them they left me behind so I and a cousin, Jimmy Hill, were boarded out in the home of a widow in Redcliffe, another suburb of Bristol. Either she was very mean or she was not being paid much—or both. For she kept us on very short rations. I remember breakfast always consisted of bread and margarine or bread and jam. Never bread, marge *and* jam. At first, we tried asking for bread and marge and, having got that, to wheedle a bit of jam out of her—but we never succeeded.

It was during this period that I had my only sustained schooling, at St Mary Redcliffe, Bristol. Though I could read well enough, I was very backward in other subjects; but I discovered that I had an aptitude for drawing and painting. I concentrated on them and was, as least, able to shine in class at something. In 1954 I paid a visit to that school. My old headmaster had long since retired, of course, but I actually sat in a desk in my old classroom—though it was a bit of a tight squeeze. I think I became popular with the boys because I asked the then headmaster to give them a day's holiday—which he did—and I gave all the pupils five shillings each. What a change it was then from my days at the school.

For a time I had to go there in bare feet—apparently my foster-mother could not afford to buy me a new pair of shoes when the ones I had wore out. I vividly remember the humiliation, because the other children used to step on my feet in the playground. My teacher must have found out about this, for she let me out of class a few minutes early so I could escape from my tormentors.

After about a year at St Mary Redcliffe, which proved to be the longest time I would ever attend one school, my mother sent for me and I made the long journey to Toronto, where they had settled. It took ten days by sea and three more on the train. The journey was a nightmare. The vaccinations, which everyone had to have before being allowed into Canada, made me ill and I spent most of the time aboard ship in my cabin—or, rather, in the one I shared with eight others.

Life in Canada was a big change both from the dusty heat of Cape Town and from the rolling green hills of the English West Country. My stepfather had a job as a salesman with the Toronto Gas Company and we lived in a little frame house on Yonge Street on the city outskirts. It was only the second house my mother and I had lived in, and for the first time in my life I was able to keep pets—four pigeons which I housed in a 'loft' made from a packing case. The harsh Canadian winters were a shock, and a delight. I walked along streets where the snow was banked on both sides higher than my head, and travelled in trams heated by wood-fired stoves. Often I even skated to school.

This was a wooden building about two miles from our house, and all I liked about it was the journey there—and especially back—on my skates. At that time British immigrants were not popular in Canada. Many of them arrived broke and took jobs for less money than the Canadians would accept. Generally, they must have been a disgruntled lot—the Canadians had nicknamed them 'Broncos', because they were always kicking against their conditions. And at school, I had an additional handicap as well as that of being British. I still could not speak English too well, and with my dropped aitches and West Country burr I must have sounded exceedingly odd. My teacher took a delight in making me stand up in class to recite a poem or read a passage from a book to the accompaniment of derisory giggles from the rest of the pupils. Naturally, I hated it.

This unhappiness, coupled with the fact that we needed money at home, prompted me to leave school when I was twelve. And that was the end of my formal education. It had lasted on and off for five years in about ten different schools.

My first job was with a firm that collected waste paper and baled and resold it. I was paid two dollars a week to deliver the cheques in payment for the paper after it had been collected and weighed. I suspect I got the job for two reasons—both connected with my size. Because I was small for twelve I could travel half-fare on the trams. The second reason was more subtle: it often happened that what appeared to be a huge amount of paper did not weigh very much and, consequently, the payment for it was much less than the seller expected. When I arrived with a cheque, often for only a few cents, the sellers were disappointed. But because I looked such a child, I think my employers banked on people not arguing with me—or venting their anger and probably their fists on me—as they might have on someone bigger.

Their psychology seemed to be right, for I never had any serious trouble. I received plenty of dark looks, though, and reached the stage where I felt I was taking my life in my hands every time I knocked on a door. However, I did not stay in the

41

job long, for I was always looking out for something better. Eventually I became a messenger boy at Eaton's, Toronto's largest store. It paid twice as much and was less risky.

It also had another advantage, for it enabled me to spend more time reading. I had not left school long before I realized my lack of education and I determined to catch up. I got books on history and geography from the library, and devoured any newspapers or magazines I could find.

I worked in the stock rooms across the road from the store in Queen Street. They were linked by an underground tunnel and it was my task to deliver goods to the sales departments by means of a large wickerwork trolley. Often I had time to spare between making deliveries and I spent it reading. Whenever I was out with my trolley I was eager to get back.

One day, while pushing the trolley along the tunnel, I thought, 'If I had some roller skates I could push this much faster.' I bought a pair and the idea worked. The round trip to the main building and back took about a third of the time. Soon I was scooting along at a fair old lick and, in the time saved, I was able to read a great deal more. But then disaster struck. On one trip I bumped into the wall and broke a trolley wheel. I fully expected a ticking off, or even the sack, but the manager did not realize the real reason behind my roller-skate idea. He thought I was showing initiative and efficiency and gave me a rise of fifty cents. And to make the trolley easier to push he had it fitted with larger wheels.

My roller skating is still remembered at Eaton's to this day. When I visited Toronto in 1976, Fred—the son of the Mr Eaton I had worked for—presented me with a pair of skates at a Variety Club function given in my honour. I told Fred jokingly, 'After working for your company I decided I would never work for anyone else again.'

When I was fifteen I moved to the leather department, which had a large order from the French government for gun harnesses. I was with about twenty Russians who did not speak English. The work mainly consisted of hand stitching using two needles at the same time, one in each hand. It was a tricky job until you mastered the technique. We worked about

42

nine hours a day, and then went on to overtime. At 5.30 we were given the equivalent of a shilling, and an hour off for tea—I spent a quarter of my tea money on ice-cream and the rest on a ticket for the Bioscope.

I was ambitious to move on; so I decided to use my aptitude for drawing and painting and become a commercial artist. Twice a week I studied art at night school, and eventually got myself transferred to the art department at Eaton's. Here I helped to draw the black-and-white advertisements which Eaton's booked every day of the week for the back page of the *Toronto Evening Mail*. As the youngest and least experienced member of the department, though, I was restricted to drawing the easiest objects. Articles of furniture and bottles of medicine were my main contribution.

My memories of Eaton's are warm and grateful. In Britain, whenever people asked me where I was educated, I always replied, 'Eaton's.' They invariably thought I meant Eton College and from the odd looks they gave me I suspect they felt the place had done a poor job on me. One of the best aspects of working for the company was being able to visit their summer camp, which gave me the first real holidays I'd known. Going there in the summer of 1914 I little realized that I would never see the place again. But a few weeks after my fifteenth birthday I joined the Canadian Army, saying I was seventeen.

I must confess that this action was not quite as patriotic as it might seem—it was an accident. It happened when two of my colleagues in the art department, a few years older than myself, had their imaginations fired by illustrations in a glossy magazine of British Army motor cycle despatch riders on the Western front dashing heroically through the mounted Uhlans (a crack German cavalry regiment). My friends decided they would like to become despatch riders and went off to volunteer. But at the time the Canadian Army had its full quota of despatch riders, so the pair were told they would be called when needed. Meanwhile, they were each given a badge to wear which proclaimed they had volunteered and were awaiting call-up.

I thought I would like one of those badges, so down I went to the recruiting office. The sergeant eyed me suspiciously when I walked in, for I was a short unmilitary figure. Undeterred, I boldly told him, 'I want to join the Army.' Unfortunately, I forgot to add that I wanted to be a despatch rider. I filled in some forms and waited for my badge. But all the sergeant said was, 'Come back tomorrow to be fitted for your uniform.'

Then the truth dawned on me: I had enlisted.

3

'*Billy was a drummer boy*'

'**H**EY, you with the jumper. Come here!' The command came from an irate and bemused sergeant in the drill hall where I was being kitted out with my uniform as a private in the Canadian Army. The 'jumper' he was referring to was my greatcoat.

I had been in trouble from the start, for the suppliers of uniforms to the Canadian Army had not envisaged anyone of my size. I was given the smallest uniform to be found, but I was still lost inside it. The cap had to be stuffed with paper to stop it falling down over my face and I had to do the same to the boots which were like boats on me. The tunic hung down below my knees, making me look like a Russian peasant, the trousers completely covered my feet and the greatcoat was so long I kept treading on it. There was nothing I could do except cut the trousers and coat to fit. So I borrowed a pair of scissors and set to work.

First the trousers. They looked fine once I had cut a foot off the bottom and wrapped my puttees around them. Next, the greatcoat. I put it on and bent over to make a mark at a suitable height from the ground. I took it off, spread it on the floor and cut along the line I had made. Unfortunately, I had not allowed for the fact that I had measured it while bending down; when I put the coat on again it hardly covered my backside. Hence the sergeant's caustic form of address.

Brushing aside my protests that everything was too big, he

ordered me to get the coat lengthened before next morning and to make sure I was properly dressed. So off I went home in my incongruous uniform to break the news to my parents that I had joined the Army—for I had been too scared to tell my mother and step-father the night before. Now I worried that they might not only be angry; I feared they would tell the Army my real age and have my enlistment cancelled.

To my surprise and relief neither of these things happened, though my mother shed a tear or two as she lengthened my greatcoat with part of the material I had cut off, and made a few alterations to the rest of my uniform.

They were not too concerned, I think, because neither dreamed that the Army would use a youngster like me. In any case, they believed the war would be over before I had been trained. When eventually I was posted overseas they tried to get me discharged—but by then it was too late.

However, I was young enough to like the idea of being in the Army. I was earning more ($1.50 a day) than I had been at Eaton's—and all found, of course. At fifteen I was full of the spirit of adventure and my only worry was that the war would be over before I could get to France. So with a light heart and a better-fitting uniform, I reported for duty next morning.

My innocent enthusiasm was promptly dampened when I was debited ten dollars for a new greatcoat—which I never received. I felt that was one of the first real injustices of my life. Whether it was an administrative slip-up or a bit of fiddling I never discovered. I suspect the latter, for repeatedly we poor rookies had stoppages made from our pay for broken windows and other damages supposedly done to the barracks, an old school. I never noticed any of the damage being repaired. More likely the money went on beer for the NCOs.

Though conditions were tough, I found my first few weeks in the Army pleasant enough, mainly because I was put in the bugle band, which consisted of thirty 'musicians' with bugles and drums. I was a bugler and laboriously learned to play a few notes. Of course, I could not read music—and I suspect that the drum major couldn't, either.

The band's main function was to take part in recruiting

meetings, marching behind the recruiting officer and then standing on the stage of a local theatre while he painted a horrific picture of the beastly Germans destroying homes, raping girls and torturing women. Listening to him I felt very much an adult soldier about to go off and fight for civilization. The recruiting officer was an estate agent in peace time, and he was the most blood-thirsty man I ever knew. His only ambition, or so he vowed, was to get to France and kill Germans. His enthusiasm was so catching, his exhortations so rousing, that he raised several battalions—though he never did go overseas himself.

What was perhaps more important to a small, insignificant-looking fifteen-year-old was that the uniform proved a great attraction to the girls—far better than the I-have-volunteered-badges worn by my colleagues at Eaton's. Not that my uniform was perfect, even after being altered by a tailor. My cap looked particularly odd, having been pinched in and tucked to make it fit. Generally, while I looked all right from the front, my rear view left much to be desired.

Nevertheless, I went back to Eaton's to swank; while I was wandering round the store I saw a very pretty young girl with a fresh complexion and beautiful golden-ginger hair. Full of soldierly bravado I started talking to her, and found that her name was Jean Coombes. She was fourteen, and had not been working at Eaton's very long. To my delight, she was very impressed by my uniform and from then on we spent nearly all our spare time in each other's company. We went to the pictures together and both roared with laughter at the antics of a funny little man: he was Charlie Chaplin, then at the beginning of his rise to fame.

After the heady glamour of the recruiting meetings came the cold realism of square-bashing, and then we were posted to our first camp at Borden. I was put into the 170th Battalion, but was later transferred to the Bantam Battalion as bugler and drummer boy. By then I had learned the rudiments of both instruments and could beat out a lively rat-tat-a-tat and blow various bugle calls. Jean wrote regularly, and she sent me food parcels while I was overseas; I carred her photograph

47

throughout the war. She was the first girl I had ever loved.

After I left Canada for good she married, becoming a Mrs Rose, and had a daughter who grew up to be the image of the Jean I had known. In the early Fifties Jean visited Britain, and I was delighted to have her stay at Filey Camp. When Eamonn Andrews did a *This Is Your Life* television programme on me in 1959 she was flown to Britain to appear on it—much to my surprise and pleasure.

A couple of years after that reunion—in 1961—a writer whose work appeared under the initials LFL wrote some verse to accompany a drawing of me by Roth in the London *Evening News* which recalled those long-lost days:

> *Billy was a drummer boy when he was just fifteen*
> *He's wasted very little time in all those years between*
> *Years that were mostly kind to him*
> *Though they've filled out his figure*
> *The drum he beats these days, of course, is also*
> *   somewhat bigger*

To return to my time as a drummer boy: it was winter and we lived under canvas in bitter cold conditions, with snow seeping into the tents. Hot water was scarce and I was glad I had not started shaving. But one morning on parade the inspecting officer glared at my chin and barked, 'Get that fluff off.' So I bought a razor and began shaving once a week. Frankly, about this time I began to wonder if it had been such a good idea to join the Army.

These harsh conditions were not made any more bearable by the fact that there was no sign of us being sent overseas. I had become friendly with a young chap called Jim Little and we were both worried that the war would be over before we could get to France and win a few medals. So eventually we decided to desert. Not to get away from the Army, but to join another unit in Hamilton, Ontario, which we had heard was soon to embark for England. Our first problem was to find some civilian clothes for, when we had been kitted out, we had sold ours to a dealer for three shillings each. However, we managed to buy a couple of old suits, and changed into them in the woods behind the camp, burying our uniforms in the snow-covered ground.

Next came the problem of getting to Hamilton—about forty miles away. We did not have enough money for the rail fare, so the only way was to 'ride the rods' on the freight trains, in the traditional manner of the American hoboes. It was not a style of transport I would recommend, but there was a warm spirit of friendship among the hoboes. Every now and then along the railway line there were ramshackle camps where they met up to warm themselves by a huge fire and eat a hot meal. Where the food came from I never discovered, but Jim and I were made welcome and had a real tuck-in. At Hamilton, we discovered that the unit we planned to join was a cavalry regiment. Neither of us had ridden before, but we were so keen to get overseas we refused to let a little matter like that deter us. Once again we enlisted.

Naturally, we had to be taught to ride and as the regiment was due to embark in a few days, we were given a crash course. Round and round a large drill hall we went for hours at a time, stopping only for meals. It was an excruciatingly painful experience, made worse by innoculations that had been pumped into the very part of our anatomy suffering the most. After a couple of days it was agony to sit down or stand up. In addition, one of my arms was painfully swollen and I felt as though I was running a temperature.

Among the various other things we were taught was how to give medicine to a horse. This involved feeding it a pill which you blew down the animal's throat. You made a paper tube and while someone else opened the horse's mouth, you inserted the tube, dropped a pill about the size of a marble down it—and blew. I tried this only once, but the horse knew more about it than I did and blew first. I have often wondered since whether some of the old-timers in the battalion guessed that this might happen and laid on the lesson as a joke. If so, it was not much of a joke as far as I was concerned—I did not need a laxative for about three weeks.

After all the trouble we had taken to get overseas, we now

heard that the regiment's departure had been delayed for some time. We were disenchanted with horses, and so Jim and I decided to return to our old unit and take our punishment. We had not been with our new regiment long enough to get paid, so again we did not have our rail fare. We hated the thought of riding the rods once more, for it is a terrible form of travel during a Canadian winter. But how could we obtain enough money for the fare?

We decided to appeal to a local clergyman and, presenting ourselves as brothers, we told him a tear-jerking story about our mother dying in Toronto. But we got neither money nor sympathy. We had picked a pretty tough character, the most villainous-looking clergyman I have ever seen; though, in all fairness, he had probably had many similar requests that winter. Times were hard for everyone. The towns were flooded with unemployed and there were no dole or welfare payments to cushion them. Many of the unemployed were only saved from starvation by street-corner charity soup kitchens where they queued for hours for a bowl of broth.

So it was back to our previous method of transport. Our reception at Borden was as cold as the weather, and we were both sentenced to twenty-one days in the glasshouse. My mother and stepfather, who had been informed of the escapade, managed to impress upon the colonel my youthfulness and my sentence was reduced to one week. I can still remember looking through the barred window of my cell and seeing my parents standing sadly outside. That was a bigger punishment than anything the colonel could impose. He had been blunt with me: 'You'll never do any good in life,' he told me firmly. Nevertheless, I must have rehabilitated myself somewhat, because by the time we went overseas a few months later I had been promoted to lance-corporal.

That journey to England was long and tedious. We were two weeks in the train travelling the eight hundred or so miles from Toronto to Halifax, Nova Scotia, because we were repeatedly held up in order not to arrive before our convoy assembled. Several times during the journey the railway line ran close to the US border and whenever we stopped on these occasions a number of American volunteers deserted. These were fair-weather soldiers—they had probably joined up because they had been unemployed, and then found Army life not to their liking. But if we had known what lay ahead of us I think a few Canadians might have done the same!

When we eventually got aboard ship, we discovered that we had to sleep in hammocks—it took most of us the best part of the twelve-day voyage to master the knack of using them. Three days out of Liverpool we were joined by three Royal Navy destroyers, and I really began to feel I was a part of the war as I watched them weaving in and out of the convoy of merchantmen.

In my section I was the only one who had been to England and I was amused at the reaction to the country by my Canadian friends. They were all amazed at the smallness and compactness of everything, and they laughed outright at the size of the railway engines compared to the huge monsters with their cow-catchers on the front they had been used to in Canada. They were surprised by how fast these engines went, though.

We were stationed at Sandgate Camp, near Folkestone, Kent, where we spent several miserable weeks in quarantine behind barbed wire fences. For three days all we had to eat were biscuits and jam. The camp had no canteen so we were all delighted when, during our second week, an officer and a sergeant appeared to take orders for cigarettes and chocolate. They collected the money, wrote down our names meticulously and arranged to return next day with our purchases. We never saw them again. Later we discovered that they were a couple of opportunist privates. About a week later we were caught by a similar trick. This time it was a photographer offering to take pictures of us to send to our folks back home. Foolishly we paid in advance and once again never saw anything for our money.

The camp catering officer was a Major Hughie Green, who was once the target of a protest by some of us. It arose because the fish we were served was often bad and we thought he was responsible. So the members of the bugle band decided to do something about it. We took a stinking fish from the cookhouse and marched round the camp, playing our instruments and dragging the fish behind us on a tray. (Major Green was the father of another Hughie, who—thirty years later—would appear as a famous entertainer at a Butlin Luxury Holiday Camp.)

Meanwhile, our training continued. We practised regularly on the rifle range at Hythe, starting out at dawn to march the eight miles there. We also learned how to dig trenches—though I later found that when we had to do the real thing in France we did the job a lot quicker. Shells had a way of speeding you up. (We dug trenches without the help of an ingenious Canadian invention that had been issued to us before embarking. It looked like an ordinary spade, but it had a hole in the centre of the metal part. The idea was that if we were attacked while digging we could use the spade as a shield and fire our rifles through the hole.)

At Sandgate the horrors of war were still camouflaged for us by a romantic idealism. We saw very few wounded soldiers and had little or no idea of what awaited us, even when we witnessed one of the early Zeppelin attacks on Folkestone. And when the detonator of a hand grenade exploded in my face during a lecture, for several days I was blind and lay in hospital sick with fear not so much at the thought of becoming blind permanently but because I might not get well soon enough to go to France with my pals and win a medal. Luckily my eyesight returned, the wound healed and I was able to stay with the men I had trained with.

It was about this time that I discovered the game of crown and anchor. This is played on a board marked off in six squares, two bearing the crown and anchor symbols and the other four the suits of playing cards. You place your bets on the squares of your choice and then the owner of the board rolls three dice marked with the same symbols as those on the board. If you symbol comes up you win, if not the banker or owner of the board keeps the stake. We were introduced to the game, for neither I nor the Canadians had known it before, by some British troops stationed nearby. After losing my first week's pay of 6s. a day (the British 'Tommy' was paid only 1s.) I realized the banker nearly always came out ahead, and so I decided to go into the crown and anchor business myself.

I found it difficult to obtain a board because none of the British, who naturally wanted to keep their monopoly, was willing to sell me one. Eventually, I got one from an aunt (another of my mother's sisters, Lottie Coneley, who—after the War—would help me again).

Pretty soon I was running a highly profitable game. Being so small I always took the precaution of having two hefty pals along in case of trouble, but in fact my size was an asset. There had been several cases of bankers refusing to pay out winnings and many prospective punters were wary of playing the game. But, probably because I looked so young and innocent, they seemed to trust me. I ran my crown and anchor game at every opportunity all the time I was in the Army—but after the first few weeks I always played with men outside my unit. I didn't want to make enemies by taking money from my own comrades.

I prospered so well I could afford to pay people to make my life easier: I had one bloke to clean my rifle, another to clean my boots and polish my buttons and a third to fetch my breakfast. I was so well off I didn't draw my Army pay for fourteen months—it helped that I neither drank nor smoked—and sent most of it home to my mother.

When I was on leave, though, I spent money taking out girls and generally enjoying myself—and this eventually brought me a cropper. It happened whilst I was on leave in Bristol, where my fairground relatives spent the winter. At that time, the Canadians were not strong on discipline and many of the soldiers stayed on leave until they were caught. Being youthfully impressionable, I did the same. One day, I was walking down Old Market Street, Bristol, in uniform, my collar undone and a girl on each arm, when I was spotted by two Military Police and taken back to camp. That is how I lost my lance-corporal's stripe.

We finally arrived in France as reinforcements for the 4th CMRs (Canadian Mounted Rifles) in the 3rd Canadian

Division; after my riding experience in Hamilton, I was relieved to find that we had no horse. In fact, we seemed to spend most of our time marching all over northern France, for we were a 'flying corps', constantly being shuttled from one hard-pressed point to another. We took part in the second battle of Vimy Ridge and were at Ypres, Arras and the second battle of Cambrai. Here, to our amazement, we saw tanks for the first time: one had lumbered over the top of our trench during the night, but we were so exhausted we were not even aware of it amid the clamour of guns and exploding shells. Only next morning did we notice its tracks which were little more than a foot from where I had been sleeping standing up.

During the two years I was at the Front I never fired a shot in anger, but I vividly recall the horrors of trench warfare. There were times when I would willingly have parted with a leg to escape from it all. And I swore I would work for nothing forever, if only I could get back to 'Civvy Street'. But it was not to be and I slogged on as a stretcher-bearer, collecting the wounded, often under shell-fire, and burying the dead. It is not so much the danger I remember, but the mud and the lice—our 'next of skin' as we wryly called them.

Once a month we came out of the 'line' for a bath and to have our underwear and uniforms fumigated. We got our own uniforms back, but never the same underwear, and it was a grim and grisly feeling to see lice—other men's lice—still glistening in the pants and vests. We spent hours cracking the lice one by one.

I discovered later that I was one of the youngest soldiers to have served in France but, despite the horror of them, those years were the making of me. I have been broke a few times in my business career and in my private life I have known disappointment, pain and heartbreak. But after my experiences in France, I have always been able to say to myself, 'You're not as badly off as you have been.'

And I survived, where many did not, to be given the opportunity of putting the hard-learned lessons of war into peace-time practice. For instance, I had learned how to judge and pick men. War certainly sifts the men from the boys. The

54

one who looks every inch a hero at base camp can crumble at the first sign of danger, while the insignificant, unassuming and quiet one often proves to have the guts, courage and ability to inspire his comrades.

When Armistice Day eventually arrived, we were stationed just outside Mons in some ruined stables. It should have been a joyful day, but for me it was one of the most miserable of the war. My mates went into Mons to celebrate, but as I still did not drink I did not feel like going with them. So I stayed in camp, imagining the celebrations back in Canada, and feeling very homesick.

But though it was a miserable day for me, it was a tragic one for others. For in Mons the floor of an upstairs dance hall collapsed, throwing the revellers on to the ground below. A number were killed and several of our unit were badly injured. I was one of those who rushed to the scene to help and it was a heartbreaking business moving dead and injured men who had survived so much—only to be trapped by Fate when they thought they were safe. And as I worked I could not escape the chill feeling that had I gone with my mates I might easily have been a casualty too.

The war was over, and I was anxious to return home as quickly as possible. My stepfather had died in 1917 and my mother was now alone, supporting herself by working as a saleswoman in the wallpaper department of Eaton's store. But unfortunately we kicked our heels in France and then in a camp near Liverpool, and the mood of many Canadian soldiers became ugly. The resentment of the private soldier at the delay in sending him home was focused on the NCOs who represented authority, and there were a number of instances where they were physically attacked. As a result some NCOs were sent home ahead of the lower ranks for their own safety, and one of these was our own Sergeant-Major Alf Pavey. He had been with us since our training days at Sandgate and a very tough taskmaster he had been—though no tougher than he had to be, I suppose. But many of us harboured dark thoughts about what we would like to do to him after the war. It was the wishful dream of many a lowly private that in civilian life he would be in a position of authority over one of his NCOs or officers—a situation that Irving Berlin encapsulated after the Second World War in his song 'I've Got My Captain Working For Me Now'.

For me, this dream would come true. In 1936 Alfred Pavey came to Britain on his way back from visiting the Vimy Ridge battlefield, where so many Canadians had died. He read about my Skegness holiday camp and came to see me. 'Will you give me a job?' he asked. 'I think you know I'm a good organizer.' I must admit it was a situation that gave me some pleasure. Here was the man who had often made my life a misery, come to me for a job. But the feeling of hatred for him and the authority he had once stood for was only fleeting. The years had passed and I had changed. Indeed, Pavey was probably responsible for some of the character I had developed in the Army and which had served me well since. I gave him a job and he worked for me until the war started in 1939 when he retired and returned to Canada.

But in England in 1919, waiting to return to Canada, I went on leave to London. There I had two very different experiences that made a big impact on me. I had been through a war and had learned to look after myself, but in some vital aspects of life I was still a naïve nineteen-year-old.

For instance, I had never been in a posh restaurant. So when I found myself in Piccadilly Circus, I decided to go into the nearby Trocadero, then one of the grandest restaurants in London. I was overwhelmed by the opulence, the crisp linen table cloths, the bewildering array of knives and forks and the aloof waiters in dinner jackets. I was apprehensive and somewhat on the defensive, but I was determined to go through with it.

When the waiter approached and politely inquired, 'What can I get you, sir?' I thought I was being patronized. Panicking, I ordered the first thing that came into my head.

'Eggs and chips,' I said.

'How many eggs, sir?'

'Five,' I told him firmly.

He took the order without a flicker of surprise. I had no difficulty in downing five eggs and chips—eggs had been a luxury for too many years, and in any case I was hungry. Then the waiter came to take away my plate, and for some unaccountable reason I felt he was trying to get rid of me. So when he said, 'Is there anything more I can get you, sir?' I promptly replied, 'Yes. Same again. Five eggs and chips.'

This time it was more of a struggle to eat them, but I was not going to be beaten. Finally I had a clean plate and the bill was politely presented. I looked at it with astonishment. It was ridiculously small for the amount of food I had eaten.

Suddenly, I realized that the waiter had deliberately given me a small bill. Today I still wonder why he did it. Had he spotted how unused I was to that class of restaurant and felt I might not be able to pay the bill? Or had he taken pity on me? Had I reminded him of his own son, perhaps one he had lost in the war? Whatever the reason I have never forgotten his kindness and the way he helped me cross what was to me then a big social barrier.

Two days later came my second experience in the art of growing up; this one was much more pleasant. Her name was Joy and I met her in a Paddington pub. She was pretty and young, but very worldly and, though I have no idea how old she was, I think she felt sorry for me because I looked so young and inexperienced.

She took me back to her little room and I spent two wonderful days and nights with her. After the personal loneliness of the last two years and the horrors of the trenches I was totally captivated by her warm, feminine companionship. I suppose I fell madly in love with her and in a state of rosy euphoria I asked her to join me in Canada.

'I can't give you an answer now,' she said, 'but let's keep in touch with each other when you go back to Canada and I'll let you know then.'

Happily believing her, I returned to camp. For the next two weeks I dreamed of her constantly. Then, one day, I visited a nearby town, turned a corner and there she was, laughing and beautiful, on the arm of a Canadian officer. When she saw me she looked the other way. My adolescent heart was shattered, but fortunately my misery was soon dispelled. For at last we embarked for home.

We arrived in Toronto at night and, as one of the first units to return from France, we were given a big reception. The torch-lit streets were lined with a guard of honour and the pavements packed with people. And there, among them, I spotted my mother, waving, cheering and crying all at the same time. Without a moment's hesitation I dropped out of the marching ranks and ran to her. I never went back to the Army. Despite this sudden and unofficial end to my chequered military career, I have, in fact, maintained stronger connections with the Canadian Army than most ex-Servicemen. For in 1960 I set up a £100,000 Trust Fund to provide financial help to Canadian Veterans of both World Wars who forfeited the right to an official pension by staying on in Britain. It has always warmed and touched me that, at its annual dinner, the British branch of the Canadian Veterans' Association toasts me as 'Our Best Friend'.

Back in 1919, my first concern was what I could do for a living. Like a lot of ex-soldiers I wanted a secure job with a pension, and the best way I knew of getting that was to work for the city council. Unfortunately, I had no qualifications beyond my art training for, at a time when other young men were learning a trade or profession, I had been in the Army. The council had no call for artists, and the only jobs a City Hall official could offer me were as a street sweeper or lavatory attendant. He gave me a form to fill up—but I did not get either job. If I had, I might now be a retired street sweeper or lavatory attendant.

I went back to night school, studying commercial art four nights a week and I was able to get my old job back in the advertising department at Eaton's. It began to look as though I was getting a sense of direction and purpose in my life.

Eighteen months after my return home, in my twentieth year, I began to feel restless. Though I was only six years older, I was a vastly different person from the callow youth who had gone to the recruiting office for his 'I-have-volunteered' badge. Most of my older colleagues in the department were the same people who had been there when I had left to join the Army. Now many of them were round-shouldered, bespectacled, wore anxious expressions and seemed set in their ways. I began to wonder how I would look in ten years' time, and I decided that was not the future for me.

I am not one to dramatize my emotions, but at the age of twenty I had a strong feeling that I would be a success in life. What was less clear was how I would achieve that success. The first hint of the shape of things to come emerged in 1920 with the opening of the Toronto National Exhibition. I went to the fair adjoining it and, walking around, I noticed there was no darts stall. The fairs I remembered in England had always had one, and they were very popular. So I took my holidays from Eaton's and opened a darts stall at the fair, offering kewpie dolls as prizes.

It was a success—and so I told my department manager at Eaton's that I was leaving. Very cocky I was, but not as clever as I thought. One day a stranger introduced himself and talked in glowing terms about a carnival he was setting up in the town of Renfrew, Ottawa. 'You're doing well here,' he said. 'Why don't you have a stall at my carnival?'

I jumped at the suggestion and paid in advance for two sites, spending almost every dollar I had made—a total of about £400. I borrowed the rail fair, and with bubbling hopes set off for Renfrew; but when I arrived there was no trace of my sites or of the con-man who had sold them to me. If only I had remembered the lesson I had learned at Sandgate camp in England. Chastened, my high hopes punctured, I returned to Eaton's and humbly asked for my job back in the art department.

But this experience made me realize how attracted I was to the life of a fairground showman. Those early days I spent travelling the West Country fairs with my mother had made their impact. Or perhaps it was simply that I had a showman's blood in my veins. Whatever the reason, I began to remember nostalgically the friendly community of the travelling showman. The idea of an open-air life, not tied to a desk or an artist's easel, also attracted me. And in addition I recalled the good times I had had in England as a Canadian soldier. Perhaps unlike the British 'Tommy', we had the time of our lives when we went on leave—I suppose I thought it would always be like that.

So I made up my mind to return to England and join my fairground relations. It was an unusual decision for a young man to make at that time, for countless thousands of ambitious Britons were following the adage 'Go west, young man' and starting new lives in Canada.

My mother wrote to her sister Lottie Coneley—their four brothers were travelling showmen—and I knew they would make me welcome in England. But first I had to get there. I did not have the boat fare, so I had to work my passage. My mother, who was still working at Eaton's, gave me a few dollars and once again I 'rode the rods' on the freight trains.

This time I headed for Halifax, Nova Scotia, where I had heard it was often possible to get a berth because so many British seamen jumped ship when they arrived in Canada. Cattle boats, in particular, would usually take on untrained men to feed, water and 'muck out' the cattle.

A few questions along the waterfront and I landed a berth on just such a boat, the *Scandinavia*. It was a rough trip and most of the way across the Atlantic I was terribly sick. The poor cows nearly starved. At Liverpool I was paid off with £5—all the money I had in the world.

It was 17 February, 1921.

4

'Small profits and quick returns'

IT is called Locke's Yard now, and it lies sandwiched between a dairy and the Enterprise public house in Parson Street, Bedminster, a suburb of Bristol. During the winter it is jammed with caravans and lorries, for it is the off-season home of many West Country travelling showmen.

When I knew it more than sixty years ago, it was called Dorney's Yard and it was much bigger than it is now. It still served the same purpose, though. For as soon as October was over, the travelling showmen headed for the Yard to spend the winter there and prepare for the spring. In the sheds that fringed the Yard, they repaired and re-painted their stalls and 'rides'.

I had visited it whilst on leave during the war when I went to see my mother's sister, Aunt Lottie Coneley, and my four travelling showman uncles. Now, having arrived in Liverpool, I headed there again. Showmen are incorrigible optimists— indeed they need to be to survive—and being a showman at heart I have always had plenty of optimism. I certainly needed it that cold February morning when I set out on the road south.

I had spent the night in a seaman's hostel in Liverpool and, wanting to keep most of my precious £5, I decided to hitch-hike to Bristol. Hitch-hikers are common enough today, but they were rare birds then for the simple reason that there was so little traffic on the road to provide the lifts. What drivers there were proved kind and helpful, but even so it took me five days to reach Bristol. The rigours of my long journey, however, were quickly forgotten when I pushed open the big, black-painted double gates at the entrance to the Yard and saw and heard again the familiar sights and sounds. There were forty or fifty families living there. The Yard was crammed with maroon-painted white-topped caravans, or 'living wagons', and the vans, which carried the equipment. Everything had to be pulled by traction engines or horses—there were no lorries. I have seen traction engines hauling as many as sixteen vans at once, but after the First World War the limit was set at four, because as more traffic came on the roads these 'trains' proved a safety hazard. The Yard was also littered with wheels, timber and large sheets of canvas stretched out on the ground. There were children running around, women hanging out the washing—and pervading this scene the thump of hammers and the sharp smell of paint as the fairground roundabouts were repaired and repainted.

It was a bitterly cold February afternoon. I was very hungry, as I had eaten little in order to save money. I was also very dirty. On previous visits, Aunt Lottie's caravan had always been the first on the right as I entered the Yard and I headed in this direction. I had only taken a few steps when she spotted me. She ran up, hugged me and cried: 'Here's Bertha's boy.' I immediately felt at home. I was given a bunk in a wagon shared by three others, and though it was cramped I have never felt more comfortable anywhere in my life.

Having arrived, I next had to decide what I was going to do. I asked my Uncle Marshall, the head of the Hill family, for his advice. 'Pack up and go back to Canada,' he said with forthright candour. It was sincere and probably sound advice, for he knew just how hard was a showman's life. But it was impractical. For, while I had not burned my bridges exactly, it would certainly have been difficult for me to go back. There was no chance of being able to work my passage again, as there were plenty of out-of-work crewmen at Bristol ports and, in any case, to get a ship from Britain you needed a seaman's ticket. The only way I could have gone back to Canada would have been as a fare-paying passenger—and in my state of wealth it seemed unlikely I would be able to afford that for a long time.

No, what I wanted to do was to become a showman; and when they saw my determination, my uncles helped me to acquire a small hoop-la stall for thirty shillings and let me have some 'swag'—the showman's term for prizes—to be paid for later.

The first fair of the season was just before Easter and was held on the Friday and Saturday at Axebridge, between Bristol and Bridgewater. I travelled there by train with my portable stall. My other equipment, the blocks for the prizes to stand on and the throwing rings—five for twopence—I carried in a wicker hamper.

At Axebridge I learned something that was to become the cornerstone of my success. Everyone knows that the ring you throw at a hoop-la stall must not only slot over the prize itself, but also over the block that it stands on. Fairground folklore has it that I shrewdly made my blocks smaller than the normal size. This not only made the prizes easier to win, but also encourged people to play more. It proved to be good business.

That first day all my prizes, which had cost me £10, were won—but I took £20 in tuppences. In those days, most stallholders tried to give away as few prizes as possible. They would have the same prizes for years. Not the same *kind* of prizes, but the very same ones. Alarm clocks and metal vases, for instance, were kept so long they went rusty, and had to be constantly cleaned with metal polish.

On this day, as usual, the other stallholders hardly lost any prizes, but they only took £5-£6 each. I had lost £10 worth of prizes, but I had made a profit of £10. It was obvious who had done the better business. That day I discovered the benefit of small profits and quick returns—which is something I have practised successfully ever since.

The legend is only partially true: for I did not make my blocks smaller deliberately. To economize, I cut them myself; and they turned out smaller for the simple reason that I made a mistake with the measurements.

Axebridge was a two-day fair and, though my mistake with the blocks proved a long-term blessing in disguise, it left me with no swag for the second day. But, because of the spirit of fellowship among travelling showmen, I had no difficulty in borrowing enough prizes to see me through. Once again I lost them all, but once again I made a good profit.

Naturally, before the next fair at Yeovil I had to buy more swag. The swag merchants were in London and congregated in a long lane in Houndsditch. There you could buy pepper-pots for sixpence, watches for 1s 3d to 2s 6d, alarm clocks for 3s and heavy metal or china vases for a few shillings each. So up to London I went. My task was not easy, for I needed to get most of my swag on credit. How I thought a total stranger, speaking in a curious mixture of West Country and Canadian English, would be trusted with credit I do not know. But fortunately, after trying and failing with a couple of merchants, I came across a Mr Alfred Myers, whose firm is still in business today.

He knew some of my West Country friends and let me have £50 worth of swag for a small down-payment. It proved to be a good investment for him, for in the next few years we did many thousand pounds worth of business. I arranged to collect the goods next morning, and then began to think about a bed for the night. I could not afford a hotel but, luckily, it was a mild spring evening, so I curled up on a bench in St James's Park. It is not a form of accommodation I would recommend, but with the resilience of youth I slept well enough.

Next morning, having picked up my swag, it was back to the West Country and the fairground circuit. From Yeovil we went to Exeter and the Easter Fair at St Thomas's. On the second leg of the circuit we travelled through Herefordshire, calling at Hereford, Ludlow, Leominster, Craven Arms and other small towns.

That first summer passed quickly as I learned the business. The hoop-la stall continued to do well, but I was constantly in debt to Mr Myers. Nonetheless I always paid, and gradually I was able to increase my credit. It was a hard, but interesting and often exciting life, 'catching' the various fairs, finding digs for 2s 6d a night and then setting up your stall. It was important to fix your digs first because after working on the fairground you were dirty and dishevelled and landladies would often refuse to take you in. When you had arranged your accommodation, you did not return until after the fair had closed at night—and this practice once led me to a strange encounter in Ludlow.

It was midnight when I got back to my room, ready to drop straight into the comfortable double bed. But as I put on the light I saw another man asleep in it. I was in no mood for any confrontation—and in any case, as the one in possession, he might have refused to budge, leaving me the option of the floor. So I quietly climbed in beside him.

Next morning I discovered my unexpected bed-fellow was an Italian onion-seller who cycled from town to town with strings of them hanging from the handle-bars. His name was Joe Romaine and he frequented the fairs because he found he sold more onions there than by going from house to house. Joe became one of my best friends, and eventually he gave up onions to become a travelling showman. Twelve years later, when I opened my amusement park at Bognor, he was one of my first tenants.

During those early years I made many friends. At that time travelling showmen were often looked upon as roving vagabonds, but they were—and are—wonderful people. They were tough, though, and very useful in a scrap. During the winter some of them earned a living as boxers. One showman, Johnny Grattan, became a West Country champion. Another was a man called Frankham, a half-brother of Joe Beckett, the British Heavyweight Champion, who was beaten by Georges Carpentier. I always thought that Frankham was a better boxer than Beckett, but he stopped fighting after he killed a man in the ring.

Most travelling fairs had a boxing booth, where the fighters stood out in front on a platform challenging anyone in the crowd to go two or three rounds of three minutes with one of them for 10s or £1. On the West Country circuit the booth was run by a man called Sam McKeon, who acted both as referee

65

and time-keeper. This was a most useful combination for, if the challenger was a good scrapper, Sam would make the rounds a short three minutes so that whether his man won (which he usually did because he was a pro) or lost, he did so with the minimum of physical damage to himself.

If there were no volunteers or challengers one of the fairground showmen helped out by stepping up and pretending to be one of the public. They would put on a show without hurting each other. Even I used to step up as a challenger when there was a shortage of volunteers, though Sam made sure I was matched with someone who was not too big or too tough. Those fights gave me useful experience because you certainly had to learn to look after yourself on the fairgrounds. Late at night you usually got some tough character, full of beer and bravado, looking for trouble.

Showmen always came to the aid of one another when anyone had an ugly customer. One night at Avonmouth, near Bristol, I had a nasty experience when a couple of drunken Irish seamen, who looked about eight feet tall, staggered up to my hoop-la stall, just as I was closing. They clearly were big trouble and I looked anxiously around for help but I always stayed open until the last possible minute—and there were no other showmen in sight. I told the seamen I was closed, but one of them insisted on playing and threatened to smash up the stall if I didn't let him. In the hope that someone would appear before it came to a showdown I gave him five rings and asked for the twopence charge. 'I'll owe you it,' he said, giving two rings to his mate.

Whereupon he clambered over the outside rail of the stall and placed a ring over one of the smaller prizes. His mate did the same, and then they both loudly demanded their prizes. I gave them with foreboding because I guessed that their next stop would be to place their ring over the big prizes at the back of the stall.

Desperately I looked round for help and was relieved to see a showman I did not know because he had just joined the fair, approaching quietly. He motioned to me to ignore him. Calmly he drew from his sleeve what looked like a two-foot length of rubber hose pipe. He crept up and walloped both men on the back of the head. They collapsed, out cold. My saviour (a Londoner called Jack Harvey) shouted for some other showmen and they dragged the men to the fairground gates where they threw two buckets of water over them and sent them staggering off into the night.

Because they often get drunk on shore leave, sailors invariably created trouble when we were near a Royal Navy establishment. In the autumn, we always attended the Portland Fair, near Portsmouth, and when the Fleet was in we expected—and got—what is now called 'aggro'.

I never experienced any real trouble myself, though one night a drunken sailor climbed over the outside rail of my hoop-la stall, lay down among the prizes and fell asleep. I shook him and tugged at him, but he snored on blissfully, so I had no option but to let him lie there and carry on using the rest of the stall. It was an incongruous sight with people throwing their rings on either side of him. Actually, it was good for business because word got around and people soon flocked to look and giggle and usually had tuppence-worth of rings. Every now and then a sailor would come along, climb over the rail and look at the sleeping man's cap to see which ship he came from; finding he was not a shipmate, they all left him there. He slept on until closing time when some of my fellow showmen helped me to move him. We made him comfortable under one of the wagons and went to bed. He had gone in the morning.

Most fairgrounds were rented by the owners of the big attractions or 'rides', who were known as 'riding masters'. They then let the sites or 'ground' for the side shows and stalls to the stallholders, although sometimes stallholders rented 'ground' direct from the local council.

In the Twenties, these council fairgrounds were often plagued with tricksters and con-men who gave genuine travelling showmen a bad name. In fact, at fairs controlled by the riding masters, they were banned. For these villains were far worse than the old-time fairground dentists, who at least gave people something for their money even if it was only a mouthful of blood. They ran all kinds of games and swindles, where there was little or no chance of the public winning.

There was the 'cobbler'. Imagine a table with an upright peg in the centre; at each end of the table is an upright linked by a bar across the top from which is suspended a wooden ball. The aim of the game is to swing the ball past the peg and knock it down as it swings back. If you think about it, you can see that this is extremely difficult to achieve, for the ball invariably swings back on a trajectory, which brings it past the peg on the other side. The cobbler's operator showed how it could be done. While he poured out his patter, he swung the ball and as he did so he leaned very slightly on the table which had the effect of making the peg move sideways. As the ball swung back he eased the pressure so that the peg returned to its original position and was hit by the ball. It looked easy when he did it, but when the punter tried he soon found otherwise.

Then there was 'cover the spot'. All you had to do was completely cover a red spot nine inches in diameter with five apparently circular discs six inches in diameter. As with all these crooked games the con-man running it demonstrated that it could be done. But there was only one way it could be done and that involved trickery. One of the 'discs' was very slightly oval, but not noticeably so at a glance. To cover the spot completely you had to place this 'disc' down last. But when the punter came to try he was led into putting it down first. Instead of being given the five discs together which would have enabled him to put them down in any order, he was handed them separately and the first one he received was the oval one. He was not given another disc until he had placed that and, of course, once he had done so, it was impossible for him to win.

The 'windbag merchants' were another unsavoury lot. They worked as a team of four or five men, a salesman and several 'gees' pretending to be customers, and as a precaution they frequently changed roles. They had earned their nickname for two reasons—they relied on the gift of the gab to trick people and they sold at a huge profit bags or envelopes which contained little more than air.

The salesman's spiel went something like this: 'Now I'm here today, ladies and gentlemen, to give you an opportunity which will never occur again. I've been commissioned to advertise these watches and that's the only reason why they're going for a song, so to speak.' He then produced half a dozen watches, put each one of them inside an envelope and sealed it. 'Now I'll tell you what I'm going to do,' he would say. 'In this suitcase here I have a number of other sealed envelopes. They don't all contain watches, but they do contain a prize. Now I'm gonna put these envelopes containing the watches—and, ladies and gentlemen, the envelopes are identical and unmarked—into the suitcase. And then, for one shilling I'm gonna let you buy one of these envelopes. I can't guarantee you'll all get a watch—but you'll get something. Now that's worth a gamble, ain't it? Who'll be the first to try their luck?'

Of course, the first to buy the envelopes were the 'gees', and they always got the one containing a watch—which they excitedly showed to the crowd. This invariably tempted other customers forward, but as they received their envelopes, the salesman would suggest that people didn't open them till the end of the sale—so as not to spoil the fun. 'I tell you what I'll do. Anybody who's got an unopened envelope at the end of the sale will receive an extra present.'

With this carrot, most envelopes naturally remained unopened, which, of course, prevented the mugs from discovering that instead of a watch they had got some worthless trinket for their shilling. When the sale ended, the salesman grandly handed out the 'extra prize' which was something like a pencil, worth less than a penny. And then, as people started to open their envelopes, he closed his case and quickly walked away, with the 'gees' forming a surreptitious bodyguard.

Travelling showmen united against these unwanted intruders, but amongst themselves there was fierce competition for good sites at the fairs. At some places it was customary for a stallholder to claim the site he wanted by laying down the front pole of his stall on it. Sometimes, however, the issue was only settled with a fight. But though showmen would work like hell to beat each other if they wanted a particular piece of ground, they would never play dirty. And if you were ever in trouble they were the most kind and helpful of people. It was, in fact, a community that could only survive through mutual help. Perhaps this community spirit sprang from the unpredictability of the life we led. For you never knew what awaited you. On the big day of a fair you had all been waiting for, it could rain and your takings would be practically nil.

That was bad enough when you only had yourself to support, but when you employed others, you often could not pay them, and they had to wait for their money. It was very much an up-one-day-and-down-another way of life. When the weather was good you did very nicely; when it was bad you did not eat very well. And, of course, you also had to make enough money to keep you through the winter.

That first summer, I earned an average of about £25 a week, and though that was a lot of money in 1921, it was still not enough to allow me to save for the rainy days of the winter. When winter finally arrived I went hungry more than once. Next winter, I told myself, I would have to earn some money. But how? In the Britain of the Twenties jobs were scarce, particularly for unskilled men. However, the showman's world is a small one and news and gossip spreads quickly. In this way I heard that Bertram Mills had started a Christmas circus at Olympia in London where he would let stalls and side-shows.

So, when Christmas arrived, I went to London to have a look. Mingling with the crowds I noticed that there was a certain part of Olympia where people gathered while waiting to enter the Big Top and where all the stalls faced inwards. With all these potential customers this was obviously the best place for a stall and I decided that the following winter I would have one just there.

At that time the Bertram Mills Circus was the biggest winter circus in Britain. Mills himself was originally an undertaker in the days of horse-drawn hearses. He became such an expert on horses that he was a frequent judge at shows all over Europe. Immediately after the First World War he attended a circus at

Olympia and thought, 'I can do better than that'—and he did.

But for me, deciding to have a stall at Olympia was one thing, having enough money to rent one was another. To get it I needed to increase my income during the season, so in 1922 I opened a second stall and hired a seventeen-year-old lad called Tom Bridgwater—because he came from that small country town—to run it for me. I paid him £1 a week.

This expansion meant I needed transport of my own instead of travelling by train which was, in any case, time-consuming and tiring. I bought an ex-American Army four-wheel-drive lorry for £50. I had never driven before, but the man who sold it to me gave me a quick lesson and I blithely set off. Unfortunately, I drove the first few miles with the hand-brake on—which did not help matters. The lorry itself was in pretty poor condition generally and it frequently broke down. I learned so much about the mechanics of motor vehicles through trying to keep it running, that a few years later when I had acquired five similar lorries, I saved myself thousands of pounds in the cost of repairs.

That summer saw two further developments. I added goldfish to my prizes and put Tom and myself in white coats with a 'B' embroidered on the breast pocket. At a time when most of the stallholders wore everyday working clothes and mufflers, the Butlin's 'uniform' gave an impression of an efficient, well-run stall where you got a fair deal. I also started making my stall look more distinctive—while the riding masters had introduced bigger and better attractions to the fairgrounds, the stallholders had hardly changed their type of stall and methods of working over fifty years. Coming into the business with a fresh outlook I saw the advantages of making the stalls look different and as bright and substantial as possible. They were all painted red and white, and I began building them with box pillars instead of poles; though this meant harder work erecting and pulling down, it paid off because people were attracted by them.

By the end of 1922 I was enjoying the life of a showman so much that I abandoned the idea which had occurred to me from time to time during those first two hard years, of going back to Canada. My big desire now was to earn enough to enable me to bring my mother back to England and to give her a happy and comfortable life.

The additional stall run by Tom Bridgwater had boosted my profits enough for me to be in a position to hire a site at Olympia, so at the end of the season I went again to London. I discovered that the sites were let by Mills's secretary, Miss Agnes Moore in August of each year.

Yes, for £40 I could have a small round stall, eighteen feet in diameter, for the six-week run of the circus. But I did not want just any stall, I wanted one in a special position. Miss Moore clearly could not see why I was so specific, but yes, all right, I could have one in that position. It was a vital step in my progress and I have never forgotten Miss Moore's kindness.

I was confident that I had made a good move, but not everyone agreed. Many of my fellow West Country showmen thought I would come a cropper. Indeed, I was the only travelling showman to have a stall at Olympia that year. All the other stallholders there were from seaside resorts, a different breed from the showmen I had known, and they were generally new to the business. They were what we called 'flatties'. Many of them seemed prosperous, however, and the realization of this fact was later to have a dramatic influence on my life.

Meeting these other stallholders confirmed that this was no ordinary country fair I was at. This was Olympia, London. And the customers would undoubtedly be more sophisticated and more difficult to attract.

'What you need,' I told myself, 'is something special for prizes—something better than wrist watches, alarm clocks or goldfish.' What I needed, in present-day jargon, was a gimmick. It was then I remembered Chapman's, a shop in London's Tottenham Court Road. Each time I passed it I was fascinated, for the window was full of beutiful multicoloured budgerigars, twittering and chattering away. In the cages they were often in pairs and I was touched by the affection they showed each other, real love birds.

Love Birds. Little Love Birds. Better still Lucky Little Love

72

Birds. Suddenly I knew I had found what I had been looking for. Promptly, I bought a hundred at two shillings each. They were one of the best investments I ever made. At Olympia I kept them in a large round cage in the centre of the stall and they were just as powerful an attraction as they had been in Chapman's window.

That Christmas I changed my stall in another way. Instead of customers trying to lassoo prizes with rings, they could now attempt to toss balls into coloured bowls. A ball landing in a green bowl won a small box of chocolates and in a blue bowl, a larger box. And if it plopped into a yellow bowl the prize was a Lucky Little Love Bird.

I made a profit of more than £200—a small fortune to a young man who would otherwise have been marooned in Dorney's Yard eating into his meagre savings. My judgement had proved right and the stall was a success. Ever since I have always studied the behaviour of people in relation to their surroundings before making a big decision. This practice has played a major part in my success.

But the Lucky Little Love Birds certainly played their part. Over the years I must have given away more than a million in prizes, and I may well have been responsible for the huge popularity of budgerigars in Britain today. Birds have always fascinated me and when I lived in Windlesham Lodge I kept many birds in the grounds, including cranes and pheasants. Now at my home in Jersey, peacocks freely roam the lawns and I also have more than twelve hundred budgies of all colours.

Many people believe that you should never let budgerigars out of their cages into the open air. This can be risky if you have a solitary bird, but when there are several they invariably return, guided by the song of the budgies in the aviary. I first discovered this through giving my Lucky Little Love Birds as prizes. People tried to win them for their children, and when they did the bird cage was often given to the child to carry. Sometimes, the child, excited, let the cage door open and the budgie escaped. Generally it would head back to the other birds on my stall. I felt sorry for the kiddies when this happened

73

and if the customers came back to me with an empty cage I gave them another bird.

The year after introducing my Lucky Little Love Birds I began casting around for a new gimmick to use at Olympia. Once again I thought of pets and during a Sunday morning walk I found the answer. Or so I thought. But this time my idea backfired, and I found myself in trouble with the great Mr Bertram Mills himself.

5

'Hurrah! It's Butlin's!'

BERTRAM Mills, resplendent in topper and morning suit, a blue carnation in his button hole, glowered down at me. 'Get these bloody things out of here,' he boomed.

The 'bloody things' were lovable little puppies in a basket on my hoop-la stall at Bertram Mills's Circus of 1924. They were the successors to my Lucky Little Love Birds and I had hoped they would be equally popular prizes.

I had had the idea strolling down Club Row in Shoreditch, where dogs of all kinds were bought and sold. I often spent happy hours there on a Sunday morning, admiring them, and particularly the puppies. There was something magnetic about these cuddly playful creatures, with their large innocent eyes—they were always surrounded by people. Obviously puppies had that magical something that made people want to own one, or buy one for their children. They seemed to be perfect prizes. So on my next visit to Club Row I bought twenty 'Lovable Little Puppies', and the following day presented them at Olympia.

It is general practice among showmen, when they first open for the day, to increase the customer's chances of winning the big prizes. The successful ones will then usually walk about the fair with their trophies creating interest and at the same time unwittingly advertising the stalls. At Olympia that morning I put out more yellow bowls—the ones the ball had to land in to win the top prize. Soon ten of the puppies had been won. And, as I had hoped, the winners were walking about Olympia with the cuddly little darlings, being the focus of much fuss and attention. It seemed that my latest 'gimmick' was going to be a big success. Unfortunately, I had overlooked one important fact: young puppies have a tendency to misbehave themselves. Which is precisely what they did.

In those days at Olympia it was quite common to see women visitors wearing expensive fur coats. Not surprisingly they did not take kindly to puppies, no matter how endearing, misbehaving themselves all over their clothes. It was not long before a number of very irate customers, including two ladies in fur coats, presented themselves at my stall and complained about puppies that were not coat-trained. Someone had also complained to Bertram Mills himself—hence the appearance of the great man at my stall, like the wrath of God, peremptorily ordering me to get rid of the animals. Some were brusquely handed back to me—so I had almost all twenty to dispose of again.

I decided to give them away, but that proved more easily decided than done. For while people love a bargain, they are highly suspicious of anything being offered free. They think there is a catch somewhere. For hours I stood in front of my stall trying to give puppies away.

'Anyone want a puppy?' I cried. 'They're free. Take one home for the kiddies.' But not one single person accepted my offer. In the end I had to take my lovely little puppies to the Battersea Dogs' Home.

That winter is memorable, however, for a happier event. For by the end of the Olympia season I could afford to bring my mother over from Canada. I bought a luxury caravan or 'living van' for £600 on the 'never never' and together we toured the fairs, towing the caravan with the four-wheel-drive American ex-Army truck. It was like old times—except that it was a faster and less strenuous way of travelling than in the old gypsy caravan pulled by Blackbird.

Unhappily, this new life-style did not last long. While going down a step hill, the lorry's brakes failed. I managed to navigate a couple of corners, but as we careered round another bend the caravan tore away from its couplings. It dived into a deep gully and was smashed beyond repair. As Mother and I looked sadly at the wreck I suddenly realized that, with the obstinacy for which I seem to be notorious, I had ignored the advice of my fellow showmen to insure the van.

Mother was a greater asset than perhaps at that moment I seemed to her. With her great experience of fairgrounds she was able to take over my other stall and within three years I had four stalls and six people working for me. But before I reached this stage, something happened that was nearly to finish me as a showman.

Very soon after I began travelling the fairgrounds I realized that the stallholders, the people who ran the hoop-las and the roll-a-penny boards, were getting a raw deal from the riding masters who usually controlled the letting of the 'ground' at the fairs. The riding masters were grouped in families. Perhaps the most famous was the Collins family, headed by Pat Collins, who later became an MP. They controlled most of the fairgrounds in the Midlands and operated several complete fairs. Also in the Midlands were the Thurstons and the Farrars. In the West Country were the Hills, the Heals, the Andertons and the Rowlands. The Studs, the Whites and Danters controlled Wales, the Cordonas were big in Scotland, and in the London area there were the Wilsons, the Bolsworths, the Grays and the Nicholls.

If these families were the aristocrats of the fairgrounds, the stallholders were the serfs. And, like the serfs of olden times, they were at the mercy of their masters. In the early Twenties, some riding masters started charging stallholders rents that made it difficult for them to earn a living. On the fairgrounds feelings grew. At night, after the customers had left, there were fights between stallholders and the riding masters' workmen. Gangs from both sides roamed about, smashing caravan windows with long poles. It was getting nasty.

I have always been an independent character. Ever since I left the Army I have hated taking orders, and I have never liked my livelihood to depend on others. So it was natural that I rebelled against the unfair dominance of the riding masters. Or perhaps it was simply that I had no more sense. But whatever the reason, I became the leader of the West of England stallholders in their fights. To give ourselves strength in numbers we formed the Stallholders Association, but the riding masters proved too powerful for us. They retaliated where it hurt by refusing to let 'ground' at any price to members of the Association. One by one the stallholders, faced with ruin, gave in. After three months the Association collapsed. But it was not the end of the affair for me. In today's industrial jargon I was victimized. For the riding masters refused to let me 'ground'.

To continue in business, I had to find fairgrounds not controlled by the big riding masters. This meant the smaller fairs, church fêtes and the like—and so I returned to the West Country. Yet these little fairs proved highly profitable, and soon I had more stalls than I could get 'ground' for. This led me to form my own fair, complete with a small family circus which I hired.

It was an exciting but exhausting life. We were up at dawn and on our way to the next fair by eight or nine o'clock. There we spent more back-breaking hours erecting the stalls, the rides and the circus tent. Sometimes I went several days and nights with almost no sleep. But I was young and resilient and I enjoyed it all. And I still had enough energy left to take an interest in the girls.

One night in 1924, at the start of the autumn fair in the small Devon town of Tiverton, I noticed a good-looking brown-haired girl standing by the 'spinner' I was operating. A spinner is a stall with a large arrow which in those days the operator swung by hand round a circle of numbers. You bought a threepenny numbered ticket and if the arrow stopped at your number you won a prize.

The girl did not buy many tickets, but she came and stood by the stall every night. Eventually we began to talk and I learned that her name was Dolly. She was a pleasant Devonshire girl, bubbly and good company, and I liked her

78

very much. One night I walked her home to her parents' fish and chip shop where she lived with them and her three other sisters.

When we moved to the next fair about thirty miles away I drove to see her each day. Even when we were back in Dorney's Yard I visited her regularly. We fell in love and in 1925 we married in Tiverton Parish Church.

The next summer I operated some hoop-la stalls as a concessionaire at an amusement park run by the White Brothers on Barry Island where the idea of my English holiday camps had come to me. Mother stayed at Barry to run the stalls there, and Dolly and I went back to tour the West Country fairgrounds with our stalls. Life was good. My business was developing and I was happy with Dolly in our little 'living wagon'. I whistled at the wheel of my ex-Army lorry. Gradually, by taking out from my profits only enough to live on and ploughing back the remainder, I expanded until I had five lorries and a score of men working for me. Like my stalls the lorries were painted red and white, with BUTLIN'S painted in bold gold lettering on the side.

About this time I also added the slogan 'Hurrah! It's Butlin's' on the side of my vans. I have always felt that when you have a good slogan people tend to say it aloud when they read it. That certainly happened with mine. Whenever we rolled into a town the kids would run alongside the lorries shouting 'Hurrah! It's Butlin's!'

Later this was emblazoned on the banners which adorned my 'rides' and it hung over the entrances to all my amusement parks.

These innovations, however, did not endear me to some of the old-time showmen—and this lead to trouble for me within the Showmen's Guild of Great Britain. The Guild, which was founded by my uncle, Marshall Hill and Pat Collins (the riding master who became an MP), is a close-knit and powerful association of travelling showmen. Unless you are a member there are many fairs at which you cannot hire 'ground'. With the help of Uncle Marshall I had become a member, though normally only those born in a caravan were eligible. I had not been, of course, but Uncle fought for me. 'All right,' he said, 'he wasn't born in a caravan, but his mother was, and he spent many of his early years in one.' With his support I was elected and I have always been deeply grateful to him.

For many years Uncle Marshall was Vice President of the Guild, with Pat Collins as President. When Marshall became seriously ill, Pat Collins stood down to enable Marshall to end his days as President—a touching gesture, and one that is typical of the spirit among showmen. It is, however, a spirit that can evaporate under the heat of competition and I experienced this in the mid-Twenties. Though I was a member of the Guild, some veteran showmen always regarded me as a newcomer, calling me a 'flattie'. And when my new-style methods began to hit their business a few of them tried to have me expelled from the Guild on the grounds that I was providing 'unfair competition'. Luckily for me, the move got no support from other Guild members.

As the Twenties ticked by I noticed a change in the fairs we visited. Many of them were held on Bank or local holidays, big events in the life of the district, and had always been attended by large crowds. But gradually the crowds were beginning to dwindle. This was worrying, for we relied on these fairs for the major part of our takings. What was happening? Were fairs becoming less popular? Were we losing customers to the picture houses? It did not take much probing to discover the cause.

It was the charabanc, that early lumbering product of the motor age, the predecessor of today's luxury, air-conditioned, all 'mod-con' coaches. With the arrival of the charabanc people were escaping from their often dismal surroundings to spend a day at the seaside. It occurred to me that it would be good business to follow them.

As with many things in life the impetus to translate thought into action came about accidentally. It happened during the 1926/27 season at Olympia, and a man with the unlikely name of Albert Cronkshaw was the unwitting cause of it all.

I first noticed him in one of the bars in Olympia, where he was a regular customer. Obviously he was not short of a bob or two, which suggested he had a good business somewhere. Over a drink he had no objection to telling me where—he was a 'flattie', and he did not have the competitiveness of the showman born and bred.

Albert Cronkshaw came from Skegness. I had never heard of the place. From the sound of it I thought it must be in Scotland. But when I met another man in the bar called Alfie Smith, and discovered he also had stalls in Skegness, I decided to have a look at the place.

'I was no longer a travelling showman'

S KEGNESS turned out to be not in Scotland at all, but on the Lincolnshire coast just north of The Wash. It was reached on the old London and North Eastern Railway from King's Cross. As soon as the Olympia season ended I took a train there. I sat in the carriage wondering what kind of place it would be, for I was going to a part of the country totally new to me. The view from the window, as we steamed north through the London suburbs and on to Peterborough and Grantham revealed scenes vastly different from those I had known in the west of England. There was more industry; there were more people—and the countryside itself was not as beautiful. Whilst I realized this was not the industrial north, it gave me an inkling of why people wanted to get away from their homes and factories to the seaside.

When we reached Lincolnshire, the character of the landscape changed, and we rattled on and on through flat featureless fields stretching into the distance on either side. We stopped at Boston and Sleaford and tiny places with names like Hubberts Bridge and Swineshead. Was Skegness at the back of beyond? I began to have doubts about the whole idea.

Skegness itself didn't do much to ease my doubts. It consisted of little more than two streets and a short promenade called the Grand Parade. There was Lumley Road which ran from the railway station as far as the Queen

Victoria Memorial Clock Tower on the Parade, and the High Street which ran parallel. On one side of the clock tower there were about twenty small hotels and boarding houses. On the other, where the road ran alongside sand dunes, there was a pier and a small wooden theatre. Later I would come to know George Burrows, the owner of this theatre, well. As Skegness and my enterprises expanded, he helped me to run several carnivals and national brass band festivals.

My 'flattie' friends from Olympia had a number of stalls on this road. Beyond were more sand dunes and behind them nothing but fields, a farm and an area known locally as 'The Jungle'. The whole town was so small you could stand outside the station and see cows grazing in the fields.

It was a chilly, grey winter's day with gusts of rain driving along the front and it seemed impossible that anywhere could look so dreary. But as I tried to imagine the place in summer, I sensed that it could have a big future. For with the growth of charabanc trips and motoring it could easily become a popular centre for trippers and holiday makers, drawing particularly from the teeming North and Midlands. My instinct was right: within ten years Skegness was transformed into a bustling, thriving resort with a sea front as impressive as any in the country. Today it has a population of 14,000 and attracts 1,500,000 visitors a year. 'The Jungle' is now a built-up area of residential houses and hotels.

Before catching the train back to London that bleak February day in 1927, I decided to have a permanent amusement site in Skegness. I had scouted along the sea front opposite The Jungle, and picked out a place. Inquiries had led me to a firm of solicitors who informed me that the land, including the sand-dunes, belonged to the Earl of Scarborough. 'Oh, the Earl would never dream of letting the land for a fairground, even if the council gave consent,' I was told firmly, as soon as I had outlined my plans for an amusement park.

However, on the principle of nothing ventured, I approached the Earl direct. He soon appreciated that my ideas could bring additional prosperity to the town and instructed his agent, a Mr Foster, to lease for the summer a stretch in front of The Jungle, about a hundred yards long, for £50. It consisted mainly of sand dunes and before it could be used as an amusement site the dunes had to be levelled. This was a sizeable job and I could not afford to pay to have it done, for I would have no income until the season started at Easter.

How could I get the sand removed cheaply or, better still, for nothing? Thinking about it, I realized that sand was a comparatively expensive necessity for some people—builders, for instance. So I advertised the sand at five shillings a lorryload, provided the buyer moved it himself. It was such a bargain that builders from all over Lincolnshire took up the offer. In a couple of months my stretch of sand dunes was levelled.

In August 1977—to leap forward for a moment—I was invited to switch on the famous Skegness illuminations which had grown from the first few coloured electric lights I'd put up on the promenade. I stayed at the County Hotel; this stands in part of what was once The Jungle, where I had my first stalls. Looking out from the County now you see a broad expanse of gardens and the smooth, green swards of bowling and putting greens that fringe the large solarium.

I had been invited to perform the switching-on ceremony, I was told, because of the part I had played in putting Skegness on the map. Certainly I helped it by attracting people to the camp and by publicizing its name, but there were many others who contributed towards its spectacular development—particularly the Borough Surveyor in the Twenties and Thirties, Roland Jenkins, and a lively bunch of councillors. It was their vision that created most of the Skegness we know today.

There was also, of course, the artist John Hassall whose famous poster, showing a jolly, round fisherman leaping along the sand above the slogan 'Skegness is so bracing', helped greatly to publicize the town. The poster had originally been commissioned by the Great Northern Railway in 1908 and was adopted by Skegness later. I liked it so much I had a metal buttonhole badge made of the figure for campers to wear.

84

Though Hassall became closely associated with Skegness as a result of the poster he never visited the town until I met him at a London club in 1936. When I discovered this remarkable fact I said, 'You'd better come and have a look at the place.'

But at Easter in 1927 I opened at Skegness with four hoop-la stalls, a tower slide (where you careered down a spiral chute on a mat), a home-made haunted house, and a small electric car track. The following year, 1928, I added a scenic railway from France, and acquired my second site. It was at Mablethorpe just along the coast. I was no longer a travelling showman, though I still lived like one sharing with Dolly a caravan parked in a field near the clock tower. Mother lived in another wagon parked alongside. The days were as long and hard as though we were still on the road. Every morning, we piled into my silver and red Daimler and went to the site. It was usually midnight before we returned.

It was a period of fast expansion. Within a few years the council granted me a bigger and better site, with the sole concession for the amusements, providing I allocated space to the other showmen who had booths and shacks straggling the promenade. Soon I was employing thirty men, and then fifty. At week-ends, with part-timers we called 'strappers', I had about a hundred working for me.

Such a work-force created its own problems, for there were always a few dishonest ones who tried to fiddle the takings. With all the stalls standing on the beach, one favourite trick was to drop coins into the sand and recover them early in the morning. To beat this fiddle, my cousin Trevor Watts and I used to return to the site after everyone had gone and search the sand. We usually found £2 or £3 worth of coins, a lot of money in those days when the games only cost one old penny or tuppence a go.

Of course, there were all kinds of tricks for the light-fingered and I was engaged in a constant battle of wits to counter them. There was one man who came to work on a bike and kept his trouser clips on all the time. One night as he was leaving I made him take them off and out from the bottom of his trousers fell a cascade of coins. Another chap pulled a similar trick by wearing an open-necked shirt and a very tight belt around the top of his trousers. Pretending to scratch his chest he would drop coins down inside his shirt and they were caught in the top of the tightly-belted trousers. I stopped that one by making him fasten his collar and wear a tie.

I soon learned that one way to cut down the fiddling was to stop people having an excuse to put their hands in their pockets. So I made it a rule that cigarette packets and matches had to be kept out in the open on the stall counters. Eventually all my fairground employees wore pocketless jackets which came down to below their trouser pockets.

As the amount of money scraped up from the sand indicates, these fiddles could add up to a sizeable sum; but they also represented a worrying human problem. Most of the men would begin fiddling just a little and then gradually step up their thefts as they got greedy. I tried to catch them in the early stages, when they could be let off with a warning, rather than allow them to reach the stage where I had no option but to sack them. But it was very unusual for any of my employees to leave me of their own accord. I always made a point of paying good wages, for when you have staff dealing direct with the public it is essential to keep them happy. They are the ones who mix with and talk to the customers, and they can quickly sour the atmosphere.

Throughout these years of growth, I put every pound I earned into new equipment, and to attract customers I engaged various performers to give free shows. They included Dare-Devil Peggy, a one-legged diver who plunged into a tank of water ten feet deep from a height of sixty feet, a team of trick cyclists and a German girl who did gymnastics on top of a fifty-foot pole. She fell and was killed soon after leaving me.

Someone else who met an equally sad fate was more foolish than brave. The Reverend Harold Davidson, the Rector of Stiffkey, a little Norfolk village, was one of the scandalous figures of the Thirties, so much so that he pushed the rise of Hitler and unemployment off the front pages of the popular newspapers. A dapper little silver-haired man, an Oxford MA who entered the Church from the stage, he regularly went to

86

London, where, wearing a winged collar and a homburg hat and smoking a sixpenny cigar, he strolled about the West End chatting up young girls—some of whom were prostitutes. Eventually his conduct was exposed in a Sunday newspaper. He was dubbed the 'Prostitutes' Padre' and as a result of all the fuss he was 'tried' by the Church in 1932, charged with pinching the bottoms of waitresses in Lyons teashops, embracing a female in a Chinese restaurant and generally pestering girls. He was found guilty and defrocked.

To make a living he cashed in on his notoriety and became one of the freak sideshows at Blackpool, sitting in a barrel and fasting. After that he turned up at Skegness, wearing his dog-collar, with a lion called Freddy in a cage. Though the side-show was not on my site, I remember Freddy well. He was a friendly lion who loved to have his stomach tickled. Unfortunately, the former cleric had a habit of poking Freddy with a walking stick, and one day he poked Freddy once too often—the lion hit back with his paw, breaking Mr Stiffkey's neck.

Like all seaside resorts, Skegness had its dubious side-shows. There was 'The World's Biggest Pig', for instance. It was owned by an Australian called Joe Gardener who had come to Skegness, hired a site from another showman and started banging the big drum about this big pig. He created a lot of interest by announcing that it had a bad tooth which was causing the animal pain and he was going to have the offending molar removed and replaced with a gold one. Nobody had actually seen this remarkable pig, though he said it would be arriving by road shortly. But a week before Whitsuntide, as the fair was due to open, he came to me and asked, 'Where can I buy a big pig?'

I was unable to help him, but he found one in the area—though it certainly was not the biggest in the world. Nevertheless he managed to fool people that it was, by the simple expedient of standing it on a raised platform within a circular barrier. From outside the show you could not see the pig, but you could see the people who had paid to go in looking upwards. Thus were you led to believe that it must be a big pig, and moved to purchase a ticket to see for yourself.

The same illusion—in reverse this time—was used later to convince people they were seeing 'The World's Smallest Pony'. This was merely an ordinary Shetland Pony with its shaggy coat cropped very short—making an already small pony look even smaller. It stood in a pit in deep straw where people looked down on it. Again they could be seen from outside, giving the impression that they were observing a very small pony indeed.

Such memories are part of the kaleidoscope of my early years at Skegness leading up to the War. Yet one event dominates all others—the building of my first holiday camp. And the wherewithal to achieve this long-cherished ambition came from the Dodgems.

Shortly after arriving in Skegness, I had built my first big ride: a track around which small, battery-operated cars, called 'Custer Cars', were driven. The following Christmas at Olympia I met an American manufacturer of fairground rides. He told me about a completely new attraction called Dodgems and sketched me details. They were a big advance on 'cars' I had seen in Toronto after the First World War. The nearest equivalent we had in Britain were electric-powered runabouts shaped like a tub and encircled with steel buffers. You steered them with a wheel, but they went in the opposite direction from the way you turned it. 'Dodgem Cars' however, were miniature motor cars with all-round buffers and a conventional steering wheel. Their big attraction was the way in which the drivers could biff other cars, or use their skill to avoid being bumped themselves. I quickly saw that this combination of jovial aggression and fun, as well as all that dodging and bumping, would make them a popular attraction.

So I returned to my caravan and counted out my capital. It amounted to £1,800, but my American friend told me I would need at least £2,000 for a batch of Dodgems. I borrowed the remaining £200 and wrote off to the manufacturers. As a result, the first Dodgems in Britain bumped and weaved at Skegness at Whitsun, 1928. They were an immediate success and, spotting a winner, I sought—and fortunately acquired—the sole agency for selling them in Europe.

News of the Dodgems quickly spread through the fairgrounds and I sold hundreds of cars. I also put them into fairs on a share basis, supplying the cars free for a share of the takings. On one occasion, I gave some Dodgems to a friend on the understanding that he paid for them when he could. That friend was Billy Smart, who in those days was a travelling showman with various stalls and small rides in a tent. Billy's success with the Dodgems helped him on his way to starting his famous circus.

The Dodgems were also a major turning point in my life, for with their success I came into the really big money. It was from this point that I was on the way towards realizing my holiday camp dream. I was becoming a man of substance and also of property. For at the age of thirty I was living in a house of my own, instead of a caravan, for the first time since I had left my mother's home in Toronto.

Over the next few years I built up a chain of seaside amusement parks. After Mablethorpe came Hayling Island, then Bognor, Felixstowe, Portsmouth, Bexhill and the Isle of Man. My mother ran the park at Bognor and later moved to Hayling Island. Even so, I spent little time in my new home.

Keeping in touch with all the sites meant travelling some two thousand miles a week, sometimes working all day at one site and then travelling through the night to the next. I was losing a lot of sleep this way, so I bought an ambulance, fitted it with a bed and slept while I was driven through the night. It was a big improvement—except that when we went round a bend fast, I fell out of bed!

In addition to the Dodgems I now began to acquire a number of big rides, like the Big Dipper or Figure Eight. I bought this in France and copied two more from it. Most of my rides were bought on the 'never never' and I was constantly stretched to the limit financially. At this time everything was going well, apart from one disaster when an amusement park which I had fitted out at a cost of over £10,000 burned down. Because I'd had to scratch around for every penny, I had had nothing to spare for insurance. Alas, I had ignored a salutory lesson from the time when my uninsured caravan had crashed some years before, but after this experience I never did again!

In 1930 I needed to borrow £5,000 to pay part of the rent of my sites at Olympia, Kelvin Hall, Glasgow and Waverley Hall, Edinburgh. My bank manager explained that he could not lend that amount of money without the permission of head office—and that would take some time. However, I needed the loan immediately.

When I told my old friend Bob Larkin of my probem he said, 'Why don't you go to my bank in Streatham? If necessary I'll guarantee the loan.'

I was not too hopeful of getting such a big loan from a bank where I was not known, even with Bob's guarantee, but I went along to Barclays Bank at 123, Mitcham Lane and saw the manager, Mr Howard Roberts. It was a well-omened meeting, for Mr Roberts loaned me the £5,000. Years later he revealed why he had taken such a risk.

> Young Butlin ambled into my office looking like one of his own workmen. He did not try to hide the fact, either. I could not afford to make any mistakes, but there was little doubt in my mind about his character. What most impressed me was the fact that he had brought along the electric motor which worked the Big Dipper he was erecting on a fairground in London. He had it outside in the back seat of his car. He had it with him because if the motor was fitted incorrectly it could cause an accident. Butlin was making sure it would not be fitted in his absence. I had to respect that sort of man, and we hit it off together immediately. I knew he was going places.

Howard Roberts died around 1961, but I am still grateful to him for his faith in me. I repaid it by moving my personal and business accounts to his branch. In fact, I kept my personal account there until I retired to Jersey in 1968, and the company account stayed at the branch until Butlin's was sold to the Rank Organization in 1972. Something like £400 million must have passed through those accounts. When I first went to see Howard Roberts his bank was a small branch, but ten years later it had been rebuilt and greatly expanded—solely to cope with the immense amount of Butlin business.

To help provide work for the men who operated my fairgrounds during the summer, I started Christmas fairs. For the same reason I opened nine amusement centres with Dodgems, stalls and pin-table machines in various parts of London. One of these sites was in a large building that had previously been a department store in Coventry Street, just off Piccadilly Circus, and this led to my involvement in what the newspapers called 'The Battle of Piccadilly'. Most of the clubs and entertainment sites in the area were then controlled by Mrs Meyrick, the legendary 'Nightclub Queen' of the Twenties. Maybe she disliked a stranger moving into her territory, though whether she really was behind what happened I don't know. What I do know is that one night my amusement centre was taken over by a gang of former Irish Guardsmen engaged by, of all people, a manager I had fired a few months before. They barricaded the place and when I arrived there the following morning I couldn't get in. Naturally, I took legal advice right away, but I was told that action through the courts would be long-winded. I don't like to be beaten at anything, particularly by barefaced thuggery, so somewhat reluctantly I decided to do something about it myself.

I organized my own gang, which included a few beefy fairground men, and we broke into the place that night and regained possession. The following morning, when the other gang came back, they tried to throw us out and a stiff battle ensued before we sent them packing.

This was all very unpleasant, but it had its lighter side. In the centre of the site was a large cage, containing about fifty monkeys, and during the struggle someone opened the doors. In no time monkeys were gleefully scrambling all over the place, and most of them escaped into Piccadilly Circus. They climbed over roofs and on to windowsills. Some even swung on the famous electric signs. Hundreds of people gathered to watch their antics and for a while traffic had to be diverted. Catching them was easier said than done and, although we trapped a few, the rest scattered all over London. For weeks afterwards there were repercussions. It seemed that everyone in London who had a broken vase brought it to me, claiming it was the work of one of my monkeys which had invaded their house.

My main interests however, were still my steadily-increasing seaside amusement parks, and they constantly needed new attractions. One of my most exciting 'finds' was the Wall of Death, where a motor cyclist hurtles round a perpendicular wooden track. The first one in Britain came from Australia and I saw it at the 1935 Newcastle Exhibition. It was certainly thrilling, and it looked highly dangerous. But I had done a lot of motor cycling myself as a boy in Canada and I felt it was not as dangerous as it looked.

So I had a Wall of my own built, bought an Indian motor bike and tried it out. As I suspected, it was mainly a question of nerve and confidence. But, as I did not propose to spend my time as a Wall of Death rider, I had to convince others. I brought together a number of young men who worked for me, and gave them a demonstration. Eighteen agreed to let me train them to become 'Death Defying' riders. They performed on the nine Walls of Death I had had constructed, which were sent out on 'shares' to various fairgrounds.

My most foolhardy do-it-yourself exercise, however, was when I trained a group of six young lions during my early days at Skegness. I have always been fond of animals, but I suspect that half the attraction here was the opportunity to wear the lion tamer's uniform of breeches, red coat and top hat. Not to mention the fact that lion tamers are admired for their courage and skill particularly by the ladies!

Like riding the Wall of Death, lion taming not only demands skill, but a lot of confidence. For lions have extraordinary keen perception and quickly sense a person's frame of mind merely from his physical movements. If a trainer walks into the cage in a confident manner, the lions treat him with respect. They appreciate they have met their master.

But let the trainer enter nervously or hesitantly, and they will promptly play him up. The natural instinct of a lion is to test his trainer by rushing at him. If he stands his ground, the lion is confused and does not press home his attack. It is vital—indeed, a matter of life and death—to make clear who is boss.

Training these young lions was a fascinating experience and one I thoroughly enjoyed—though I am not suggesting I was in the same league as a professional. But I did teach them to do a few simple tricks.

Perhaps I had a particularly amiable set of lions. I even persuaded one of them into the back seat of my Austin Seven and drove it around Skegness. But despite fancying myself in my uniform, my lion taming career did not last long. This was not due to the lions but to some Polar Bears which were also in my Skegness Zoo. Polar Bears are dangerous animals because they are not intelligent enough to understand what their trainer is trying to teach them. Indeed, these particular bears turned on their trainer and killed him. After that, I decided to leave animal training to the professionals.

Nevertheless, the Skegness Zoo was so successful that I opened others in my various amusement parks. This was a venture that eventually led me to my only brush with the law, and to the inside of a prison cell.

It all began in the summer of 1933 with a lion called Rex. I had opened a small zoo at my Bognor amusement park and arranged for a lorryload of animals, including Rex, to be brought from Skegness. But when the lorry arrived there was no Rex. Somehow word got about that he had escaped. Before I could check whether Rex had actually been loaded on to the lorry at Skegness, a young local reporter asked me whether I had a lion missing.

'I don't know,' I said in all honesty, 'but we should have had one in a load of animals from Skegness. Mine is not the only zoo around here, though, and there's also a circus in the district.'

93

However, that was enough for him and he sent off a story to the national newspapers about a ferocious lion roaming about Sussex. Once it was in the papers everybody began seeing lions. I was doubtful that there was a lion on the loose but if it was Rex, I knew that he was perfectly harmless. What *was* certain was that the story was good publicity for my zoo, so I suggested we start hunting the lion. With a convoy of press cars in attendance, we dashed about Sussex; though we found no lions, we captured plenty of headlines. 'At any moment,' wrote one imaginative reporter, 'we may hear the jungle roar.'

Then suddenly, the affair took a more serious turn. A farmer telephoned me to say he had found one of his sheep mauled and dead in a field. We went to look at it and certainly it had been badly slashed about. It might have been attacked by a lion.

Now people began to get scared. The local schools were closed and the Territorials called out. One man said he slept with a twelve bore shotgun by his bed. The headlines got bigger: GREAT LION HUNT. HOLIDAY MAKERS ARMED WITH RIFLES.

By now I knew that if there was a lion roaming the countryside, it definitely was not Rex. He had not been loaded on to the lorry, and was still at Skegness. As the days ticked by, I became convinced there was no lion at all. I had gone along with the story when it seemed harmless fun, and I had not been sure whether there was a lion loose or not. But now it was clearly time to stop. However, lion hysteria had reached such a pitch that if I had tried to deny that a lion was loose, or said it never had been, nobody would have believed me. In any case they would have probably asked how I knew.

I decided, therefore, that if people wanted a lion, they could have one. Rex was brought down from Skegness at night, and I prepared to announce that he had been captured. There was only one snag. Though Rex was innocuous, he was a pretty lively lion and he certainly did not look as though he had spent several days wandering the countryside. So before the press arrived to photograph him I gave him a more bedraggled appearance by throwing a bucket of green distemper over

94

him. He looked as though he had been haunting the filthiest ditches of Sussex!

The ruse worked perfectly. Once everyone knew that Rex was safely behind bars, the hysteria subsided and everything returned to normal. That, I thought, was the end of the affair. But I was wrong, and eventually I found myself at Lewes Assizes with the reporter who started the story, my Bognor zoo manager and the farmer owner of the dead sheep, charged with 'conspiracy to commit a public mischief by certain false statements that a lion had escaped'.

My solicitor was Vernon Stokes, whom I'd first met in Portsmouth when I leased a site there. Mr Stokes later became a senior figure with the Football Association, and chairman of Portsmouth Football Club, and deputy managing director of Butlin's. But for now he was just my solicitor on a case which lasted for more than two days and on both nights all the accused were locked up in the cells at the Assizes. At least, I knew how Rex felt. I told the court the truth about my involvement and my reasons for faking the re-capture of the lion, and both I and my zoo manager were found 'Not Guilty' and given costs. The jury decided that the reporter had blown up the story and that he and the farmer had planted the dead sheep. They were fined £30 and £10 respectively for 'effecting public mischief'.

Summing up, the judge, Mr Justice Charles, said: 'It might have been a showman's stunt or a reporter's stunt, but so far as Butlin was concerned it was a little difficult to see what he had to gain by such ridiculous nonsense. What he had to lose was pretty obvious.'

Greatly relieved, I sent a telegram to my mother at Olympia saying, 'Justice has been done.' She replied: 'Appeal at once.'

'Just a quiet little man'

I HAD started at Olympia in the winter of 1922-23 with one hoop-la stall. Ten years later I had Dodgems, a Big Dipper and various other rides. Now I was ambitious to obtain the sole rights to supply all the rides and main attractions at Olympia for the next season.

Soon after Christmas I made up my mind to tackle Bertram Mills about it. I climbed the stairs to his office in the roof of Olympia and walked along a corridor to a door marked 'Private'. I knocked and went in. The great man motioned me to a chair. I had told my foreman I would be away for no more than half an hour. It was about two hours later before I finally left Mills's office, but for £10,000—a far cry from the £40 I paid for my first stall—I had the concession for the next Christmas fair.

In this era of television and ever-more sophisticated entertainment it is interesting to recall what a funfair of the Thirties was like. An excerpt from an article in the *Sunday Express* of 15 January 1933, by Cedric Belfrage evokes the atmosphere of Olympia, then the biggest winter fair in the country, far better than I can.

> A tour of the side-shows at Olympia is much the same as a visit to one of those Dreamlands which are to be found on fronts and piers of seaside resorts. You are brought once again face to face with those strange wandering folk,

the fair showmen who sojourn only a few weeks under Bertram Mills's capacious Kensington roof-tree and then are off again for the long spring, summer and autumn peregrination around the fairs of the country. . . .

Yet Olympia this year, and other fair grounds the country over, show how the old type of fair showman is gradually disappearing. At Olympia you find all the regulation freaks—the tatooed lady, the giantesses, the midget, the sword-swallower (Professor Wolowski), the fat lady, and 'England's premier snake-charmer'—bunched together in one booth and on view at a sixpenny piece for the lot.

There are fewer of the old-fashioned side-shows—ring and dart-throwing, fortune telling, shooting galleries and the like—than ever before. Taking their place are mammoth novelty rides and up-to-date diversions of all kinds: ghost trains, mirror mazes, 'Dodgems', whoopee speedways, Graf Zeppelin flying rides and the like.

In the middle of it all a lone flea circus impresario plies his trade, using the same quaint patter in encouraging his tiny charges as he has used for many years, and his father before him. Nearby is Zimmy, who lost both his legs in his youth in a street accident and has toured the world as the 'Legless Swimmer'. At Olympia he found this billing did not pull in the public, so he changed it to 'The Human Fish—A Puzzle of Medical Science', and receipts immediately bounded up.

The brisk business being done by the flea circus and by Zimmy under his new billing show that the fair-going public is still to a considerable extent hooey-minded, still fond of the naïve, exaggerated quality inherent in fair tradition.

But Big Business has entered the world of the fair, and the public is being taught to demand big value for money spent. A 'human fish' may extract the money from their pockets more easily than a legless swimmer, but when they get inside they want to see something pretty good, and if Zimmy could not provide it he would go out of business.

After painting this vivid and changing scene, Belfrage was kind enough to devote the remainder of his article to me. I reproduce it here not for any egotistical reasons, but because it gives a pithy picture of where I stood in 1933:

Big Business has come into the English fair world in the person of Billy Butlin. . . . From the start he was the perfect successful man in embryo, for while the old-fashioned showmen who set up their booths alongside him merely saw their business as a means of making a modest income, Butlin visualized it as the potential source of a magnate's fortune. Not for him the hand-to-mouth gipsy life, the crazy hooey and ballyhoo by which other showmen generally bluffed a willing public out of coppers.

'I worked on a fair profit basis, and always gave the public value for money spent,' says Billy drily. 'To that I attribute my success.'

He can already, at thirty-three, present to open-mouthed reporters as impresive a collection of statistics and facts about his enterprises as any big business mogul in the country. He has 900 men in his permanent employ, and 2,000 during the six-months' summer season. Not one of them has ever worked for any other showman. He has his own workshops and specialists for designing ever-newer and more up-to-date rides and side-shows. By means of his special weekly carnivals at seaside resorts he has raised nearly £20,000 for charity.

Five hundred thousand pounds of capital is involved in the various enterprises under his control, which earn him an annual profit of between £20,000 and £25,000. The 'Dodgem' rides, of which he has many, alone cost £2,500 each.

And thus it is that Big Business is modernising the fair, erasing the curious traditions of the fairground which have been handed down from past centuries. The cry 'Boys—are you sports?' will soon be a dim echo in the fairgrounds of England, and William E. Butlin, the spirit of common sense, fair play and the value of money will soar on to ever greater heights of glory, building as he goes another monument to the imperishable saga of British enterprise.

Some of Mr Belfrage's eulogy is embarrassing, but journalistic exaggeration apart, he accurately pin-pointed changes that were taking place in the fairground world.

The newspapers seemed fascinated by the fact that I was not a raucous, flamboyant fairground barker but, as the London *Evening News* of 23 August 1933 put it, 'just a quiet little man, inclined to be shy and still quite young enough to enjoy a ride on one of his own roundabouts'.

In addition to running the Olympia fair, I now had a chain of seaside amusement parks. What kind of entertainment did they provide?

At Skegness in the summer of 1935, eight ever-expanding years after I had opened my first small fair on the levelled sand-dunes there, I had various big rides, a ghost train, a Noah's Ark roundabout and—of course—the Dodgems.

There were the Skeggy Mystic Water Caverns, where you sailed in small boats through a series of caves, a crazy house with distorting mirrors and a wind trap, a mirror maze and a cakewalk.

By 1935 most of my amusement parks also contained a zoo, and I was particularly proud of the one at Skegness. Among the animals I had collected were six lions, three bears—one of them a fine black fellow who danced all day—a leopard, a black panther, a kangaroo, a zebra, several seals, various kinds of monkeys and a mongoose which went for a constitutional with its keeper every morning. There was also a pond with a variety of water birds, including penguins, flamingoes, pelicans and Chinese geese, and a well-stocked aquarium.

And then there were the side-shows: Professor Rousseau's Performing Flea Circus, Madame Hart's Mental Telepathy

Show, an American gangster's car and an African Village complete with Naomi, the snake charmer.

What memories they all evoke—memories of another age, indeed another world. In 1935 these things were my life. My private life was not as successful as all this might suggest; one cause of great unhappiness was my mother's death in 1933. She had been in Scotland, looking after my Christmas fairs in Glasgow and Edinburgh, and she was taken ill just as they were closing.

I arranged for her to return to London by overnight sleeper, and met her at the station. She was obviously very ill, and I had her admitted to the Princess Beatrice Hospital straight away. I gave blood for three transfusions, but she died a few days later from peritonitis.

Mother was a remarkable person as well as being a practical, level-headed and shrewd businesswomen. She was always dressed in black alpaca, with a bunch of keys dangling from a gold chain around her waist, and gave the impression of being a woman not to be trifled with. It is a tradition among showmen that the women look after the money, and Mother certainly looked after mine. In the early years, if we hit a losing streak or bad weather slashed the takings, she could always be relied on to produce a few pounds she had hidden away to see us through. Nevertheless, she was very strict with me; indeed, no accountant could have been stricter. Whenever I wanted cash to expand I always had great difficulty persuading her to let me have it, for she had a constant fear that I would over-reach myself. But the cautious thriftiness I learned from her undoubtedly played an important part in my early success.

How I wish she could have lived another three years . . .

THE LATE BOB LAKIN, A LONG-TIME FRIEND, RECALLED BUTLIN'S EARLY YEARS:
I first met Billy Butlin in Dorney's Yard, Bristol, towards the end of 1921. I was working as a foreman-joiner for Orton, Sons and Spooner of Burton-on-Trent, the biggest makers of fairground roundabouts in Britain, and I was there to carry

out alterations to a switchback owned by Bill's Uncle, Marshall Hill.

I noticed this little chap building a hoop-la stall and I thought he was a real chump, for no showman made his own equipment. But even then Bill had strong ideas of his own and when he wanted a job doing he found the best way was to do it himself. Watching him work, I never dreamed I was seeing the beginnings of a gigantic fairground empire.

At that time stalls were simple affairs consisting of four poles and some canvas, but Bill set out to alter that and he was the first showman to have more substantial and colourfully-decorated stalls.

He also quickly showed a flair for publicity and advertising, putting up posters in advance of the fair announcing his forthcoming arrival and advertising his various attractions like the Kentucky Derby, Rolling the Tank and Stop the Clock.

By 1926 he had enough stalls to fill several lorries, and it was about then he bought his first big, spectacular motor car: a second-hand Daimler which he and I sprayed bright red and silver. He was as pleased as Punch with it, for he felt it was solid evidence he was a successful showman.

As a showman he was always honest in his business dealings and expected others to be the same. Once he ordered a ride from a well-known supplier of amusement equipment and the price was agreed on. But when Bill went to collect it, the chap demanded a higher price. Bill needed that roundabout, so he paid. Many years later when he had the sole British distribution rights of the Dodgems, this man tried to buy some. Needless to say, he did not get any.

Bill was ambitious, thought big and gave careful consideration to every step he took. In later years if he saw a ride taking good money, he had to have a dozen like it. Whatever he did had to be bigger and better. As a result he was always stretched to the limit financially.

During the Torquay Regatta in 1927, he and I were strolling along the pier one night. There were some magnificent yachts in the bay and Bill turned to me and said: 'One day I'll own a yacht like one of those big ones out there.' I little realized then that one day he would be able to buy half a dozen yachts if he wanted.

He was always a very quiet fellow and easy to get along with. Occasionally we went to Paris together to look for new rides. It was there he bought his first Figure Eight. I well remember going with Bill for a trial ride on it at 7 o'clock in the morning after negotiating with the owner late into the night on a diet of snails and brandy.

On one of our Paris visits he bought himself a Maurice Chevalier style straw hat. Bill was delighted with it and was proudly wearing it when he came to my home shortly afterwards. He put the hat down on the table just behind the cage of a parrot we had. And unbeknown to us all the parrot nibbled quite a few chunks out of the brim.

Bill was decidedly put out when he saw the damage, but he was determined not to part with his beloved hat. He borrowed a pair of scissors from my wife and trimmed the brim all round until it was more or less even. Frankly, the hat did not look so good, but Bill happily went off wearing it.

PART **2**

Expansion

8

'None of us knew anything about holiday camps'

E began building the first Butlin's Luxury Holiday Camp at Skegness in October 1935 and opened it to 500 campers on Easter Saturday, 1936. In the months between—and for quite a few afterwards—we had enough trials and tribulations to last a lifetime. None of us knew anything about holiday camps.

My plans were for a site to accommodate 1,000 people in 600 chalets with electricity and running water, dining and recreation halls, a theatre, a gymnasium, a rhododendron-bordered swimming-pool with cascades at either end and a boating lake. In the landscaped grounds there were to be tennis courts, bowling and putting greens and cricket pitches.

One major improvement on the camps then in existence were the modern sanitary arrangements, which included 250 bathrooms. The camp was to have an independent water supply, a sewage system with two miles of drains and its own electricity generating plant. All this, including the drainage system and the interiors of the main buildings, I designed myself. Much of the 300-strong labour force consisted of men who worked in my amusement parks during the summer.

The local paper wrote glowingly, 'Campers in this Arcadia will not be disturbed by storms of wind or rain, by shortage of drinking water, by lack of illuminations, by crude sanitary arrangements or by other inconveniences to which the average outdoor camper is subject.'

This was my dream and it came true in the end, but there were times when those glowing newspaper phrases seemed positively ironic. I received my first nasty jolt about two months after we had started building when a local farmer, Bob Stowe, brought me two old photographs showing the entire camp area under water. Flooding was the one thing that had not occurred to me.

'I've been in Skegness nearly ten years now and there's no sign of flooding,' I told him.

'Ah, well, you see it only happens about every fifteen years,' he said.

'When did it last happen?' I enquired.

'About fourteen years ago.'

What my face showed I do not know but, inside, my stomach was sinking. Bob's news was disastrous in its implications. Here I was with £50,000 of my own money, another £25,000 borrowed from the bank, and many thousands of pounds worth of building materials unpaid for, all tied up in a project that could be ruined by flooding perhaps as soon as next year.

Clearly the sand dunes must be reinforced, but this could be an expensive job which might easily break my tight budget. What could I do? I wandered disconsolately around the site, and suddenly I had the answer: I would enlarge the boating lake and use the earth to bank up and strengthen the sand dunes.

The reinforced sand dunes did their job well and we had no flooding until the winter of 1953. Even then our own wall held, but the sea broke through two miles north of the camp and flooded down *behind* the dunes, submerging the chalets in nine feet of icy, muddy water which climbed half-way up the walls of the theatre. For three nights I worked alongside my men trying to stem the torrent. When the water finally subsided we found nine bodies from the surrounding districts.

The camp itself presented a heart-breaking sight. There was a foot-deep carpet of mud everywhere. Chalet doors, windows and main beams had been burst and broken by the pressure of the water. And all the carp in the lake were killed by sea water. I had one of the biggest stuffed and hung in my office.

We washed away the mud with fire hoses, a process that took weeks. Drying out the chalets seemed an insoluble nightmare, but we finally succeeded with hot-air blowers used for heating aircraft hangars, which we borrowed from the RAF.

But, back in 1936, it was—strangely enough—water that was also the cause of the next big threat to my plans. This time it was the lack of it. As there were no water mains in the district all the farmers got their water from artesian wells, and I did not expect any trouble finding water for the camp when we started drilling five months before the camp was due to open. Generally, water had been found about thirty feet down, but we soon passed that depth with no sign of it. The days ticked by, the drill dug deeper until we were a mere month away from the Easter opening date—and still we had not struck the vital liquid, to me more precious than oil. I am not by nature a worrier, but I began to get worried then, very worried indeed.

For by June, a thousand campers a week were booked in. Because we were all so inexperienced in running a holiday camp, I had limited the numbers of campers to five hundred a week at first to allow for trial and error. But even my optimism had not envisaged the tremendous public enthusiasm.

To launch the camp I had booked a £500 half-page advertisement in the *Daily Express*, offering holidays with three meals a day and free entertainment from 35 shillings to £3 a week, according to the time of the season. Within a few days more than ten thousand inquiries poured in, along with many bookings which necessitated a ten-shilling deposit. I was so unprepared for this massive flood that I had only hired an office staff of four. For weeks they laboured long into the night, handling bookings and sending out thousands upon thousands of brochures. When we finished we found the camp was practically full for the season.

But though everything looked sunny on the surface, I was fighting a desperate battle behind the scenes to prevent my dream disintegrating. For I began to run out of money.

Eventually, I was virtually broke—with a queue of creditors as long as Skegness pier. With the bookings already made I knew the camp would be successful—as long as I could get it completed and opened. But if even one of my creditors pressed for payment before then and brought bankruptcy proceedings, I would be finished.

Realizing my situation, the late Bill Needham, for many years advertising director of the *Daily Express*, told me that there was no need to pay for the advert until the camp opened. Clearly, I desperately needed the same assurances from my other creditors. But getting these assurances would be exceedingly tricky. For creditors can be like sharks; once they smelt blood—in this case any suggestion I was short of cash—they would all home in for their pound of flesh. How could I avoid this?

Eventually I got an idea. Scraping together enough cash for a deposit, I bought a Rolls Royce on the 'never' and esconced in this symbol of wealth I drove to see all my creditors.

'I can't pay you just now,' I explained, 'because all my capital is tied up. But the camp is fully booked and your money is safe. I guarantee you will be paid during the summer.'

Without exception everyone agreed to wait for their money. To this day I wonder what would have happened if I had called upon them in my Austin Seven.

Meanwhile the nightmare of the water supply continued. We drilled on and on, with opening day getting ever nearer. Finally Easter Saturday dawned and the nightmare became a reality. The only water we had found was brackish and undrinkable. How on earth was I to overcome this problem? We could use the water we had found for toilets, baths, wash-basins and general domestic cleaning—but we still needed pure water for drinking and cooking. There was only one source: Skegness's own water supply. Hastily I sent out an SOS to the council, and they agreed to let me take from the town's mains enough for my requirements.

So every night three Austin trucks loaded with milk churns shuttled back and forth between the camp and my house, where they were filled from every available tap. And every time a truck went into the town during the day, it took and filled as many milk churns as it could carry. This enabled us to survive—but still we did not locate drinkable water. Then the crunch came. Skegness Council warned me that my nightly demands on the town's water supply could not go on much longer. When they turned off the tap, the camp would close.

I began to face up to the bitter prospect of financial ruin. Sadly I wandered around the camp, remembering the dream and all the hard work. And then one day, three harrowing weeks after we had opened, one of my senior men, Norman Bradford, dashed up to me. 'Water! Water!' he gasped. 'They've found it.'

They had found it about four hundred feet down. Why we had to drill so deep I have never understood, unless it was because I had foolishly agreed to pay the contractor for every foot he drilled. Perhaps he did not want to find water at thirty feet. All I know is that we later drilled a number of bore holes and reached water very quickly. Today, Skegness uses about two-and-a-half million gallons of water a week, and half of it is still pumped from bore holes.

Another vital service that caused trouble at the beginning was the sewage system. It was not very efficient that first summer—I had not built a sewage farm before—and it was a bit offensive. I had sited it away from the camp and surrounded it with a high wall, so campers were not normally aware of it. But to discourage any inquisitive people I put up a large notice declaring: Beware of the Dog. One day a camper came up to me and said, 'You know that dog down there—it does smell.'

Not surprisingly the actual opening day had its share of crises. Indeed, so did the day before. We were having lunch when the bus which passed the camp entrance stopped, and out got a woman carrying a suitcase. She looked uncertainly about her and then walked towards the glass-fronted reception block which bore the sign: OUR TRUE INTENT IS ALL FOR YOUR DELIGHT.

We looked at each other, puzzled. Who was she? Had she come seeking a job? Or, heaven forbid, were we about to come face-to-face with our first camper? Nobody volunteered to find out, as I think we were all a bit apprehensive. Finally, Fred Coppin, the camp manager said, 'I'd better go and see who she is.'

Anxiously, we watched him talking to her, and then to our dismay he picked up her case and carried it into the reception building. She was indeed our first camper, arrived a day early. Her name was Freda Monk and she came from Nottingham. Of course, we fixed her up with food and a chalet, though what she thought of the chaos around her I shudder to think. She must have enjoyed her stay, however, for she became one of our regular campers, returning each year up to the War and for two years afterwards.

Incidentally, I have often been asked how I came to put up the sign 'Our true intent is all for your delight'. Most of you, I am sure, will know that the phrase is a quotation from Shakespeare's *A Midsummer Night's Dream*, but I had no idea of that, In those days I had hardly heard of Shakespeare, let alone read him. No, I must confess I took the phrase from the front of a fairground organ. It stayed up throughout the war, when the camp became the Royal Navy training 'ship', *HMS Royal Arthur*, though I doubt whether many matelots who were posted there appreciated the sentiment.

Our first campers were due to arrive on Easter Saturday. My aim was to provide people with a good holiday whatever the weather. Well, the concept could not have had a more testing start. On the Saturday it actually snowed and for the rest of the week it was generally cold and overcast. I remember thinking at the time, 'How unlucky can you get?' People came to breakfast in their overcoats.

Norman Bradford, the one who had brought me the glad tidings about the water, met the campers at Skegness station, wearing—despite the bitter cold and snow—an immaculate dinner jacket, without a top coat. There were not as many arrivals as we expected, because one party had gone to Sheerness, Kent. Apparently, I was not the only one who did not know the whereabouts of Skegness!

However, we were in business; I was about to find out if my ideas about what people wanted on holiday were right. From

110

the start I had envisaged plenty of indoor recreational facilities and that first week they were a blessing. The billiard and table tennis tables were fairly well used by the men and boys, but it was heart-breaking to see the outdoor facilities, the sports field, the tennis courts and the bowling greens, into which we had put so much hard work, being little used. Entertainment in the evening was a problem, for at first I could not afford professional artistes. We made do with volunteers from the camp staff, a few local 'semi-pros'—and the campers themselves.

The dining-room doubled as the camp theatre. After dinner people picked up their chairs and placed them in front of the small stage in readiness for the show. Afterwards they helped to sweep up and put back the chairs.

These early shows were a veritable hotch-potch. We had a five-piece band, Jimmy Flaherty, a mouth organist, and Jimmy Loft, a local publican. Frank Cusworth, a carpenter who worked on the Dodgems during the summer and who later became a camp sports organizer, did a contortionist-dancing act. Norman Bradford appeared as a comic parson. We were so desperate for 'talent' that even I took part.

I came on the stage looking very sad and Norman asked me, 'Why are you looking so sad?'

'Georgie the elephant has died,' I replied.

'I didn't know you were fond of elephants?'

'I'm not,' I said, 'I've got to bury him.'

If you think that is terrible, you should have heard the camper who volunteered to sing. He appeared wearing a bowler hat and performed 'Come Into the Garden, Maude' atrociously out of tune. But such was the spirit—perhaps fortitude would be a better word—of the campers, that he was called back for an encore. Anyone watching those shows would never have dreamed that a year later we would be putting on entertainment with top stars in the camp's own theatre.

The change began when I asked my friend, show business agent Bert Aza, 'What do your artistes do on Sundays?' He told me they were either travelling or resting.

'Would any of them who are free do a Sunday show for me?' I inquired. 'I couldn't pay them their usual fee, but if they're not working anyway, it would be something extra.'

Bert agreed to ask his artistes and the reaction was favourable. Shortly afterwards we had our first Sunday Night - Celebrity Concert with the female impersonator Norman Evans, who was famous for his 'over the garden wall' monologue. He was paid £12 10s. He liked the camp so much he came to stay for a week with his wife and daughter—and so we got most of his fee back!

From then on the Sunday concerts became a regular and popular part of the camps' entertainment, with a succession of top stars. Among them in those early years were Elsie and Doris Waters, Florence Desmond, Judy Shirley—from one of the top radio shows at the time, *Monday Night at Eight*—Will Fyffe, Ted Ray ('Fiddling and Fooling'), Harry Tait, Will Hay, the Western Brothers, Albert Whelan and the old Cockney veteran Harry Champion singing 'Any Old Iron' and 'It Ain't Been a Day Too Long'. Donald Peers sang at the camps many years before he reached the top. Quite a change from Billy Butlin and his elephant gag!

We also moved on from our five-piece band. By 1938 we had two resident bands at Skegness: Mantovani and his Tipica Orchestra, and Lew Stone and his Band. They were two of the top dance orchestras in that great pre-War era of big bands. Many people were astonished to find a well-known band at a Butlin camp, still more two at the same time.

When the Clacton camp was opened in 1938 we continued and developed this big-name entertainment policy. One of our early variety shows there was broadcast on the BBC Regional programme. It included Vic Oliver, the singer Hildegarde, George Robey, Elsie and Doris Waters and Will Fyffe, along with the orchestras of Mantovani and Lew Stone. Of it the *Daily Express* radio reporter wrote, 'To put that collection of stars in a studio would cost about £1,500.' What would an equivalent show cost now, I wonder?

We also began having big names in other spheres. That master of the quick-quick-slow, Victor Sylvester, gave dancing demonstrations and Len Harvey, the British light-heavyweight champion and the first of many top sportsmen to appear at the camp, gave boxing lessons. He even did an exhibition bout with a kangaroo as his opponent. Joe Davis and Horace Lindrum played snooker for a purse of a hundred guineas, while Dan Maskell coached the campers in tennis and Victor Barna in table tennis. When Maxie Baer, who clowned his way to becoming heavyweight champion of the world, came to Britain in 1938 to fight our own Tommy Farr, he trained at the Skegness camp with his brother Buddy. Tommy trained at Clacton, so we were sure of having the winner at Butlin's. Jack Doyle, the colourful Irish boxer and singer, also trained at Skegness for about six weeks.

In those pre-War days, all kinds of VIPS accepted invitations to visit us as the camps became more widely known. One of the first, I remember, was Amy Johnson, the courageous woman aviator, who had just set up a new record for a solo flight from England to Australia. Gracie Fields was the first really big star to entertain at the camp—at the time she was earning £1,200 a week at the London Palladium, phenomenal money for those days. Len Hutton came to Skegness the day after he scored his record breaking 364 in the final 'Timeless' Test match at the Oval in 1939. We even had a feature film made at Skegness. It was called *Sam Small Leaves Town* and starred Stanley Holloway. Hands up anyone who remembers that!

But though big-name entertainers and personalities like these have played a big part in publicizing and popularizing the camps, the main responsibility for entertaining the campers and keeping them happy had fallen on another body of men and women whose origins go back to that first week in 1936.

In the first few days I sensed that something was missing. The campers had taken to the chalet system of accommodation, but they were not using the camp in the way I had envisaged. Many of them did not take advantage of the recreational facilities. Often they sat about aimlessly, keeping to their own family groups. Even more worrying was the fact that some of them looked bored! Wandering about the camp, watching the

113

campers and talking to them—which was to become one of my great pleasures—it became clear that we needed to involve them more in the life of the place. It was not enough to provide facilities: people obviously had to be encouraged to use them.

I could still recall the happy camaraderie of that far-off Canadian summer camp which had inspired my venture. What we needed was some way of getting the campers to mix. On the third day of that first week I said to Norman Bradford, 'How about livening them up a bit?' So after dinner that night he went on stage and in his usual jovial manner joked with the campers and told them about the various facilities and activities. Then he said: 'Now I want everyone to turn to the person on your right, introduce yourself and shake hands.' There was a bit of embarrassment at first, but people did so, laughing or smiling shyly. 'Now,' continued Norman, 'turn to the person on your left and do the same.' This time people did it with more gusto and friendliness. The ice had been broken. Throughout the dining-room people began talking to each other. This made a great difference to the atmosphere of the place.

'This is what we've been missing,' I said to myself. 'A few more friendly people around, like Norman, would work wonders.' Thinking about it, I realized that if these were to be friendly focal points, they would need to be easily identified.

'Go and buy yourself a distinctive blazer,' I told Norman. He returned with one in blue, primrose yellow and white—the camp's colour scheme. But somehow it did not seem quite right. I did not want an outfit that looked like a uniform, for that would have given a wrong impression. What I was searching for was something bright, cheerful and holiday-looking. This line of thought led me to choose a red blazer and white flannels. We had them made by a local tailor and before the first week was over Norman bounced on to the stage at breakfast-time wearing the outfit. 'Good morning, campers,' he shouted. 'Good morning,' everyone shouted back.

As I heard this reaction I felt a flutter of excitement, which increased as Norman went on to outline some of the day's activities. It was noticeable that people on holiday, among a lot

114

of strangers, liked to have someone they felt was a friend, someone who could give them information and advice. I quickly realized that they liked to have entertainment, sports and competitions laid on for them. But I also realized they must be left to decide for themselves whether they would take it or leave it. They must not be pressurized into anything.

That same day I ordered more red blazers and white flannels, and picked ten friendly members of the camp staff, five men and five girls, to wear them.

The Butlin Redcoats were born.

9

'Come and join us . . .'

Please put a penny on the drum
We only want a tanner
To buy a new pianer
So please put a penny on the drum
Come and join us
Come and join our happy party
Come and join us
Come and join our happy throng

HOW many millions, I wonder, have sung that ditty to the tune of an old Salvation Army song, winding around a Butlin bar in a follow-my-leader crocodile? It is, of course, impossible to say, but certainly the 'Penny on the Drum' routine quickly became as much a part of camp life as the Redcoats themselves.

The idea came from two of the first Redcoats, Norman Bradford and Frank Cusworth. With entertainment in the bar late at night we soon found difficulty getting people to leave when 'Time' was called. For unlike an ordinary pub, our customers lived on the premises and many of them did not expect to have to go until they were ready. They frequently stayed on in the bar talking well into the night. What we needed was a painless, friendly way of emptying the bar which would not spoil the atmosphere and make people feel they were being bullied or turned out.

116

As often happens, the answer came accidentally. One evening Frank and Norman went to the cinema to see a film called *Chain Gang*, and when they returned they had a drink at the bar. 'Time' was called and, in obvious good spirits, Norman put his hands on Frank's shoulders and they shuffled across the floor one behind the other, in the manner of an American prison chain gang. To their surprise, a number of other people in the bar joined them and soon there was a line of dancing, jigging campers. With admirable quick-wittedness, Frank took the group into the ballroom, where it was joined by many others. Then he led the way outside. In no time at all, and in great good humour, both the bar and ballroom had been largely and painlessly emptied.

Next day we talked about the success of this spontaneous operation, and we agreed it was a wonderful way of closing down for the night. It was then that Frank came up with the idea of the crocodile snaking along to the Salvation Army song 'Come and Join Us'. It was an inspired thought, not only because the song was well known to most people, but also it invited them to take part. And that, thinking of the Salvation Army, gave him the idea of having a man beating a drum at the head of the column.

These additions turned the idea into an even bigger success. Indeed, it is difficult now to imagine just how spontaneous and enthusiastic were the campers' reactions. The reason, I think, was that they felt they were joining in something new and were pleased to be a part of it. It was that pioneering spirit, shared by us all, which led to one innovation and alteration after another during the first two summers of the Skegness camp. For instance, one day a camper called Gladys Painter came to see me. 'I'm all in favour of physical jerks,' she said, 'but at the moment the exercises are designed for men. There should be some suitable for women.'

I thought it was an excellent suggestion and Gladys organized a class. It was so successful that she stayed on at the camp to become a Redcoat and Games Leader under the physical training instructor Captain ('Cappy') J. T. Bond, who became Director of Physical Education for all the camps.

117

Gladys later formed the teams of attractive girl gymnasts who performed at soccer grounds throughout Britain in the winter months.

Another outstanding example of campers helping to innovate routines that became part of camp life was the famous 'Hi-di-hi! Ho-di-ho!' chant exchanged between the Redcoats and the campers. It happened half-way through the first season. That summer an American film was going the rounds in which, I seem to recall, the chant was volleyed back and forth between squads of marching soldiers. The film has long since been forgotten, but the chant caught on in Britain. One day, addressing campers from the stage, Norman Bradford shouted 'Hi-di-Hi!' and was greeted with a spontaneous answering roar of 'Ho-di-Ho!' The practice caught on with the same speed as the penny-on-the-drum routine.

But while we learned and developed as we went along, it was clear that generally we were giving people what they wanted. Throughout the summer I kept enlarging the camp and by September we could accommodate about twelve hundred people. During the winter I spent another £40,000 to increase the capacity to two thousand, adding another dining-hall, a theatre and a gymnasium. At last the camp was really fulfilling my dream. Today Skegness can accommodate ten thousand campers.

I have come to believe that what people call 'luck' depends mainly on doing the right thing at the right time and this certainly proved to be the case with my holiday camps. Until the late Thirties only about three million people in Britain had holidays with pay. But in 1938 Parliament passed legislation giving a week's paid holiday a year to all industrial workers. This naturally resulted in a huge increase in the number of people who could afford to take a holiday. By 1946, some eight million workers would be able, and seemingly determined, to have a holiday by the seaside. Butlin camps were tailor-made to take advantage of that demand, but though I had not envisaged such a situation when I opened Skegness, I soon appreciated the wisdom of helping the movement towards holidays with pay, and I actively lobbied Members of Parliament.

When this long-overdue reform took place I came out with the slogan: 'Holidays with pay: Holidays with play: A week's holiday for a week's wage.' In those days the average weekly wage was about £3 10s (£3.50) a week.

But even by 1937 it was obvious that the Butlin-style holiday camp had caught on, and Skegness needed to be enlarged further. For my philosophy had always been that the more people I could cater for, the more facilities and entertainment I could provide. From the beginning I had persuaded the London and North Eastern Railway, with a vested interest in promoting holiday attractions on the east coast, to pay half of my camp advertising. Now we were both keen to open a second camp, and I chose Clacton-on-Sea, also on the LNER line, as the site for it.

All these plans needed money, of course, and after taking advice from my bankers and sounding out friends, I decided to turn Butlin's into a public company. The prospectus of Butlin's Limited was published on Monday, 8 February 1937 and five minutes after the list was opened the issue was over-subscribed.* It was just nine days short of sixteen years since I had disembarked at Liverpool with my £5. In an editorial in its issue of February 13, the showman's newspaper, the *World's Fair* commented: 'Truly it all reads like a fairy story.' It certainly seemed like one to me.

For the way that the public took to this new style of holiday was remarkable, and it showed that the British are not as reserved as they are painted. For instance, more than ten

---

Editor's footnote: The share capital of the company was £220,000 in 880,000 Ordinary Shares of 5s. each offered at 6s. per share, with a loan capital of £100,000 5½% First Mortgage Debenture Stock. The total assets of the new company, which included freehold properties valued at £146,499, were £297,035. The prospectus revealed what a thriving business Butlin had built up. In 1935, his various concerns made a profit of £39,509 and in 1936, £55,785.

He retained control of the new company, receiving £118,000 in fully paid-up Ordinary Shares, in addition to £123,000 in cash. Against this, however, he had to discharge obligations to various of his old companies amounting to £80,000. He also became Managing Director with a salary of £3,000-a-year. After the war this was increased to £5,000.

thousand had turned up at our first campers' reunion at the National Hall in Olympia on New Year's Eve, 1936. 'Whoopee Night at Olympia' was how one newspaper headline described it. To look after the guests there were a hundred stewards and a hundred 'Nippies'—the popular name for waitresses in those days—and when the evening was over, thousands of balloons and parachutes supporting packages of gifts floated from a roof spangled with a mass of fairy lights. In 1938, when we held a ball at Earls Court, with Mantovani and his Orchestra and two other sixteen-piece bands providing the dance music, so many people tried to get there that the roads for a mile were jammed with traffic. Several hundred people never arrived at all.

Reading today some of the many articles written about the camps both before and after the Second World War, you can see, among all the praise and admiration, the slightly-mocking it's-all-right-for-the-masses attitude which I must admit was held by many people. Invariably, though, those who sneered at the Wakey-Wakey-Rise-and-Shine atmosphere and the 'enforced mateyness' and so-called 'regimentation' of camp life, had never been to a Butlin camp.

I have always argued that these charges were greatly exaggerated. After the war, particularly, it was not good business to regiment people—too many of my customers had spent too many years being regimented to stand for taking orders on holiday.

But with several thousand people in a camp (today the camps hold from 6,000 to 12,000 with up to 2,000 staff) we have to be well organized ourselves. Meals have to be prepared and put on the table at the proper times. All entertainments have to take place at the times announced.

Today, with the trend towards self-catering, more flexible eating arrangements and the general toning-down of the role of the Redcoats to meet our customers' changing tastes, the kind of criticism I have described has virtually disappeared.

So, too, has another insidious form of criticism that was

thrown at us for years, particularly in the more straight-laced Thirties. Holiday camps, it was alleged, were nothing more than hives of immorality. This kind of lip-smacking gossip was put about, again by people who had never visited the camps, or by such competitors as hotels and boarding houses, wanting to give us a bad reputation. An article in the *Sunday Pictorial* (now the *Sunday Mirror*) of 4 July 1937 talked about the loose morals of campers and declared that 'painted ladies' were often among the visitors. I was angered by this, for the criticism lumped permanent, properly-run holiday camps like Butlin's with badly or totally unsupervised hole-in-a-field affairs. I wrote to the *Pictorial*, denying this totally untrue allegation and then tackled the question of immorality in the camps. It is important here, I think, to remember that I am using the word in the context of 1937 when people were infinitely more straight-laced than now.

'It is ridiculous,' I wrote, 'to lay sweeping charges of immorality against holiday campers. You have only to see one of the open-air church services at our camp to realize the absurdity of any such charge. A fortnight ago we were honoured by the Bishop of Grimsby conducting our service and last week we had the Bishop of Lincoln; both these eminent ecclesiastics expressed their whole-hearted approval of the camp. Is there any hotel in the country that can say the same?' And I finished: 'The patron of the permanent holiday camp is the average clean-minded family man who would make unpleasant people so uncomfortable that they would clear out of their own accord to avoid being thrown out by the management.'

This kind of criticism cropped up regularly during the early years of the camps. In fact, whenever I announced plans to open a new camp there were cries that the area would be ruined through being inundated with hordes of noisy undesirables. Often these charges were made by those who were opposed to the camps for selfish and business reasons. But I always took a great deal of trouble to explain and outline my plans to the residents and the local council. Right from the start, however, I found that once the camp was opened people

121

realized that the tone of the town was not lowered and that as a result of my activities the town benefited from the increased number of visitors.

Clacton Camp was officially opened early in 1938—and what a difference a couple of years had made. At Skegness we had no idea how people would react to the camp. I had been confident, but that confidence had been severely strained at the beginning. Now my instincts had been overwhelmingly supported by the people who mattered: the customers.

The change was reflected by the style of the Clacton opening. We had had no formal opening at Skegness—we were grateful to open at all. At Clacton there was a slap-up ceremony attended by some five hundred guests, with Lord Strabolgi performing the formal opening. There was a large party of Press men there, among them the famous *Sunday Express* columnist Lord Castlerosse, who, no doubt carried away by the euphoria of the occasion, told the audience: 'Billy Butlin has done more for England than St George.'

Castlerosse was a first-class card player and on the train journey back to London he played for high stakes with a group of strangers who had no idea who he was. So successful was he that when the train reached King's Cross, one irate and presumably financially hard-hit opponent tried to have him arrested as a card sharper!

Can you imagine the scene? There I was standing on a busy platform of Edinburgh's Waverley Street railway station in my socks, trousers and vest, desperately putting on the rest of my clothes.

This scene took place many times during the spring, summer and autumn of 1938. What on earth was I doing half undressed on a railway station platform? The answer is that I was changing trains for Glasgow after travelling on the overnight sleeper. And the reason why I was making so many visits to Glasgow was that after the opening of the Clacton camp I had embarked on another exciting project. Against competition from all the major European showmen I had secured the sole rights to create and operate the amusement park at the Empire Exhibition in Glasgow.

During the two months it took to build the funfair and the six months, from May to October, it was open, I often travelled to Glasgow from London where I now lived in a Park Lane flat, usually by way of one of the East-coast camps. Generally, I went up one night and returned the next. I was working seven days a week and became so tired I often overslept, leaving myself with insufficient time to get dressed properly before the train stopped at Edinburgh. As a result I would be bundled on to the platform in a state of disarray.

The Exhibition amusement park was a gigantic undertaking, covering 16 acres and involving an outlay for Butlin's of £225,000. One end of the park was dominated by a hundred-foot-high scenic railway, the largest ever built in Britain, which was decorated with snow-capped peaks, ornamental crags and caverns. The ride was about a mile long and the five trains reached a speed of up to thirty miles an hour.

To make the fair as spectacular as possible I bought in new equipment from all over the world. Among them were two aeroplane rides, one in which you looped the loop, stopping for a heart-churning moment at the top of the loop upside down, and another which consisted of a small plane suspended on the end of a long arm which moved the plane up and down creating a flying motion. There was also a Rocket Railway which was a modern Wall of Death ride, with rocket-shaped cars, each carrying twelve passengers, hurtling around a circular wall. There was a new type of electric speedway, where you drove miniature racing cars on a twisting, banked race track. If you were particularly skilful you could reach twenty-five miles an hour—some speed on that track. And a huge Dodgem track which could accommodate fifty cars. By now I was manufacturing these cars under licence in Britain. All-in-all it was a far cry from those West Country fairs I once knew and it gave me a big thrill to walk round it.

Unfortunately, the opening was marred with tragedy, for on the second day two drunks managed to get on the Big Wheel. They stood up when their car reached the top of its circle, fell out and were killed. Over the years I had ten of these Big Wheels, and this was the only accident. Fairground accidents are rare and those caused by faults in the rides are even rarer. For the Showman's Guild insists that all the attractions are insured and the insurance companies make frequent and thorough inspections. Rides which are part of travelling fairs are usually very safe, for they are dismantled and erected every few days and any breakages or wear are spotted quickly.

In June, the Duke and Duchess of Kent visited the Exhibition and spent a couple of hours in the amusement park, going on practically everything from the scenic railways—the Duke returned for a second trip on that—to the electric speedway. The attendant on the scenic railway told them, 'If you want the biggest thrill from the ride, sit in the last seat of the car,' and they did.

With that informality typical of the Royal Family, they happily went into the Krazy House, where visitors are assaulted by all manner of surprises. There was a rolling floor and when the Duchess stepped on to it, she was thrown against a padded wall and her hat was knocked askew. But she was not caught out by a gust of wind on a moving stairs which played havoc with ladies' skirts. The Duchess walked up an adjoining fixed staircase.

'That's the wrong way,' called the Duke as he stepped on the escalator.

'I know,' she replied with a grin.

The final night of the Exhibition was a moving and memorable occasion despite heavy rain. There was a hushed silence as a voice boomed out the farewell message of the Spirit of the Exhibition: 'I am the embodiment of all that made for Glasgow this memorable achievement . . . I live tonight; I die tonight. May memories of me abide in your hearts.'

Then, in the glare from a dozen searchlights, while loudspeakers broadcast Big Ben chiming midnight in London, the Exhibition flag was slowly lowered. The searchlights snapped off. A great experience was over.

Meanwhile the camps were booming. In 1938 we had 50,000 visitors at Skegness and Clacton and the following year we catered for nearly 100,000. Then, of course, came the War.

Like Lord Beaverbrook, whose *Daily Express* had been proclaiming 'There will be no war', I too was convinced there would be no war—and I told everybody so. My optimism was reflected by the campers themselves. Though a number of people such as government officials, reservists, school teachers and air-raid wardens had to cancel their holidays, we still had 6,000 visitors at the two camps when the war began on 3 September. Only two days previously the *Butlin Times* had carried the optimistic front page headline:

BYE-BYE BLUES AT BUTLIN'S
Campers Forget the Crisis
Are we downhearted? No!!!

The paper also printed a list of Butlin's reunions for that autumn, with the slogan, 'Summer lasts longer at Butlin's'. But summer was about to end abruptly and none of us realized that the winter was going to last a long, long time.

While Neville Chamberlain was making his fateful broadcast at 11 o'clock on Sunday morning announcing that we were at war with Germany, I was travelling from Clacton to Skegness. I arrived there ignorant of what had happened. The manager met me and his first words were, 'What do you think of things?'

'Don't worry,' I told him. 'There'll be no war.' He looked at me as though I was crazy.

Once I learned the grim news, however, I had little doubt that the camps would be taken over by the Services. Immediately after Chamberlain had returned from Munich, waving a piece of paper and declaring that there would be 'Peace in our Time', top-ranking Service officers from Britain and France had made an inspection tour of the camps.

That Sunday evening comedian Izzy Bonn topped the bill at the camp concert. The following day Skegness was taken over by the Royal Navy, and Clacton by the Army.

We had to ask all the campers to leave immediately. To soften the blow we gave them their money back, along with a coupon promising them a free holiday after the war. I was astonished how many people took me up on that offer when the camps eventually reopened.

In my heart, though, I was convinced that day would never come. I was equally sure that my fairgrounds, too, would be closed, for they were all situated on coastal sites. I felt utterly desolate. It seemed like the end of the world for me. Fairgrounds and holiday camps were my life and the only thing I knew anything about. But like millions of others I was soon to find myself absorbed in a totally different way of life.

10

'You're the only man in Britain . . .'

THOUGH the first week of the war was a sad one for me with my camps and my amusement parks being closed down, there was one happy event to lighten the gloom: I was presented with a second daughter. Her mother was Norah, the younger sister of my wife Dolly.

My marriage to Dolly began to deteriorate in the early Thirties. I have to admit that my ambition and my business resulted in me leaving Dolly alone a lot, and she began to drink heavily. As I hardly drank at all in those days, this led to increasingly bitter rows between us. Eventually, we were making each other so unhappy that we decided to part.

I gave her a good allowance, and with our daughter, Shirley, she went to live in Reading. Later I bought her a small hotel, the Lorna Doone, in her home town of Tiverton.

After Dolly's father died, Norah and her mother had come to live with us in Skegness; and when Dolly and I split up, Norah took on the job of looking after me. She used to cycle to the amusement park with my lunch.

For some years she led her own life, but soon after I moved to London in 1938 she became my housekeeper and hostess. She was an extremely beautiful and vivacious young woman, and we got on well together. As my business career and my public life expanded, with all their social obligations, she seemed to be the perfect partner for me. But we were unable to marry because Dolly refused to give me a divorce, though I

127

asked her to do so on a number of occasions. So for many years Norah and I lived together unmarried, and had three children: Cherry, Sandra and Bobby.

When Cherry was born in that first week of the war, all of us in Britain were gripped by the fear of German bombing, so I decided to take Norah and the baby out of London. I still owned the converted ambulance I had used for travelling overnight between my various amusement sites, and it was an ideal form of transport for this occasion. As soon as Norah and the baby were ready to travel, I collected them from the maternity home.

I drove westwards through the blackout and once we had left London I stopped at a hotel, but it was full. So was the next one and the one after that. By now it was late and I was becoming worried about Norah and the child. Eventually, we came to Cheltenham, where I know some business associates were staying at the Queen's Hotel. And there, at last, I was able to find accommodation. Next day I drove the ambulance back to London and returned to Cheltenham by car.

At the time I had two lovely motors: a Delahaye, and the American Aubern which I drove back to Cheltenham. It was a lovely-looking car, long, sleek and white and, if anything, I liked it more than the Delahaye. That night, when Norah and the baby were asleep, I sat talking with my business friends. In those days my London offices were in Wardour Street, and then, as now, it was the centre of the British film industry. Not surprisingly, therefore, I had entered the film business myself, as one of the backers of *The Stars Look Down*, starring Michael Redgrave, and directed by Carol Reed. (Another backer was Monty Banks, then the husband of Gracie Fields. Monty was an Italian, and when Italy entered the war on the side of Hitler, he went to the United States to avoid being interned. Gracie went with him—an agonizing decision for her to make. She hated leaving Britain at such a time, but she felt she had to be with her husband. Monty had taken the negative of *The Stars Look Down* with him, and it helped him to get started in business over there.)

After my friends and I had talked for a while in the Queens

128

My grandfather, the Reverend William Heygate Butlin

My mother, Bertha, shortly after her marriage. She is about 17

Showmen, including uncles Coneley and Hill and Jimmy Chipperfield

Aunt Lottie Coneley, the first to greet me on my arrival from Canada

I was about four when this photo was taken of Mother, Binkie and me

On leave in 1917. Left to right are Uncle Marshall Hill, me, Jimmy Hill and Uncle Bernard Hill

In 1928, when this picture was taken at Skegness, I already had quite a staff

One of my early 'gimmicks' at Felixstowe in 1933

Skegness, 1937: me with my Auburn car and a bevy of beauties (Fox Photos)

Clacton, 1940: survivors of Dunkirk marching with dignity into the camp (Fox Photos)

*Tommy Handley, holding my daughter Cherrie's hand, visiting Filey in 1946
with members of the ITMA cast*

*Big Charlie at Filey. Once we got him there, he was a great favourite with the
children*

Back to school in Bristol in 1954. It seemed a long time since I had gone there barefoot (Bristol Evening Post)

Back to Jersey after the 1969 Trans-Atlantic Race, to be welcomed by my children Bill and Jacquie

Showing the Queen and Duke of Edinburgh around Pwllheli Camp in 1963. As HMS Glendower, it was a training ship for many — including the Duke

Celebrating my knighthood in 1964, by driving into Battersea Park in a truck just like the one I'd had as a young travelling showman

*Handing over to Bobby when I retired. We didn't always see
eye-to-eye, but he has done a good job with the company* (Fox Photos)

With Bill, Sheila and Jacquie on the happiest day of my life — our wedding day

Hotel that evening, we started playing poker. Before long I had lost all the money I had on me, and was ready to pull out of the game.

'Tell you what we'll do, Bill,' said Howard Welch, one of the players. 'How about putting up that car of yours?'

I was anxious to stay in the game and win back some of my losses, so I staked the Aubern. But it was not my night. Eventually Howard Welch won the car, and I sadly handed over the keys. Next morning I suffered a further indignity. Whilst I was out for a stroll, Howard swept past me in the Aubern, grinning broadly and upping two fingers at me in a vulgar gesture.

That night we played poker again and with a run of better luck I won back my beloved Aubern. I ran it throughout the war, but as I used it mainly on Government business, its gleaming white body had to be painted in green and brown camouflage. When the war was over, it was resprayed white again and I often drove it to the camps. One day at Clacton, my good friend, the comedian Leon Cortez, who was a keen motorist, said: 'Bill, I love your car. What do you want for it?'

'I don't know,' I replied. 'I've no idea what it's worth.'

'I'll give you £350,' retorted Leon, which was a good price then.

'No,' I said, trying to put him off. 'I don't want to sell it.'

But Leon was not going to be put off. 'Well, if you don't want to sell it, let's toss for it: If I lose, I'll give you £450. If you lose, you give me the car.'

With so many friends looking on, it was an offer I could not refuse, so we tossed a coin. I lost. Leon drove that car for many years.

Back to 1939: during those first few months of war, I had plenty to do. All the rides and equipment at my seaside amusement parks had to be dismantled, greased and packed away. So too, had the rides from the 1939 Liège Exhibition in Belgium, where, against world-wide competition, I had obtained the concession to supply all the rides and sideshows.

In Britain, the big rides at the amusement parks were mothballed, but many of the stalls were merely closed and left standing as they were. At Bognor one was a shooting range with the heads of Nazi leaders like Hitler, Goering, Goebbels and Ribbentrop as targets. I never gave the stall any thought until after Dunkirk and the threat of a German invasion. Suddenly, I remembered those targets! 'If the Germans take over Britain and find them,' I thought, 'I'll be up before a firing squad.' I had no faith in the German sense of humour, or lack of it. So on the principle of better safe than sorry, I dashed down to Bognor and painted out the heads.

Another major task at the start of the war was to fix with the Services the rents for their use of the Skegness and Clacton camps. The figure finally agreed was 25 per cent of our last year's profits, but it was not enough to pay the company's debenture holders. They received no dividends until after the War. In 1939 I had just begun to build a third camp at Filey, and I was resigned to it staying in its unfinished state until the war was over. Then, suddenly, the War Minister, Hore Belisha, who is perhaps better known for introducing the 'Belisha Beacon' pedestrian crossing when he was Transport Minister, sent for me. I had known him for some time, having been introduced by Lord Southwood, head of Odhams Press, the newspaper (*Daily Herald*) and magazine (*John Bull, Illustrated, Woman*) combine. He was Governor of Great Ormond Street Hospital in London and I had helped him to raise money for it. For instance, we allowed visitors into the camps on Sunday for a shilling a time, and all the proceeds went to the hospital.

Hore Belisha told me that the Skegness and Clacton camps had proved so successful as Service establishments that he would like me to quote a price for completing Filey for the Army. From him I learned that it cost the Army £250 per occupant to build a camp. I estimated that I could do the job for £175 per head, and I quoted that price. I made one important stipulation, though: I should be given the opportunity of buying the camp back at the end of the war for three-fifths of the cost. This was agreed. On the surface it seemed a good deal for Butlin's, but it was, in fact, quite a gamble. for I had no idea what condition the camp would be in at war's end. It could be destroyed completely. There was also the worry that I might have difficulty in raising the necessary finance to buy it back when the time came. But, if all went well, the deal meant that Butlin's would have a ready-made camp at a time when there would be great demand for holiday accommodation.

It was also a good deal for the government. After the First World War the cost of demolishing the Service camps and rehabilitating the land was more than the price of building them. For that reason alone, it was later acknowledged that the arrangement was one of the best deals the Service departments made in those hectic days of expansion.

My old friend Harry Warner took over the job of completing Filey. Harry had been a captain in the First World War and so he also took over command of the camp's Home Guard. Former Lance-Corporal Butlin enlisted as a private.

I was at Filey one Sunday when the unit was to be visited by a General. Just before his arrival, the men were 'fell-in' for his inspection.

'You'd better fall in, Bill,' said Harry.

'What are you going to do?' I asked him.

'I'm going to walk round with the General and inspect the troops,' he replied.

'Well, I'm going to walk round with the General and inspect the troops,' I said. 'After all,' I thought to myself, 'it is my camp!' Unfortunately, there was no time for Harry to introduce me. From the puzzled looks the visiting General gave me, it was obvious that he could not understand why this solitary private was a member of the inspection party.

A few months after the Skegness camp had been turned into the training establishment *HMS Royal Arthur*, I forced myself to visit it—and what a sad occasion it was, I even had to obtain a permit to enter.

I stood beside the ship's captain on the 'quarter deck' as he took the salute at the Sunday morning march-past, and remembered the carefree Sunday parades when lads no older than these young matelots had strolled past laughing, arm-in-arm with their girl-friends. Where I was standing had been partly the children's playground and partly the skating-rink.

Would they ever return? Would *HMS Royal Arthur*, named after a cruiser built in 1889, ever be transformed back to a happy holiday haven? These depressing thoughts entered my mind as I stood to attention, my teeth chattering in the bitter wind blowing off the North Sea.

Before lunch I was given a generous tot of Navy rum—Nelson's Blood—in the Petty Officers' Mess and we toasted Lord Haw-Haw, the traitorous Englishman who broadcast propaganda from German—his nasally 'Jairmany calling' was known throughout the land—in the hope of spreading fear and despondency in Britain. And we laughed, remembering how, a little time earlier, he had boasted that *HMS Royal Arthur* had been sunk with all hands!

You can imagine my feelings as I walked round the camp to find that the dining-rooms, once called York, Gloucester and Kent, were now known as the Forecastle, Top and Quarterdeck Divisions. The Tyrolean Beer Garden, where many thousands had spent happy hours singing along with an accordion band, was now the Sick Bay waiting-room and the Fortune Teller's Parlour was the dentist's clinic. The Viennese Dance Hall where Mantovani's Orchestra used to play had become an armoury with stacks of rifles.

In the billiards-room the tables had been set end-to-end and covered with a flat wooden top. Here the new recruits piled their personal kit and marked every item with a rubber stamp. Oh, there were so many changes. Air-raid shelters where the rose beds used to be, for instance. But the main difference, of course, was in the atmosphere. Where only a few months before there had been carefree laughter and the happy cries of children splashing in the swimming-pool, now there was strict Navy discipline. As a civilian, I was not allowed to walk across the 'quarter deck' and every rating had to salute the flag staff when passing. All the saluting and standing to attention, and only speaking when spoken to by an officer, was such a contrast to the relaxed, friendly atmosphere I had striven to create.

Clacton Camp, taken over by the Army, had changed even more. At first it was intended to be a camp for prisoners-of-war, and barbed wire had immediately been put up around the perimeter. This had involved knocking down some chalets so that the wire could stretch in a straight line. A row of floodlights were erected and these were kept on all night—beacons in an otherwise blacked-out countryside. There were loud protests from the citizens of Clacton, who rightly felt the lights made them a target for marauding German bombers. But the lights stayed on until the first Christmas of the War when finally someone in authority showed a bit of sense. It was all particularly silly because in that quiet period known as the 'Phoney War' there were hardly any prisoners to put in the camp. Eventually it became a training centre for the Pioneer Corps.

Once again the sad transformation was made. The ballroom became a repair depot for Bren guns, the tennis courts were turned into the Parade Ground and the bathing pool, where swim-suited girls had paraded on a Sunday afternoon in the Holiday Lovelies Contest, was used for training Commandos in full kit.

Whilst we were still completing Filey, I was asked by the Admiralty to build another 'Skegness' on the south coast—on the same financial terms as Filey. I immediately began searching for a site, but before I had found it, Dunkirk was evacuated. Hitler now controlled the entire north coast of France and was threatening to cross the Channel. The project was scrapped, and the Admiralty looked to the less vulnerable area of North Wales, where the BBC had established many of its programme departments in Llandudno. Would I reconnoitre this area?

It meant frequent visits to that ruggedly beautiful part of Britain, and to save time I drove from Filey, where my presence was still needed, through the night in my old Austin 10. I vividly remember those nightmare journeys of 260 miles. Many a time I found myself nodding at the wheel, and jerked myself awake to find the car perilously near a ditch or a wall. All that driving in the blackout affected my eyesight and I had to wear glasses for a time. I didn't recognize myself! It was a laborious task, but finally I found a site just outside the little town of Pwllheli. It was nothing but a series of fields leading down to the sea with the mountains in the background, but it would enable us to build a spacious camp from the beginning instead of adapting a site already in existence.

The Admiralty approved my choice and a deal was made to purchase the land. So far so good, but—and for me it was a big 'but'—there was no water. Again I went searching, and eventually, to my intense relief, I discovered a spring about five miles from the site. The Admiralty sent an expert, a colonel in the Marines, who made elaborate tests and finally pronounced there were enough underground springs in the area to provide a sufficient and inexhaustible water supply. A reservoir was constructed, a pipeline laid and building began. We had only been working three weeks when 8,000 ratings arrived to live under canvas. *HMS Glendower* was launched.

So rapidly was the Navy expanding that before we had finished Pwllheli, the Admiralty asked me to build another training centre in Scotland. I chose a site on the coast near Ayr, looking out towards the Isle of Arran. This became *HMS Scotia*. As with Filey and Pwllheli, I was given the opportunity to buy it back at the end of the war for three-fifths of what it cost to build. *HMS Scotia* is now Butlin's at Ayr. The gamble I took in those dark days, when none of us knew what lay ahead, paid off. But it could easily have been a very different story.

Once the construction of these camps was running smoothly, I began to look around for another job. After an uninteresting few months with Northern Command at York, Lord Beaverbrook asked me to see him at the Ministry of Supply. Following his success at the Ministry of Aircraft Production, where he had slashed through bureaucratic red tape and bottle-necks to produce the Hurricanes and Spitfires that enabled 'The Few' to win the Battle of Britain, the 'Beaver' had moved to the Ministry of Supply, where he was responsible for the rapidly-increasing number of armament factories.

These factories, many of them in isolated areas, employed about fifty thousand women and girls who had been directed into war work. They lived in hurriedly-built hostels which were dreary beyound description. As a result they were deserting them in their thousands. The government was unwilling to wield the big stick against them for fear of upsetting their menfolk in the Services, but this constant drain from the hostels was creating a serious labour crisis in the factories. This was the problem Beaverbrook wanted to talk to me about. It did not take us long to find that we understood each other completely. We both spoke the kind of language the other appreciated. Neither of us had any use for 'bumf', red tape, fools or incompetents.

'We've got to do something to stop these women leaving the hostels,' said Beaverbrook. His eyes twinkled, and he added, 'Mr Butlin, we have fifty thousand women in these hostels, and I'm told you're the only man in Britain who can satisfy them.'

I replied, 'My lord, I'm a Canadian, not an American,' referring to the reputation with the ladies being acquired by the American GIs who were beginning to arrive in Britain.

The 'Beaver' appreciated the reply with a flicker of a smile, but he was in a serious mood and he continued, 'I want you to find out what is wrong with these hostels and tell me how they can be made more attractive for the women living in them. I'll give you a week.'

It was just before Whitsun and I said, 'Right, I'll start immediately after the holiday.'

'No, you won't,' said Beaverbrook. 'I want you to start now—and phone me every night during the next week to tell me what you've found out, and what you suggest.'

Beaverbrook was not a man to argue with, so I immediately arranged to visit the hostels. They were worse than I had expected, usually surrounded by barbed wire fences and looking more like internment camps than hostels. There was practically nothing for the women to do during their off-duty hours. I phoned Beaverbrook every night, and after a week reported back to him with my recommendations. He listened, grunted and said: 'I want you to be my Director General of Hostels.'

It was a project that greatly interested me, but after a moment's thought I had to say, 'I'm sorry, but I can't accept.

135

It's a full-time job; and I'm still building two Service camps, and I have a post with Northern Command.'

Beaverbrook was not amused. 'Other people can build camps,' he replied, 'and whatever you're doing in Northern Command can't be as important as this. It's a job that must be done—and it's right up your street.'

Once again I realized it was fruitless arguing with Beaverbrook, so next day I moved into Shell Mex House in the Strand, where the Ministry of Supply was based. One of the basic troubles, I discovered, was that many of the hostels were run by volunteers who, though anxious to help and meaning well, had little idea of how to organize on a large scale. But clearly the overriding priority was to brighten up the appearance of the places.

The hostels were camouflaged on the outside and we were not allowed to touch that. But inside we covered the depressing dingy brown paint with bright colours.

If you had been working in a factory all day, it did nothing for your morale to return to somewhere that looked like another factory. Next we changed their names from 'Hostels' to Residential Clubs and allowed the women to invite men friends. Until then, to my utter astonishment, they had been absolutely forbidden to invite any men over the threshold, not even a husband or brother. Mind you, the atmosphere of the places would have put many of them off anyway. To get what I wanted I had constant battles with bureaucracy, but I succeeded in installing makeshift cinemas, dance floors, games rooms and tennis courts. We found that many women loved gardening and I arranged for land to be provided for them to cultivate and experts to visit and advise. In other words, I tried to provide the same kind of off-duty conditions as were enjoyed by the WRENS, WAAF, and ATS—because the women working in the factories were equally necessary to victory; and with bombing they were probably more in the front line than many of their uniformed sisters.

My efforts to allow Servicemen to attend dances at the Clubs landed me in unexpected trouble, for some of the Clubs were in areas where American GIs, including negroes, were stationed. Naturally, these coloured soldiers went to the dances like their white buddies. Nothing wrong with that, you might say, but this was the Britain of the early 1940s, and the attitude towards coloured people was less tolerant than today. Soon there were outcries of protest, and in the House of Commons I was attacked for allowing British girls to be 'seduced' by coloured men. In fairness to the critics, it has to be admitted that many of the girls came from families where they had led very sheltered lives. To defuse this criticism we brought in hand-picked 'mothers'—older, married women, who lived in the Clubs and acted as chaperones, advisers and confidantes of the girls.

I also came into conflict with the Trade Unions. We had been forced to institute head examinations of all women going to live in the Clubs, because we found some of them had lice in their hair. Our health people argued that these check-ups were essential, for the women lived in close proximity to one another and we were getting complaints from those who had picked up the parasites from other workers.

But the Unions objected to the examinations, arguing that they were an insult to the working classes. Eventually we found a compromise which satisfied the Unions and the medical staffs at the Clubs. It was agreed that all women were given a medical examination which included an ear, nose and throat inspection. While this was being carried out a discreet check on the women's hair was made. A simple enough solution—once someone had thought of it!

During this period I made a number of tours of the Clubs with Mrs Winston Churchill. Our tours would last a week at a time, and often she would insist on staying overnight in one of the Clubs. Whenever this very charming lady, normally so well dressed, visited a Club she wore a scarf over her hair instead of a hat. I regarded this as a gesture of sympathy and respect for the women who were forced to tie their hair in a scarf for safety reasons at work. I thought that was a very imaginative touch. Indeed, Mrs Churchill did much to raise the morale of women factory workers throughout the country.

I spent eighteen months at the Ministry and my changes in

the hostels seemed to be successful, as the number of women leaving was drastically reduced. For this work I was later honoured with the MBE.

But I was not happy as a Civil Servant—let's face it, in no way could I be said to have a Civil Service mind. Take, for example, the way everyone was graded in subtle ways. You could tell the status of a man by the size of his office desk and the amount of floor his carpet covered. So to cock a snook at such idiocy I fitted out my office at my own expense with the biggest desk I could find and wall-to-wall carpeting.

I have always been accustomed to using my own judgement and I found it difficult to work in committees. It was often hard to explain to someone else why I was so sure that a certain step was the right one. The Civil Service routine of memo-passing was also not my style. When I arrived at my office at eight o'clock most mornings, I found my In-tray piled with folders containing memos and reports. Most of them seemed to me to be ridiculous or totally-outdated proposals. It was impossible to comment on them. So I stuck them in the drawers of my desk. Eventually, of course, I received a memo saying 'Folder number such-and-such was sent to you on such-and-such a date and we are unable to trace it.'

I ignored these plaintive cries and continued stuffing the paperwork into my desk. Finally, every drawer was full. Now I had to take action. One morning I arrived at my office very early and took out all the folders with their mass of bumf. Then, my arms full, I wandered around Shell Mex House depositing files willy-nilly on umpteen desks. My silent protest must have made some impact somewhere in the higher echelons of bureaucracy, for the amount of paper landing on my desk was suddenly and drastically reduced.

By 1943 I had left the Ministry and Britain was now on a strict war footing. People had difficulty in getting away for holidays. Passenger trains were greatly reduced, petrol was rationed and many seaside resorts were closed to civilians. But people needed relaxation and entertainment, and so a scheme was launched to encourage towns and cities to organize Holidays At Home weeks. While I was at the Ministry of

138

Supply several places including Gloucester, Leicester and Sheffield had asked me to help them to organize their holiday weeks and I was happy to do so. I had many thousands of pounds' worth of fairground rides lying idle and I had them brought out of mothballs and loaned to various towns and cities. They were mostly operated by retired and middle-aged volunteers—and even by school children. Luckily, several like-minded men had joined the Ministry in those wartime days, and I had not been there long before I began seeking them out. They were men who I sensed, or knew, would work the same hours as I did, and not mind what they were asked to do. One of them was Major Russell Pickering, who had been such a loyal supporter during my early struggles at Olympia. His son followed his father's footsteps and did a splendid job. Another was George Ogg, whom I first met when I was dabbling in the film business just before the War. He later became a fellow director of Butlin's and we worked together for many years before he, like me, retired. George was—and still is, for that matter—a Scot with a gentle accent that is deceptive, for it hides considerable strength of character. Behind his polite glasses he was a shrewd appraiser of men and a brilliant organizer. Himself, he was a man of few words, none of them wasted.

Someone else from the same mould was Norman Maclaren, who came to look after my business affairs when I was on war work. Mac too, joined me after the war and became the very able and universally-liked company secretary. What I liked about 'Mac' was that he was unflappable in a crisis—and we had plenty of those in Butlin's after the war. It was a trait not confined to business: one day, the late Godfrey Winn, the brilliant journalist and author, was rushing by car from Filey with Mac to catch a train at York. As they entered the city they missed a head-on collision with a lorry by a proverbial hair's breadth. Godfrey, who had had a distinguished and courageous record as a war correspondent and afterwards as an Ordinary Seaman with the Navy, told me frankly that he was 'palpably shaken', but Mac was completely unperturbed. All he said was, 'It would have been a pity if we had missed the train.'

Russell, George and Mac were some of the friends I made at the Ministry of Supply, and we continued to be friends into far-distant peace-time years.

After Lord Beaverbrook left the Ministry, and I had got the Residential Clubs running smoothly, I asked to be relieved of my post in order to help the Holidays at Home project—something much nearer to my heart. I recruited my old fairground friends Billy and Charlie Manning and they formed three travelling fairs with forty-four rides between them. Among them were the galloping horses and switchback roundabouts—the latter with large decorated cars in the shape of animals, which had been so popular in the 1920s. I had always admired them and had an ambition to own one, but in those days I couldn't afford £12,000. Only the big showmen could pay that kind of money and, as a result, there were only ten or so in the country. However, new and more thrilling rides came along and the gallopers and switchbacks were abandoned in yards up and down the country. When I was asked to help with the Holidays at Home, I remembered these rides. With Bob Lakin, I went to see the various owners and to my immense delight I was able to buy every one of them for between £200 and £500. My ambition had more than been achieved, for instead of having one, I had them all.

I enjoyed visiting the fairs again as we moved from Gloucester, Stroud and Cheltenham to Derbyshire and Yorkshire. It was like old times: travelling with Charlie and his wife, stopping for a cup of char on the road with a night watchman, or washing in a basin outside the living wagon in the morning. But I was only filling in time until I started my next job.

In 1956, when my memory was fresher than it is today, I talked to Godfrey Winn about those eventful times; in his inimitable style he wrote about them, and I can do no better than to recall his words (from a book which was later abandoned). He began his story with Lieutenant-Colonel Basil Brown—a man whose future was to be closely involved with mine and the camps'—coming to see me in my Oxford Street office:

There was no premonition, no hint of peace-time collaboration when [Basil] was ushered into the Guvnor's office. This is a large room, where the man sitting behind what was once Von Ribbentrop's desk has plenty of time to study each visitor's appearance and deportment, before he reaches the chair opposite him. I always feel myself, even today, that I am advancing across the headmaster's study carpet, and this particular headmaster has a disconcerting habit of always waiting for you to speak first. This is partly shyness on his part, partly shrewdness. It gives him time to complete his impressions. For my own part, I never get quite accustomed to the contrast, between sitting alone with Bill in that great room, on the first floor, with all the different telephones on his desk (which he answers usually in monosyllables, 'Yes', 'No', 'Right') and following him, at lunch-time, out into Oxford Street, where, unrecognized in his raincoat, and wide-brimmed grey hat, he has to push his way through the crowd of potential customers.

To return upstairs to Basil Brown. Before the war he had been managing director of one of the best-known house furnishing firms in the North of England, which had held a royal appointment through three successive reigns. Also a member of the York City Council, and a freeman of the city, Basil has still found time to pursue the outside interest and hobby which absorbed him, amateur acting, and the repertory movement, in general. Anything to do with the theatre aroused his enthusiasm at once: all the same, he joined the Territorial Army too, and devoted an equal amount of his time and energy to parades and manoeuvres with the West Yorkshire Regiment.

Of course, the moment war was declared, everything else was thrust into the background, and Basil was soon out in France as a 'footslogger' with his regiment, destined to be wounded at Dunkirk, and to be twice mentioned in despatches. It is intriguing to note that at the moment when his future boss was frantically searching for a suitable site for the camp that was to become, in due course, *HMS Glendower*, Basil Brown was lying on his back, in hospital at Basingstoke. And it was there in hospital that something happened by chance, which was to bring appreciably nearer the first meeting of Basil Brown and Bill Butlin.

It happened like this. One day a senior officer, on a tour of inspection, passing by Basil's bed, stopped and asked a question. 'Are you by any chance the Basil Brown who was connected with entertainment in the north, before the war?' Whereupon the wounded officer's reply, in the affirmative, was unknowingly to settle his future for the rest of the war. For, on his discharge from hospital, and not yet fit enough to join his active unit, he found himself posted to the War Office to join the staff of Lieutenant-General Sir John Brown, who was at that time Director General of Army Welfare and Education.

During the next two years, Basil worked considerably harder than he had ever worked before the war, playing a big part in trying to get Army Entertainment properly organized, and it was his drive and imagination which created the famous 'Stars in Battledress' that possesses the proud record of having visited all the overseas battle fronts. Early in 1944, Basil Brown was appointed Assistant Director of the Army Welfare Services for the 21st Army Group, with Brigadier Medlicott as his immediate chief, and it was at the suggestion of Medlicott, that Mohammed, so to speak, came to the mountain, paying a personal visit to the Butlin Building. And what an exciting message it was that the Army's envoy had for delivery that spring afternoon, when all over the country whispers and rumours were spreading, and in the south, there were many tell-tale signs of the imminence of the coming invasion.

The return to France of Allied Troops. When, where, how? No one knew for certain, except at the highest level of all. Still plans had to be made, on the assumption that the landings, when the signal for D Day was at last given,

142

would be successful, so that after the first battles had been joined, and won, there would come the need for a respite for the battle-scarred troops to have rest and relaxation, in a series of Leave Centres, set up on the Continent. Here it was where once again the 'Holiday Camp King' came into the picture. Would he undertake one more final job? Would he become Honorary Advisor to General Montgomery and his staff, concerning everything to do with these Leave Centres, inside the 21st Army Group? . . .

Actually, the reason why the Army authorities were so anxious to enlist Butlin's unique knowledge and flair was that they had envisaged these rest camps as being situated all along the coast of France: miniature seaside camps, in fact, very much on the same lines as Skegness and Clacton, before the war. Instead, in between that first meeting, a few weeks before D Day, and the finalizing of all the plans with Butlin's distinctive touch, the war—and the invasion—had moved on so swiftly that the whole of Northern France had been virtually liberated, with Belgium, at the same time, hastily evacuated by the enemy.

So, in the end, it was to Brussels that Butlin came, the first civilian from these shores to enter the city, flown out specially in a Dakota, to attend a conference of High-Ups. No sooner had Butlin, in his usual unobtrusive grey suit, landed, than he found himself in the throes of a crisis that he completely understood from his memories of his own Army days in the First World War.

In short, the troops were browned off. Brussels had officially been turned into a Leave Centre, but there was precious little amusement of a satisfactory kind on offer to the Servicemen just come from the line.

'Mind you, there were plenty of places,' Butlin explained to me, 'being operated by extremely worthy and worthwhile organizations like the Church Army and the YMCA. But they simply hadn't got it in their power to offer the boys what they really needed.'

143

'And that was?'

'Pleasant feminine companionship.'

'Of a respectable kind?' I echoed.

'Exactly.'

'And how did you manage it?' Because it was obvious from the twinkle in his eye that he had managed.

'Well, let's start from the beginning. First of all, with Basil, and two or three other officers, I made a tour of the whole city, looking out for suitable buildings to turn into clubs. When I found them, I marked them and said, this will do when we have given it a few coats of paint, and brightened it up, and installed a band, and some nice tables and chairs, and set up a kitchen and a bar.'

'But the girls . . .'

'I'm coming to that. First, we had to get the clubs themselves running. The NAAFI guaranteed the running costs, but there simply wasn't time to wait on such decisions, we had to get cracking that minute. I remember at one conference of Brass Hats, held soon after my arrival, with me the only fellow not in uniform, I got a bit fed up with the endless talk, and said: "Look here, I believe in this scheme so much and that it will really work, that I'll guarantee it to the sum of £5,000". Basil told me the sequel. Apparently after I had gone out of the room, one of the Brass Hats commented, "The idea sounds all right, but how do we know he's got five thousand?"'

'What I couldn't guarantee was five thousand suitable girls, to act as dance partners and hostesses. But I had a jolly good shot at it. I was up against a ban straight away. No fraternization with women who had been too friendly with the Germans. Mind you, there was a good reason for the ban. Brussels, when I arrived, was absolutely overflowing with prostitutes. I decided the best way of sorting the situation out was to form a committee of well-known local women to visit all the leading shops and factories, interview the girls and ask them if they would co-operate in the scheme. The idea was explained very carefully to them, so that they didn't get any wrong ideas. That would have been fatal from the start.

'Of course,' he went on, 'it wasn't as easy as it sounds now. That committee and the others that I formed in other towns later took a lot of handling. Hardly any of the girls could speak a word of English, so we had cards printed and placed on all the tables round the first of the clubs which we named the *21 Clubs* after the 21st Army Group, not after the famous restaurant in New York.'

'And what was on the cards?' I asked.

'Why, the usual phrases, in English and Belgian: Will you dance with me? What is your name? Would you like something to drink? Once we'd broken the ice, everything went with a swing. We had as many as seven thousand girls, nice girls, mark you, offering their services in the end. And we couldn't open the clubs fast enough. Until suddenly something went wrong. We had to widen the area from which we were recruiting the girls, and now we found ourselves up against a new snag, Communism. Many of the outlying districts in Belgium were at that time full of Communist agitators who decided that here was a splendid opportunity to cause trouble and create a wedge of distrust between the liberators and the liberated. Of course, there wasn't a word of truth in their smear campaign, but unfortunately some of the papers took it up, and I found my picture on the front page one day, with this caption, in large black type underneath, THE PROCURER FOR THE BRITISH ARMY.

'Well, I've been used to the rough and tumble of life and I've learnt to take things as they come, but this was something that I hadn't reckoned with, and for once in my life I saw red. As you know, I'm not much of a talker, and less of an orator, but I was so angry, I called a press conference of British, American and Belgian representatives in the Sansivant Dancehall, and I let fly straight from the shoulder. I put it to them: which was better—that our boys should have decent girls to dance with and talk to, and relax with inside one of the 21 Clubs—mind you

145

there was a strict rule about their meeting only inside the clubs—or would you prefer that our troops, after being starved of all female company for months, should go and look for it, in the brothels, or the out of bounds parts of the city?'

But the real enemy who had either to be conquered—or won over—was the Belgian Minister for Home Affairs, and Butlin decided that his best plan of campaign was to beard his enemy in his own lair.

'I thought, at least I shall then know how I stand. If you face a man in his own office, with no side-talking, you can get at the truth. The trouble in this case was that I didn't speak a word of either French or Flemish, so that everything had to be done through an interpreter. When I first came to Brussels, an official interpreter from the 21st Army Group was assigned to me, and he became almost my shadow. His name was Captain Dennis Rake, and we soon became firm allies. Now Dennis was a very brave fellow, he had worked previously in the Underground Movement, and must have had some narrow squeaks, but I am sure he'd tell you that the day we tackled the Minister together was his worst experience.'

'What happened?' I asked.

'Oh, we won the day. The air was cleared, the Minister and I agreed to an armistice, on honourable terms and all was well, with the running of the Clubs from that time on. In the end, we had them flourishing in many other places besides Brussels. Places like Hamburg, Enschede, Eindhoven, Blankenburg and Antwerp.'

No less a figure than General Montgomery himself agreed to perform the opening ceremony of the 21st Club in Antwerp. An elaborate programme was arranged for the Commander-in-Chief. He would arrive by sea, first inspect the Harbour Defences, and then drive through the city, in a flotilla of cars, with many members of the Belgian Government as well as local officials in attendance.

Troops lined the route, and from an early hour in the

morning crowds began to assemble, in the same way as they will turn out for a royal occasion in London. After all, Monty was almost more than royal, he was the god of liberation, and as the first of the outriders appeared in sight, volleys of cheers resounded down the route, warming the hearts of the group of VIPs waiting on the steps of the Club for their great moment.

Alas, the great moment never happened. So far from the car slowing down, and stopping, so far from any presentations taking place, any inspection of the club's interior, any spate of mutual congratulations, there was a complete and devastating anti-climax. For the General's car flashed past in a second, and there they were, left behind on the steps, looking at each other, in bewilderment and dismay. Only later, was the mystery cleared up, when an ADC drove back to explain that Monty had had a rough passage in the ship, and wasn't feeling up to an opening ceremony or anything at the moment. Meanwhile, the person most unaffected by the contretemps was typically Bill Butlin himself. When an agitated senior officer, covered with scarlet tabs, turned to him, exclaiming: 'What shall we do about it?' the club's sponsor replied with the commonsense that is the core of his make-up, 'Let's have a cup of tea.'

In his evocative article, Godfrey did not make clear that the Belgian Home Affairs Minister complained that six thousand young Belgian women had membership cards to the club—and that they were being led astray by British troops. What a contrast to the time when, earlier in the war, I was accused of allowing British girls to be led astray by coloured GIs!

I felt the allegations and innuendoes were an insult to the troops in general and particularly to the Belgian girls. Of course, when an army moves into a place there will always be fraternization. But to me it was much better if this took place in pleasant, inexpensive and properly-supervised surroundings. The truth of the matter was that the campaign against the Club

147

was motivated by political and commercial reasons. There were collaborators and communists who wanted to embarrass the British, and there were owners of sleazy clip-joints who saw the Club taking away their business. As war reporter Rex North wrote in the *Daily Mirror* at the time: 'Because 75 per cent of the Allied lads spend their leaves in Service Clubs, Belgians owning night clubs are losing millions of francs. Some of them are darned sore and they've pulled strings to get the military-controlled dance-halls shut.' North pointed out that as many as two thousand people visited the Brussels Club each night and that a soldier could get 'a whole evening's fun' for about 2s. 6d. They could get tea, coffee and snacks for very modest prices—though the only liquor available was a weak lager costing about fivepence a glass. At a privately-run club Servicemen could pay ten shillings for a single drink.

The *Daily Mail*'s Courtenay Edwards saw me in the Club and quoted me as saying: 'There are no opportunities for mischief here. See for yourself. That Belgian woman in uniform over there is a welfare inspector. Seven of them are going round all the time. And there are always four Military Policemen on duty. We have not had a single complaint from any girl, or from any mother of any girl.'

Courtenay Edwards made a particular point of watching how the British boys behaved. 'Everything seems perfectly all right to me,' he commented. 'The nearest approach to familiarity I saw during the entire evening were instances of Tommies putting an arm around a partner's shoulders as they were sitting at tables taking refreshments.'

In all, we opened eight 21 Clubs in Belgium, Holland and Germany. They proved a great success and, apart from the unpleasantness in Brussels, we had no troubles with any of them.

Travelling and working in these war-torn countries, however, was often eventful. One of my most frightening experiences occurred while flying over Belgium towards the end of the war. I normally travelled from Britain to the Continent by sea, but on one occasion low-lying fog in the Channel prevented this. Aircraft were still operating, however, and as I was in a hurry, I decided to fly. Along the Belgian coast the British advance had by-passed a large pocket of well-armed German troops. We had to fly over the area and a very hot reception we got. The plane was ringed with 'flack'.

Later the pilot told me it was over that same area that the plane carrying Glenn Miller, the famous band leader, was shot down in 1944. It is generally thought that his plane crashed in the Channel, but could that be wrong?

Of course, there still remains the question: why has the plane never been found if it was shot down over land? Yet aircraft that crashed during the War are still being found. Perhaps one of these days my pilot will be proved to have been right and the mystery of Glenn Miller's disappearance will be solved.

Yet another unpleasant experience occurred in Antwerp, where we had requisitioned a dance-hall for a 21 Club. One night, two days before the opening, a nearby cinema with many British troops in the audience was hit by a V1 'flying bomb' and the death toll was heavy. Next day, after a brief visit to Brussels, I returned to Antwerp for the opening of the Club.

When I arrived, the hall was in darkness, but I knew where the light switches were and I edged carefully towards them. But there was something odd. I kept tripping over bundles. Finally I was able to switch on the lights—and realized what the bundles were. The hall was being used as a mortuary for the V1 victims.

Next door to the ballroom were the premises of a zoo—a bleak sight without the animals which had been destroyed months before because of the food shortage. When the war ended, the cages were put to another use. They became prison cells for collaborators. Looking at the cages I reflected that it must have been a particularly unpleasant experience to be arrested as a collaborator—knowing the deep hatred of your captors. At that moment I little realized that I would shortly feel that silent enmity.

It happened when I was being driven from Brussels to Hamburg where we were opening another 21 Club. There were six of us in the truck, and I was the only civilian. Once into

Germany we drove carefully because the road verges still bore signs declaring 'Not cleared', indicating that they might be mined. But, despite this caution, we knocked down and killed a young boy who dashed into the road in front of the lorry as we were passing through a village.

We carried him into a house, where we were surrounded by a group of angry, threatening Germans. I did not speak but I became aware that much of the anger seemed directed at me. Suddenly I realized what was happening. Because I was in civilian clothes the Germans assumed that I was one of them, collaborating with the British. I shall always remember the hard, cold expressions in the eyes of those Germans, and I still wonder what might have happened to us, and to me in particular, if Basil Brown had not produced his revolver and stood close beside me.

In Hamburg itself, my showman's past caught up with me. A big amusement park owned by the famous Schipper family of showmen had been taken over by the British Army to provide free entertainment for the troops. The Schippers were old friends of mine from before the war, and now I was able to bring in one of the brothers to help to run it for the British Forces. Adjoining the Schipper amusement park was the Belli Brothers Circus. The strict rules of non-fraternization with the Germans were by now being relaxed, so I organized a performance of the circus for British troops and selected Germans.

This led to a touching incident, for some of the acts in the show had appeared at the Bertram Mills Circus at Olympia before the War. When they heard I was in the audience they came to pay their respects. The famous Belli brother and sister riding team saluted me with their riding crops and several of the clowns came up and doffed their caps.

To build up the Schipper amusement park various rides that had remained undamaged in other parts of Germany were brought to Hamburg. In charge of this operation, and also of feeding the fairground and circus people, was a young Royal Artillery officer, Lieutenant Colin Johnson. When he was demobbed he joined me at Butlin's and became a senior member of the firm.

Soon after opening the 21 Club in Antwerp, I decided I could do little more for the Army Welfare Service. The troops were gradually being filtered home and no more 21 Clubs were needed. It was time for me to start thinking about my holiday camps again.

11

'Who do you think they're cheering for?'

ONE day in June 1946, I was walking through the reception hall at the Clacton camp when I saw an elderly man and woman sitting side by side.

'What are they waiting for?' I asked the receptionist.

'They want to book in for this week, but we're full up,' she replied.

We were not totally full up because there was one chalet empty—the one set aside for me. At the camps I did not have a special chalet of my own because, inevitably, it would have become better furnished than the rest and I wanted to avoid the campers thinking the ordinary chalets were not good enough for me. So whenever I visited the camps I slept in any chalet that was empty. On this occasion I had originally planned to stay the night and had been allocated a chalet. But then I decided to return to London that evening. So I said, 'Let them have my chalet.'

A few days later I was back in Clacton and I saw the old lady. 'How are you enjoying yourself?' I inquired.

'Oh, I'm having a marvellous time,' she replied. 'But tell me, who is the old gentleman who's sharing my chalet? He's stone deaf and I can't get a word out of him.'

I tell the story now because it illustrates how full the camps were in the summer of 1946. There was a tremendous demand for holiday accommodation with millions of Servicemen and -women and war workers wanting a well-earned rest. And the demand was bolstered by the eight million workers now receiving holidays with pay. My gamble at the start of the War had paid off.

After leaving my 21st Army job, my first task was to switch the camps back to the holiday business. I had an early success, for half of the Filey camp, which had been occupied by the RAF Regiment, was handed back only a few weeks after the end of the war in Europe. The camp had been well looked after, though with its blacked windows and camouflaged buildings it did not have much of a holiday atmosphere. We soon changed all that, however, with plenty of bright paint.

For obvious reasons, the biggest problem was the shortage of manpower. Old employees kept arriving as they were demobbed, but the situation was still difficult. Then I had help from an unexpected quarter. The RAF men in the Service part of the camp were waiting to be demobbed and, bored with kicking their heels, many of them offered to help put the camp back on a civilian footing. Delighted, I accepted, paying them the union rate for the job. A few days later the *Daily Mirror*, not knowing this, published a story that I was getting free labour. Acting on that information the Air Ministry stopped the men working, much to the annoyance and financial detriment of many of them.

One of the main tasks was to demolish the air raid shelters. They were about a hundred feet long by ten feet wide, with an entrance at each end; and while we were knocking them down I was reminded of a plumber we had employed during the building of the camp who had stayed on to work for the RAF. He was a fat, nervous man who, despite his bulk, was always the first when there was an air-raid warning. Once, however, this proved a disadvantage, for the throng following him into the shelter was so heavy he was pushed out of the door at the other end. Unfortunately, as he was forced backwards through the door, one of the attacking German planes was machine-gunning the camp and he received a bullet or two in his plump posterior.

Other major jobs were to clean and repaint the swimming-pool, which had two feet of mud on the bottom, and construct a boating lake. We used the parade ground for the base and built a bank around it. Any RAF men who later holidayed at the camp would no doubt recognize the spot, but others would not realize that they were rowing over the place where many thousands of men had spent hours of square-bashing.

We managed to open Filey for a short season in the summer of 1945 and catered for 50,000 campers, many of them arriving with their old Skegness and Clacton badges, not to mention the free holiday certificates I had given to those who had their holidays cut short when the camps were taken over in 1939.

Our biggest difficulty was to find staff to run the place. To help out, I advertised a holiday-while-you-work scheme which enabled people to stay at the camp for the bargain price of £2 2s. a week—in return for four hours work a day. If they were prepared to work for more than four hours they were paid the full rate for the job. But the idea was not a success. It was a big relief when millions of men and women were demobilized and we were able to get enough staff. For running a chain of holiday camps the size of Butlin's was—still is—a complex operation of organization, staff management and military-style logistics.

Even getting the customers into the camps entailed immense organization. I have been looking at some figures I had drawn up in the early Fifties. They showed that at the bigger camps like Skegness, it was not uncommon for up to 12,000 applications to be received in one day at the height of the season. All of them were acknowledged within twenty-four hours. On Saturday we often handled 12,000 people—6,000 leaving and 6,000 newcomers.

Then there was the formidable task of catering for 1,000,000 campers in a summer. At a camp accommodating 5,000 visitors, for instance, the *daily* consumption of potatoes was four tons. We needed 9,000 bed sheets a week, enough to cover the area of a large airstrip, not to mention pillow slips. We held a stock of 88,250 blankets, which to use another analogy, would have covered fifty-five football pitches. Crockery and cutlery were other big items. One year 9,467 cups were broken and we supplied 48,000 forks and the same number of spoons. Many were genuinely lost or damaged, but some were undoubtedly taken as souvenirs. All cutlery is engraved with the name of Butlin's. So I try to be philosophical and regard the losses in 'souvenirs' as cheap advertising.

Sports, music, dancing: they all cost money, and the figures were astronomical. The swimming-pools needed 67,000 gallons of purified, chlorinated water *at each camp*; tennis courts used 2,300 balls a season, and table tennis 5,100. About fifty table-tennis bats were broken or disappeared at each camp each year.

In the period I am writing about we needed one and a half tons of powder or crystals to grind into the ballroom floors and 400 lengths of chalk to mark the darts and sports scores. And at a big camp like Filey I spent over £2,500 each year on three thousand sports prizes while the whole Butlin organization spent £18,000. What a happy change from the early years at Skegness when we were so hard-up I asked the campers to contribute to the cost of the prizes!

Skegness and Clacton camps were 'demobbed' in time to open for the summer of 1946, and we had more than 100,000 campers. Skegness had been well maintained by the Royal Navy. Even the gardens were all cared for and though the camp had been attacked constantly by the Luftwaffe—fifty-two bombs dropped on it—the Navy rebuilt it as fast as it was knocked down.

I was pleased about the gardens because for me they have always been an important aspect of the camps. I have loved gardens ever since I was a child. In Canada we did not have one and, of course, it was not possible to have one while living in a caravan. But I always enjoyed looking at them as we travelled around and it became an obsession with me to have a garden. So when we built Skegness I immediately began planting rose trees. At first I could only afford a few, but I always felt the campers appreciated them. One evening, while walking around the camp, I met an old lady coming out of her chalet carrying a tooth-glass of water which she carefully poured around the root of a rose tree. 'I pretend it's my own tree for the week of my holiday,' she explained.

Indeed, many of the campers take a great interest in the

gardens—as this little story illustrates. At Skegness, in order to give the gardens a little more colour, I had plastic flowers wired to the front branches of the trees lining the middle road of the camp. The effect was attractive, particularly at night when the trees were floodlit. One day a lady camper stopped me and said: 'Can you please arrange for me to see your Head Gardener?'

'Certainly,' I replied. 'What's it about?'

'I want him to tell me the secret of his wonderful pruning.'

'Pruning?' I queried.

'Yes,' she said. 'It's very clever how he gets all the flowers growing only on the front of the trees.'

Clacton, which had been taken over by the Army, had fared less well than Skegness, having had many chalets demolished. It was originally a POW camp, but was never used for that purpose. Sadly, its first wartime occupants were troops who had escaped from Dunkirk—and a heart-rending sight they had made. For two days they did nothing but sleep. Later the camp was taken over by the RAF and was damaged still further. Doors were even taken from the chalets to use as table tops!

My next major step was to take over the remaining half of Filey and the camps I had built at Pwllheli and Ayr for the Navy. Under the agreement made with the Services they were bought back at three-fifths of the original building cost. With what we now blithely refer to as 'inflation', the camps were a bargain in 1946, but still necessitated a considerable financial outlay. To raise the money we made a Rights Issue.

Pwllheli became a Butlin camp in May, 1947, but not before I had overcome strong opposition and the campaign against us started as early as 1944. Heading the attack were the Welsh Nationalists. 'Butlinization', they roared, 'will ruin one of the most beautiful and unspoiled areas of Wales.'

I had my supporters locally though, for I made it clear that the camp would bring much-needed prosperity to the area. I pointed out that we would buy huge amounts of produce from the local farmers and I also promised to give work to large numbers of local people in the camp itself, which was in an area where there had always been much unemployment.

The controversy raged until 1946 when the Ministry of Town and Country Planning held an inquiry. Local unemployed and tradesmen demonstrated in favour of the camp and the inquiry itself was a lively affair. The audience kept interrupting the proceedings, usually to show support for the camp. This worried me because it could give the impression I had packed the place with my supporters—which was certainly not the case. Eventually, I stood up and told the Chairman, 'I hope you don't think these people are anything to do with me, because they're doing my cause a lot of harm.' I felt confident that I had allayed any suspicions until the lunch adjournment. As the audience filed out a fat old woman in the front row of the gallery, whom I had never seen before, called out, 'Do you want us back this afternoon, Mr Butlin?' She obviously meant it with the best of intentions, but at that moment I could happily have thrown her off the top of Mount Snowdon. Nevertheless, we won the Ministry's blessing and *HMS Glendower* became a Butlin camp.

One of the thousands of young sailors who had passed through *HMS Glendower* during the war was Lieutenant Philip Mountbatten who, of course, later became the Duke of Edinburgh and the Queen's husband. This resulted in the camp being honoured by a visit from the Queen and the Duke. Some time before this took place I had been invited to lunch at Buckingham Palace and the Queen had said to me: 'My children are always hearing about your camps and they want to know when they can visit one.' I replied that they would be very welcome any time. In fact, none of the Royal youngsters visited any of the camps, but when the Queen toured North Wales in the summer of 1963 she expressed a wish to see the camp where her husband had been stationed.

It was a nostalgic return for him and he clearly remembered the main parts of the camp. I asked him if he would tell me which chalet he had slept in. He grinned and said: 'Not bloody likely. You'll only put up a notice on it and charge more!'

The Queen had not been to a holiday camp before and she and the Duke spent several hours visiting practically every building, including the chapel and the newly-opened entertainment centre, which cost £1,750,000 to build—more than the cost of the original camp.

By the time of the Queen's visit I had come to know the Duke well through the National Playing Fields Association, of which he was a most enthusiastic President, having succeeded his uncle, Lord Mountbatten, in 1948. It has always been a pleasure to me to know that Butlin campers have contributed so much to this worth-while charity, which since 1925 has provided grants for sports fields and other facilities ranging from running tracks, pavilions and changing rooms and adventure playgrounds throughout the country.

In more recent years it has done much to help physically and mentally-handicapped children. For between 1949 and 1978 campers raised more than £200,000 and there are many playing fields and buildings all over the country bearing plaques declaring they have been donated by Butlin campers.

The Duke had his own ideas for promoting the Playing Fields Association and in 1949 he visited the Skegness camp to present a silver Challenge Trophy to be competed for by the camps every summer, the winner being the camp that collected the most per camper for the Association. For this visit he flew to an airfield about fifty miles from Skegness, where I had arranged for a Rolls to meet him. On the outskirts of Skegness I joined him and we drove through streets lined with about a hundred thousand people, including children, who had been given the day off from school and a small Union Jack to wave.

The Duke acknowledged the crowds through one window of the Rolls, while I waved through the other.

'Who do you think they're cheering for?' he asked with a grin. 'You or me?'

The competition started by the Duke's visit proved highly successful. Each year at the Butlin's reunion when we filled the Royal Albert Hall with six thousand people every night for a week, a cheque was handed to the Association and the Trophy awarded to the winning camp.

On three occasions the Duke lent his lively presence. The first time was during the Coronation Year of 1953. I stood up to

158

welcome him and found I had forgotten my speech. Greatly embarrassed, I publicly admitted my sin. The Duke grinned and quipped, 'I always carry my speech with me.'

When the Duke was next with us three years later, I reminded him and the audience about this incident. 'You'll be pleased to know, sir, that I've got my speech with me this time,' I announced, producing it from my breast pocket with a flourish. And then, while thousands watched, I felt in my breast pocket for my glasses—and discovered to my horror I had left them at home. So once again I was unable to read my speech.

But to revert to those early post-war years. In 1947, the camp I had built for the Navy at Ayr was also taken over by Butlin's. It was opened by that great Scottish comedian Sir Harry Lauder, and meeting him reminded me of the time he had performed in Toronto when I was young. Today it would be hard to believe, but he was not a success with the Scots in the area. They felt he was taking the micky out of their race in his act, and there were some acid articles in the newspapers. It is odd that a man who came to represent Scotland in the minds of millions was once not liked by some of his fellow Scots.

Shortly after the end of the War Harry Warner and I visited Paris, where we saw an impressive model of a Russian holiday camp. The Russian officials were exceedingly proud of it, so we asked if we could visit it. 'Yes, of course, we would be honoured and delighted,' they said. Some months later, after many delays and much to our surprise, we received the necessary visas. We travelled by boat to Hamburg and then took a laborious train to the East German border. And there we came to a grinding halt. No amount of waving of documents, no amount of name-dropping could get us across that border.

Later I learned why. The camp had not progressed beyond the model stage.

Whether the camp ever became a reality I never discovered, even when I did finally get into Russia many years later in 1962. That was when Lord Thomson, a Canadian and a great friend of mine who owned *The Times* and the *Sunday Times*, celebrated the first birthday of his *Sunday Times* colour magazine by taking a group of top businessmen, including myself, to Moscow. It was not only a remarkable achievement at the height of the 'Cold War', but a fascinating, though sometimes bizarre, trip.

Surprising things happened from the start. As a VIP party we did not go through Passport Control at London Airport, and as a result one distinguished personage did not realize he had forgotten his passport until we were about to embark on the Russian Tupelev 114. This was disastrous, for even though we were on an officially-sponsored visit, the political climate at the time made it highly unlikely that the Russians would let anyone into the country without a passport.

What to do? There was much scratching of heads until someone thought of an idea. The VIP was rushed off to one of those do-it-yourself photographic cubicles and then, as we winged eastwards, one of the prints was stuck on a sheet of writing paper. Underneath the photograph were typed the words you find on your passport and signed by the Home Secretary. Only on this occasion the signature was that of Roy H. Thomson. The Russians were clearly taken aback by this most unusual document, but after much conferring and telephoning the forgetful VIP was finally allowed in.

The days were full of official visits, numerous toasts and banquets. Roy Thomson pulled off a journalistic scoop by meeting Nikita Krushchev, the ebullient extrovert who was then the top man in Russia.

It was a remarkable confrontation. On one side was a dyed-in-the-wool capitalist and on the other the world's most powerful Communist. Roy later told me something about the meeting in the Kremlin. He sat across a green-baized table from Krushchev, who was flanked by portraits of Lenin and Marx, and they quickly established that their birthdays in 1894 were separated by only a few weeks. 'But you are a bit taller,' Krushchev said, pretending to be jealous.

Roy commented that though they came from vastly different social systems they had both come up in the world. 'Oh, we do,' Krushchev quipped. 'We certainly do come up.'

And when Roy commented that though he owned a

hundred newspapers, Krushchev would surely have owned two hundred if he had been a capitalist, Krushchev pretended to be conspiratorial. 'Ssh,' he said, glancing round. 'Don't say that. Communist agents may hear, and think that I *want* to own two hundred newspapers.'

They had a long and friendly talk about world affairs, during which Krushchev teased Roy about his wealth. 'What good is money to you?' he asked. 'You can't take it with you.'

He was greatly amused when Roy replied: 'Then I'm not going.'

After two-and-a-half hours Roy felt he had kept Krushchev long enough. 'We're keeping you,' he apologized. 'No,' said Krushchev. 'Everything on Saturday stops at mid-day.'

'You're working overtime, then?' joked Roy.

'It's all right,' replied Krushchev with a grin. 'I'm on piece work.'

Roy, who had a very quick and ready wit, shot back: 'But how do you spell "piece"?' Unfortunately the interpreter did not understand Roy's play on words, and so the joke was lost.

Before they parted Roy presented the Russian Premier with a battery-driven wrist watch for himself and a gold one for his wife. Kruschchev pretended to be suspicious about his own gift. 'Are you sure it is not some infernal device put together by capitalists to blow up the Communist system?' he said, poker-faced. 'I must get my wife to try it on first. A Yugoslav once told me that whenever they wanted to cross a minefield, they always let the ladies go first.'

I did not meet anyone so grand as Premier Krushchev, though I did have dinner with the British ambassador to Moscow, who was suitably impressed by Thomson's visit. 'I've been here two years and I've never met Krushchev,' he told me, 'yet Roy Thomson meets him on his first day here.'

However, I did talk to some ordinary Russians—which was more my style. I was surprised to find how many people spoke English. Moscow had a lot of hot-dog stands like those in New York and on several occasions I left official functions to visit these and talk to people. Understandably, they never said anything controversial and expressed themselves happy with life—but it was still an interesting experience.

For Roy Thomson the visit was a great and prestigious success, but I suspect it was for him marred by one thing: he was unable to buy either of Russia's leading newspapers, *Pravda* and *Izvestia*! For myself, I would have liked to have visited a Russian holiday camp, if they had any, but I received only vague generalities when I raised the subject.

Some social observers have said that Butlin's camps introduced a Brave New World democracy into Britain's social life. Certainly the camps have always been democratic, for everybody pays the same, gets the same food and accommodation and is treated the same. But I like to think there is a gulf of difference between Butlin's and the rigid regimentation you would surely get in a Communist-controlled camp.

In 1946, I began to think about expanding overseas. My first step was to form a new company, Butlin's Irish and Continental Holidays Ltd. It was financed by 300,000 Five and a Half Per Cent Cumulative Preference Shares of £1 and 4 million Ordinary shares of one shilling, and its first object was to build a Holiday Village at Mosney, some twenty-three miles north of Dublin, to accommodate 2,500 visitors. You notice I called it a Holiday Village, not a Camp—and this reflected something that had been in my mind for some time. I had always visualized my camps as self-contained villages, but I had started with the name 'Camp' in 1936 and it was difficult to change it in Britain. Starting anew in Ireland, I was able to go back to the drawing board. And to help eliminate the old-style image I began to tone down some of the more strident aspects of the original camps.

A writer in the *Financial Times*, describing a visit to Mosney, reported on 27 August 1948: 'Perhaps there is a little less loud-speaker at Mosney than in some other places. Here is Mr Butlin in his middle period—a Sixth Symphony Mr Butlin, a mellowing Mr Butlin, a Greensleeves, not a Wakey, Wakey Mr Butlin.'

By the end of the Fifties the atmosphere at the British camps

162

was also being modified and the thinking behind this was later pithily summed up by the slogan 'Butlin Land is Freedom Land', which my son Bobby introduced. In *The Times* of 12 June 1959 a Special Correspondent wrote: 'Regimentation is not exactly the word for the hearty hospitality dispensed through the broadcasting system and by the blazer brigade of hosts and hostesses. The old "Wakey, wakey" regime has been toned down.'

As people's tastes changed and became more sophisticated, we continued this toning down in the Sixties and Seventies. In 1977, Radio Butlin, as we called the camp Tannoy system, began to be phased out. There was undoubtedly much snobbery about the 'Wakey, wakey', enforced-gaiety-atmosphere of the camps. Looking back I wonder if we might have been a little too sensitive about this criticism, for perhaps all that was wrong was that the camps were ahead of their time.

But if some people turned up their noses at Butlin's in those post-war years, there were many, including distinguished people in all spheres of life, who did not. The Countess of Mountbatten and her daughter Pamela were frequent visitors, having been brought to the Skegness camp originally by Godfrey Winn. Among the politicians who came were Anthony Eden, Herbert Morrison and Hugh Dalton. When I invited well-known politicians I always took them to Filey camp because the bar there was an exact replica of one in the House of Commons. Incidentally, the magnificent chandeliers in the great ballroom used to hang in the German embassy in London. And in the realm of entertainment the top stars in the country came to the camps. Immediately after the war we re-introduced the successful policy of having big show-business names for our Sunday Celebrity Concerts. But now a new generation, indeed a new breed, of entertainer had emerged. They were the stars of radio, the artists who had kept up our morale during the dark days of the war. They were household names with familiar voices, but few people had seen them in the flesh. So with the slogan 'Stars You Have Heard – But Seldom Seen' we brought them to Butlin's.

We had no difficulty in deciding who we should have first. It had to be Tommy Handley and the cast of the most popular wartime radio comedy show, *It's That Man Again* – or *ITMA*. It coined a score of catch-phrases that became part of the nation's language. Millions still remember 'I don't mind if I do' uttered by the alcoholic Colonel Chinstrap, played by Jack Train, who became a regular and popular performer at the camps. Not to mention 'Can I do you now, sir?' and 'It's being so cheerful that keeps me going' from the office char, Mona Lott. Or the polite pair who were always saying: 'After you, Cecil,' 'No, after you, Claude.'

They were followed by Richard Murdoch and Kenneth Horne from *Much Binding in the Marsh*, another of the great wartime radio shows which was set in a mythical (thank goodness for us all) and hilariously-mismanaged RAF station. Other stars included Anona Winn, who later became even more well-known through the radio programme *Twenty Questions*; Arthur Askey, whose own catch-phrase 'I thank yew' is another one that entered the language, the ventriloquist Peter Brough with his cheeky puppet Archie Andrews and the 'Memory Man' Leslie Welch. The idea was a big success. It brought us publicity in the newspapers and gained us invaluable word-of-mouth advertising. For every Monday morning thousands of campers sent off post-cards saying, 'Guess who we saw last night?'

To raise the image of the camps still further we next moved 'up market' in the entertainment world. I hired the San Carlo Opera Company of Naples for two weeks for £10,000, and their first performance was of Puccini's *La Bohème* at Filey before 5,000 campers and specially-invited guests who included 400 VIPs from London. We took them to Filey in the Yorkshire Pullman, which had been in mothballs throughout the war. It cost £1,100 to hire, but it brought a touch of luxury to those austerity-ridden days. Unfortunately, the train caught fire outside Doncaster and we were delayed for two hours. And when we arrived at Filey I was promptly confronted with another problem which generated almost as much heat as the train fire. Two of the stars of the San Carlo were a husband

and wife and they were having a tempestuous row. They refused to sing with each other or share a chalet. So with great difficulty we juggled the accommodation lists and gave them separate chalets.

But we had no sooner settled them in when the husband came and demanded they be put together again. Apparently all was now sweetness and light. Not in all quarters, though. For when we moved certain visitors a second time, they undoubtedly thought we had all gone mad.

It was at Filey a few years later that I was involved in another embarrassing incident. I was walking round the camp one day when I noticed a man digging leisurely in one of the vegetable plots. He seemed to spend most of his time leaning on his spade and smoking a cigarette. Half an hour later I passed him again and he was still carrying on in his leisurely way. This was too much for me. Angrily I went up to him. 'I won't tolerate slackers on my staff,' I said. 'Go to the office and collect your cards and a week's money.' He looked at me in amazement. 'What are you talking about?' he asked. 'I don't work here. I'm a camper.'

'Then why are you digging here?' I demanded. 'I'm digging for worms,' he replied. 'I'm going fishing.' Collapse of a red-faced Billy Butlin.

In addition to the San Carlo, the Bristol Old Vic and the International Ballet also visited the camps. This type of entertainment surprised many people, particularly those who still looked down on holiday camps. But as was proved during the War, the appreciation of classical music, ballet and opera is not limited to any one section of the community. Even so, for some of our campers this class of entertainment was certainly a new experience—including me.

For instance, at the opening of the Pwllheli camp, the London Symphony Orchestra conducted by Stanford Robinson gave a concert and one of the works in the programme was a piano concerto, with Solomon as the soloist. The first movement of this work had a long stretch where the piano was silent. I was backstage during this part of the concert and the stage manager asked me, 'Mr Butlin, why isn't

Solomon playing?'

'It's probably because someone has forgotten to pay him,' I said poker-faced, fixing the man with a hard stare. He was quite worried and I must confess I was starting to worry myself, wondering if Solomon had actually gone on strike. Just as I was making my way to the wings to see what was happening, I was relieved to hear him start playing.

But, successful as these artistic ventures were, the main entertainment for the campers was still popular music and 'Variety'. And, while we had a regular flow of stars, much of the entertainment was increasingly provided by young, unknown artistes who had begun to realize that Butlin's offered what was described as 'probably the finest collective training ground for theatrical talent in the country today'. By appearing regularly in shows throughout the summer, many young entertainers were able to develop and polish their talent. After a season or two at the camps many of these artistes turned professional and eventually became big stars.

And then there were the Redcoats, whose ranks rapidly filled with embryonic entertainers. Many of them, too, became successful. Between them all they deserve a chapter to themselves.

166

12

'The Ladder of Fame'

ANYONE who has been in the Services will probably agree that, however good the standards of outside professional entertainment, the most popular shows are generally those put on by Servicemen and -women themselves. In the Services this was known as soldier-to-soldier entertainment and it undoubtedly accounted for the success of such shows as *Stars in Battledress* and the RAF *Gang Show*.

The same principle worked at the camps—right from the start when volunteers helped to entertain after the evening meal. When the Redcoats began to expand, those who could go on stage and entertain were always highly popular. After the war we developed this idea. When I say 'we' I include Colonel Basil Brown, who became Director of Entertainments for Butlin's after the war. In 1971 he was succeeded by Frank Mansell, an ex-comic who appeared in various Resident Revue companies.

We encouraged campers to entertain themselves through amateur talent shows like *I Want To Be an Actor* and *The Ladder of Fame*. For a time we ran a show called *In Camp Tonight* in which campers were persuaded on stage to recall their wartime experiences—and some fascinating stories we got, too. Later, when would-be entertainers began to realize that the Butlin Redcoats could be a stepping stone into show business, the Redcoat ranks were packed with aspiring talent,

167

though the majority of them had never been on a stage before. For our part, we realized that the Redcoats could be used like the soldier-to-soldier shows. Through being involved in the day-to-day life of the camps, they were regarded as friends by the campers and were able to create the same sort of togetherness as the wartime Service shows. We called the shows *Redcoats Revue* and presented them late in the week, when the campers had got to know the Redcoats. They have been immensely popular ever since—which is not surprising. For in a large camp there are anything up to a hundred Redcoats, providing a wonderful pool of talent.

And what talent! There was Charlie Drake, though at first he was a camp boxing instructor. He had boxed for the RAF during the war and he was ideal for us because we liked our instructors not to be too big. It made it easier to persuade the campers to climb into the ring with them! Charlie was at Filey and it was there he teamed up with a big female impersonator named Jack Edwards. While they were still at the camp they developed a successful television act, 'Mick and Montmorency'. During this period Charlie's first son was born and I became the child's godfather.

Des O'Connor was a Redcoat at Filey for two years and married the 1953 winner of our Holiday Princess Contest. He led the sports and social activities and met the new campers in the reception hall every Saturday. He played a very popular game with the children called 'Hunt the Pirate'. It entailed Des being chased round the swimming-pool and then thrown in. From the time he won £5 as a first prize in a talent contest, Des desperately wanted to enter show business. At Filey he was so often to be found hanging around the theatre when he should have been elsewhere that he narrowly escaped being sacked.

His efforts to be selected for the camp show failed repeatedly, but unabashed he wrote one day to a show-business agent, describing himself as 'principal comedian' of the show—and to his amazement he received a telegram saying: 'Arriving to see you Friday.' What on earth was Des to do? What he did was to draw all his savings from the Post Office, which amounted to the princely sum of £32, and bribe

168

the three comedians who *were* in the show to go missing or fall sick on the Friday. The ruse worked, for at the last minute a desperate entertainments officer remembered Des and called him in to deputize. And what is more, the agent liked him well enough to get him started on the variety halls at the end of the summer.

Dave Allen, after being a newspaper reporter in Ireland, was a Redcoat at Skegness and appeared with two established Butlin performers, Bill Martin and Dizzie Leslie in a most successful show called *Three's Company*. In the camps, however, Dave's brother, who used his own name of John Mahoney, was much better known. He was camp comic at Filey and was immensely popular.

Freddie (Parrot Face) Davies, was another Redcoat who was ambitious to have his own show, and kept asking Frank Mansell to give him a chance. One day Frank called him into the office and said: 'I'm going to give you your own show.'

'That's great,' said Freddie.

'The show will be called *Give That Man a Coconut.*' Freddie looked mystified. 'What's it about? What do I do?' he asked. Frank looked at him poker-faced and replied, 'Don't ask me. I only think up the titles.'

Freddie went away to rack his brains and a few days later came up with a comedy show in which the campers could participate. It ran successfully for the remainder of the season.

Ted Rogers, Roy Hudd, Colin Crompton, Mike Newman and Jimmy Tarbuck were all Redcoats—though Jimmy started at Butlin's as a kitchen porter. He became a Redcoat at Pwllheli, but his Liverpool accent was so strong in those days that many of the campers could not understand him. Later, of course, he became a national name through compering *Sunday Night at the Palladium* on television, and appeared on a Royal Variety Show before the Queen. A few days after that he judged the finals of one of our talent contests and he told the audience with a grin: 'You know, I was sacked from Butlin's because I couldn't speak the Queen's English.' He paused and then added, 'When I met her last week she didn't complain.'

Cliff Richard was also a Redcoat and he sang in one of the

bars at Clacton, where he later met and teamed up with a group called the Shadows. It was the first time we had introduced music into this particular bar and when the executive in charge of the bars heard Cliff he was furious. He stormed into Basil Brown's office and yelled, 'What are you trying to do? Ruin the business?' So Cliff was moved, but when he and the Shadows appeared in a *Redcoats Revue* they were a big success.

Two other Redcoat singers were Russ Hamilton, one of the big pop stars of the Fifties, who was a Kiddies' Uncle at Clacton, and Clinton Ford. Clinton was out of work in Liverpool when a musician friend, off to the Pwllheli camp for the season, suggested he tried for a job there. The entertainments manager thought he was a rock'n'roll singer and was about to turn him down, but Clinton sat on the edge of his desk, sang him some sweet songs, and got the job. Michael Holliday, another top singer of the Fifties, who died so tragically in 1963, also got his first break at Pwllheli.

And at Skegness we once had Ringo Starr, later to achieve fame as the Beatles' drummer. Ringo then played with another Liverpool group, Rory Storm and the Hurricanes. When they arrived at the camp they all sported long hair. In those days long hair was not as acceptable as it later became, and those campers who wore such a style usually proved to be trouble-makers. We gave many of them their money back and asked them to leave. So I told Rory Storm's group to get their hair cut. They all did—except Ringo. I had to threaten to sack him before he complied. When I met him years later he reminded me of the incident. 'You wouldn't be able to make me do it now,' he said.

Quite a few other now-famous artists got their early experience by working as resident entertainers at the camps. In the pop world there were the Bachelors, who were at the Mosney camp in Eire, Georgie Fame, Brian Pool and the Tremeloes, Dusty Springfield and the Beverley Sisters, who sang with Eric Winstone's band. Helen Shapiro often worked for us after winning a Butlin's talent contest.

Among the comedians were Norman Vaughan, Terry Scott,

Joe Baker, Bruce Forsyth, Benny Hill, Hugh Lloyd, Jack Douglas, Val Doonican, Hughie Green and Bill Maynard. Bill recently has had a big success on television as the entertainments officer in a holiday camp that fortunately bears no resemblance to Butlin's. He recalls being auditioned for a job at Skegness by Richard Stone, a top agent, and actor Ian Carmichael who produced the camp shows.

Working at the camps was good training for comedians because I insisted they got their laughs without resorting to dirty jokes. On the dressing-room doors of all the camps was a notice saying: 'Watch your material. Don't use blue gags. The children don't understand them, the parents don't like them. And we won't have them at any price.'

Many young artists got the chance and experience of working before big audiences by appearing on our Sunday Night Celebrity Concerts. Among them were Bruce Forsyth, Benny Hill—we paid him £15 for two shows—and Frankie Howerd, who 'died a death'. Afterwards he asked me, 'Why didn't I go over?' I told him, 'Well, your act isn't very good. If I were you I'd give up show business and get a job.' Millions of people are undoubtedly glad that he did not take my advice.

Not all of the famous names who worked at Butlin's entertained there. Some of them were on the administrative side. For instance Bill Simpson, of *Dr Finlay's Casebook* fame, was in the cashier's office at Ayr and that glorious singer Moira Anderson joined the accommodation department there. Actress Glenda Jackson was a coffee bar assistant at Filey to be near her then husband Bill Hodges, who was in the camp repertory company.

While all these people were working at the camps, we were visited by a stream of celebrities. Laurel and Hardy came to Skegness and revealed themselves as two amiable, if ageing, natural clowns. They happily fooled around on the roller-skating rink and pedalled boisterously around the camp on a tricycle. That famous old-time cowboy, Hopalong Cassidy was another visitor. He came to Britain with a group of American boys who had won a tour of the Butlin camps in a competition organized by an American Variety Club to find champion newspaper sellers. The London Variety Club arranged for a similar number of boys from public schools in this country to travel with them. It seemed a good example of Anglo-American friendship—but it boomeranged most unfortunately. The Americans were tough and worldly, and they taught the British boys a few things—like playing poker and shooting crap for money—which their headmasters did not exactly appreciate.

Many illustrious sportsmen visited the camps, among them the American heavyweight, Joe Baksi, who came to Britain to fight our own champion, the Doncaster lad, Bruce Woodcock. It was a disastrous fight for Woodcock. Baksi broke Bruce's jaw in the first round and though he struggled on bravely, he was overwhelmed. When Baksi later spent a few days at Filey, I thought that as Doncaster was only some forty miles away I would invite Bruce over to meet him. He replied with typical Yorkshire bluntness, 'I've met him.' Eventually, however, I persuaded him to meet Baksi and shake hands and they became great pals.

The summer of 1951 was enlivened by the arrival of two young American children, aged five and four, Bubba and Kathy Tongay, who were incredible swimmers. Their father, Russell, a tough, opportunistic former US Coastguard, brought them to Britain in an attempt to swim the English Channel. The newspapers promptly dubbed them 'The Water Babies'. I felt that if they succeeded, the feat would tremendously encourage swimming among British children. To help meet the expenses of the trip I paid them £1,000 to give displays at the camps. But no sooner had they arrived than I found myself in the middle of a bureaucratic wrangle. The Home Office at first refused them permission to stay, but after a last-minute effort from their father, the authorities relented. As I had partly financed the trip, I was called to the Home Office to discuss their fate. After a long discussion it was agreed that they could stay for a month if I would be responsible for them and see that the only swimming they did was in the camp pool.

A regular visitor to the camps about that time was Donald

172

Campbell, son of the great 'Speed King' Sir Malcolm Campbell who had won for Britain the world land and water speed records with his famous Bluebird car and boat. Donald was highly conscious of being Sir Malcolm's son and this drove him on to continue his father's quest for speed and more speed. One of Donald's dreams was to break the world's water speed record, and he made plans to attempt it on Lake Coniston. We became great friends and I was anxious to help him, but I did not want to give him straightforward financial support. To avoid this I put up a £5,000 prize for anyone who broke the record—confident that he would be the one who did it. I was delighted when he won the prize by reaching a speed of 276.33 mph in 1964. Tragically, in 1967 he was killed, trying to break his own record. After his death, Sir Max Aitken, myself and several others financed a scholarship in his name.

All these personalities enlivened the camps, but the backbone of the entertainment was still provided by the Redcoats, stage acts and, of course, our resident bands. Before the war such top orchestras as those of Mantovani and Lew Stone played many seasons at the camps. In the Forties and Fifties most of the major bands of that era played for us at one time or another, for each of the camps had two dance-halls and two bands. Even Mantovani, whose fame had vastly increased since pre-war days, spent two seasons at Filey. Another big name who, in fact, spent several seasons there was the irrepressible Harry Roy. And at Minehead we had Frank Weir, who had a big record success in the Fifties with his *Happy Wanderer*.

Eric Winstone and his orchestra moved into Clacton when it re-opened in 1946 and he stayed with Butlin's, playing at various camps. For a time he was at Pwllheli, where he once had a practical joke played on him. Late one night Eric retired to his chalet and when he opened the door he got the shock of his life. There, tethered to his bed, was a horse! Eric could not believe his eyes—but he could believe his nose. For the horse had misbehaved itself.

During the first seven summers he played at Butlin's, Eric lived in a chalet on the camp. 'I was,' he once told me, 'a

173

permanent tenant with ever-changing neighbours. I felt like a goldfish in a bowl. I might be half-way through shaving when there would be a knock on the door, and opening it with soap still on my face I would find myself confronted by a camper with an autograph book, or a couple wanting me to play a certain tune that evening for their anniversary.

'At first I found it annoying, but I later came to realize it had its compensations, for the dancers you played for were no longer just customers, they were people you knew personally. It is no idle boast that every camper and every member of the staff from the man at the gate to the man who swept the ballroom floor, called me Eric.'

On Saturdays, Eric sometimes stood in the reception hall watching the new campers arrive. One day, wearing flannel bags and a very much off-white roll-neck sweater, he was taken by a harassed father of three youngsters as a member of the reception staff. Handing Eric a shilling tip he instructed him to take the larger of two suitcases, and the smallest of the three boys, to such-and-such a chalet. Eric duly obliged, and felt he had earned his tip when the youngster spent his time on the walk to the chalet endeavouring to kick him in the shins. Still, he felt the entire incident was worthwhile when he saw the look on the faces of the father and mother as they entered the ballroom that evening and spotted Eric, immaculate in his tuxedo, standing before the band bathed in an amber light.

Eric was a successful composer with such hits as 'Stage Coach', his signature tune, 'Pony Express' and 'Oasis' and he wrote several 'Butlin' pieces, the 'Butlin Conga', the 'Butlin Waltz' and a song called 'Remember We Met at Butlin's', which he recorded with the Beverley Sisters.

It brought back nostalgic memories to hear it being played during the summer of 1978 on a BBC radio programme about Butlin's.

> Was it Skegness or Clacton or Filey
> Was it April, June or July?
> Remember we met at Butlin's
> I was the guy.

I wonder how many remember that being played during the summer of 1947?

In the winter Eric became 'Uncle Eric' and presented a programme broadcast from Radio Luxembourg for the 200,000 members of the Beaver Club for campers' children, which I started in 1951. Many of these children will now be adults with children of their own, but I am sure they will still remember their days as Butlin Beavers and the Beaver Code they promised to embrace:

BEAVER

B stands for: Be kind to animals.
E stands for: Eager always to help others.
A stands for: Always be clean, neat and tidy.
V stands for: Victory by fair play.
E stands for: Energetic at work and play.
R stands for: Respect for parents and all elders.

I am sure, too, they will remember the Beaver Lodges at the camps where parents were only allowed on sufferance, and the grand initiation ceremony conducted by the Camp Mayor in all his ceremonial robes. And the Christmas and birthday cards from King Beaver, or the Beaver Diploma they received when they wrote reporting having passed an 'exam' at school. And, of course, the Beaver Reunions held in all the main cities, culminating in the great get-together at the Royal Albert Hall in London, when three thousand children sang:

If you're a Butlin Beaver you're a friend of mine
If you've the Beaver spirit then the world is fine

For my part, I was always greatly moved by this occasion, particularly when there was a child whose birthday fell on the day of the reunion. If this happened we gave him or her a box for themselves, their parents and relatives, and arc lights were trained on it. Oh, the pride and pleasure of the child who received this honour.

Apart from Eric Winstone, of course, many big-name bands

played at Butlin's over the years: Billy Ternent, with his distinctive brass sound, Ivy Benson and her All Girls Band, the famous ex-RAF orchestra the Squadronaires, Syd Seymour and his Mad Hatters and Teddy Foster.

Some of the band leaders were great characters: there was Dick Denny, for instance, who fronted the first professional band at Filey after the War. Also at Filey in the early post-war years was Charles Amer and his Butlin Boys. Charles first joined Butlin's as entertainments manager at Skegness in 1937. Later he developed various business interests, but he still remained a keen musician and his band played at the camp for several years. Now he is a wealthy builder and hotel owner and chairman of Middlesbrough Football Club.

At Ayr we had Scotland's foremost band led by Ronnie Munroe, who later joined the Scottish BBC and directed the resident dance orchestra. Also at Ayr was Stanley Barnett. At Skegness was Alan Green, another great character. His band played at several Royal Variety Performances and he always appeared on the bandstand wearing white tie and tails. The tail coat was very useful for it camouflaged the bottles of Guinness he kept in his trouser pockets. And at Mosney, we had Jimmie Masson's band.

As the camp shows got bigger and better with 'Resident Revues', the weekly *Redcoats Revue* and visiting stars, we began to need theatre orchestras as distinct from dance bands and that is how Al Freid came to join us. Al conducted the number one 'pit orchestra' for the Moss Empire theatre chain and he came to Butlin's to form our first concert orchestra. He was our principal conductor for more than twenty years and always conducted the orchestra for the finals of our National Talent Contests at the London Palladium. There were two other famous orchestras which specialized in playing old time dance music at many Butlin functions—those of Harry Davidson, who originated the radio programme *Those Were The Days* and Sydney Thompson of *Take Your Partners* fame.

I cannot talk about dance bands without mentioning dancing itself, for since the early post-war years, Butlin's have played an important part in the boom in popularity of all kinds of ballroom dancing. Back in 1940, we held the Butlin Professional Dance Championship under the aegis of the Official Board of Ballroom Dancing. It was held at the Royal Opera House, Covent Garden, which during the War became a Mecca dance-hall, and was organized by Captain J. Russell Pickering (or 'Pick' as he was popularly known), who was general manager of the Opera House and a one-time director of Butlin's. A one-day event, it was a glittering success but war-time circumstances prevented it being repeated.

At Pwllheli in 1950 we organized the first national Stage Dance Festival for all types of dancing from ballet to tap. The following year it was transferred to Filey, and Harry Silvester was appointed organizer and compere. During his seventeen years in the job his genial personality and expertise helped to develop the Festival into the world's largest. Tony Tarver, formerly of the Sadlers Wells Ballet, has since taken over as organizer. Over the years many talented dancers have competed in the Festival and gone on to make their mark in ballet companies and stage musicals.

In the late Forties sequence dancing, in which large numbers of couples perform together a regular, repeated series of steps—very often they are old-time dances—began booming after the lifting of a bizarre ruling barring competitors under 30.

In 1951, I decided to hold a dance festival at Filey. Luckily, I had working for me the perfect man to organize it. Wilfred Orange had been in dancing since before the War, when he ran four ballrooms and two dancing schools. He had also been an early member and past Chairman of the Official Board of Ballroom Dancing, a body which exercises tight control over ballroom dance contests and whose permission is necessary before you can hold a championship contest. Wilfred came out of the RAF to become entertainment manager at Filey and later at Ayr, and then set up an office in Nottingham to look after Butlin's Social Clubs, assisted by two Redcoats, Bert Knott and Eddie McGuire.

His interest in dancing, however, led him to have

discussions with Philip J. Richardson, the then Chairman of the Official Board of Ballroom Dancing. As a result they organized the first Butlin's National Veleta Competition. In February 1948, after local heats throughout the country, five thousand couples took part in the finals at the Royal Albert Hall. For the record, the first winners were Mr and Mrs Joe Stead of Blackpool.

Wilfred later organized a Modern and Latin Dance Festival. It was a great success, and it still is. Today Butlin's hold all kinds of dance festivals at the camps—which with their large dance floors, stages, sound equipment and on-the-doorstep accommodation, are ideal sites. In 1978, 40,000 people attended them. They are generally recognized as being the largest dance festivals in the world.

Looking back over this chapter, I hope I have accurately reflected how Butlin-style entertainment developed in the camps and how many now-famous artists played such an important part. But there are two performers who became regulars at the camps whom I have still to mention. It is very much a case of 'Last but not least', and when I mention their names I am sure many campers will agree. For I am talking about Maurice Fogel, a most amazing mind-reader, and Peter Casson, the hypnotist.

Maurice Fogel, apart from his mind-reading, did some remarkable feats like catching a bullet in his teeth after it had been fired from a gun. But I particularly remember him for two instances of cool nerve, once when he stole an entire audience from a camp theatre and again when he hoodwinked hundreds of campers with a brilliantly-executed ploy. His piece of audience-poaching took place at Filey, where he was giving a nightly show at the camp's second theatre, the Gaiety. At the main theatre, the Empire, there was a variety show headed by Teddy Foster and his Band. Fogel was anxious for a sizeable audience because he had heard I was in the camp, but fifteen minutes before his show was due to begin the theatre was practically empty. Fogel trotted across to the Empire where his fears where confirmed. An audience of several hundreds were already seated.

As he thought of his own empty theatre, Fogel became desperate—and desperate men often perform uncharacteristic deeds. What Fogel did was boldly to mount the stage in front of the curtain and coolly announce, 'Ladies and Gentlemen, I'm sorry to have to announce that Teddy Foster and his Band have been recording a television show and through no fault of their own they have been delayed. Consequently the show will be late in starting. However, a show is about to start in the Gaiety Theatre with the amazing mind-reader Maurice Fogel. If you wish to see this show you should leave now.' A large part of the audience left for the Gaiety—and Teddy Foster never did discover why he had such a poor house that night.

Fogel's other feat was also at Filey where we had a new bar, the Regency. For some unaccountable reason it was not very popular and so Fogel was asked to stage a show which would attract people into the bar. He came up with an ingenious stunt which I did not see as I was not in the camp. Had I been I might well have stopped him, because it was in dubious taste. But from what I heard later it did no real harm.

He announced that on such-and-such a night he would eat a camper alive—and he asked for volunteers. Of course, everyone believed it was a trick and he got three men volunteers, from whom he picked one. Dead-pan, he warned him that he was totally serious and gave him an opportunity to pull out. But not believing Fogel could possibly mean it the man declared he would go ahead.

On the night the Regency Bar was packed with campers anxious to see how Fogel would get out of his impossible promise to eat a man alive. Fogel built up the drama by appearing with a bottle marked 'Ether', a large sponge and several towels. He was accompanied by a couple of assistants dressed in doctors' white coats. The volunteer stripped to the waist and with the tension mounting, Fogel daubed one of the man's shoulders with ether. And then to everyone's astonishment he began to bite into the flesh. The victim gave a loud yell. 'My God! He means it,' he cried, and dashed out of the bar. Fogel blandly addressed the audience. 'Ladies and

179

Gentlemen, I am sorry I am unable to proceed with my demonstration of eating a camper alive as the volunteer has withdrawn. But if anyone else wishes to step forward I will be happy to continue.' There were knowing guffaws and applause—but no volunteers.

And the Regency Bar? Once people had been in it, they began to use it more and the problem was solved. The camper was not hurt, for Fogel's bite had only nipped him superficially. Afterwards he saw the funny side of it all.

Peter Casson was a brilliant hypnotist who induced campers to do some hilarious antics. I once saw him put two friends of mine, eminent lawyers from Bermuda, into a trance. He told them they were two years old and making sand pies on the beach. They knelt down and with imaginary spades began filling imaginary sand into plastic bowls they had been told were buckets. Then they began squabbling like children do, hitting each other with the bowls. It was an amazing example of hypnotism. Most show-business hypnotists need their subjects up on the stage near them, but Casson's power was so strong he could influence people sitting in the second row of the theatre. Once he even hypnotised the camp commissionaire who was standing at the back of the theatre. He was found fast asleep in his office the next morning and Casson had to go along and wake him up.

Indeed, on several occasions campers he had put in a trance during his evening were still under the influence the next morning. It was an easy enough job for him to wake them up, but sometimes he had already moved on to another camp. When this happened he had to de-trance them over the telephone.

Towards the end of the Forties I could have used a hypnotist myself—to put some of my critics to sleep. For after years of consistent success both Butlin's and I ran into trouble. And in the City, where I was once one of the Stock Exchange's blue-eyed boys, the knives were out. What caused the trouble was an ambitious plan to earn much-needed dollars for Britain by moving into the American holiday market. Ironically, the idea was born when I went on holiday myself. With the opening of

Ayr we had accommodation for about 38,000 campers at any one time, and nearly 1,600,000 people were spending their holidays in my camps. I had steadily enlarged all the camps, but in addition I now began to think of expanding abroad.

BASIL BROWN RECALLS THE POST-WAR YEARS OF EXPANSION:

It was at that time that one saw the true definition of a dedicated man of tireless energy. For Billy and those around him there was no let up. In the summertime it was a matter of all day and every day for seven days a week. After a week's concentrated planning at the London Headquarters, one's office door would open on a Friday afternoon, and the Guv'nor would pop his head round it and say, 'Where are you spending this weekend?' Woe betide the reputation, and indeed sometimes the future promotion of anyone who said, 'At home.' And thus, each weekend members of the Head Office staff left London to help with the Saturday changeover, when five or six thousand holiday makers would leave, and all the essential work had to be carried out to receive the new batch–a turnover of ten or twelve thousand people on one day. It was a regime that offered ample opportunity to those who sought a successful career, but with the overriding warning that anyone who was afraid of the heat should keep out of the kitchen.

Many people have asked me how it was possible to find teams of enthusiasts who were prepared to make many sacrifices in their private family life, in order to carry out all the duties allocated to them. My answer has always been the same. It was the spirit of adventure, and an almost curious acceptance of the necessity of living up to the example set by this magnetic personality.

Expansion continued, but it was not all plain sailing. There were delays, disappointments, frustrations, and in one case failure, but throughout Bill Butlin typified himself as the man of whom Kipling wrote when he said, 'If you can meet with triumph and disaster, and treat those two impostors just the same'. For if I were asked for Billy Butlin's outstanding characteristic, I would say it was his courage in the face of adversity or disappointment.

PART **3**

Sunshine and Shadows

13

'Have you heard about The Bermuda Plan?'

THROUGHOUT my working life I was never one to take holidays—even though I spent some fifty years providing them for others. For if your work is your hobby you never feel the need to take a break. Even on the rare occasion when I did take a holiday I was unable to stop thinking about business and I had ideas that led to big developments in my life: for instance, it was during my short holiday in Barry, South Wales, in the early Twenties that I got the idea for my holiday camps when I saw families trudging around in the rain with nowhere to go. But in 1946, after the strenuous war years, I decided I needed a rest and I took a holiday in Bermuda. There were times in the next few years when I fervently wished I had stayed at home. For though my vacation led to a new, dramatic phase in my life, it eventually cost me £250,000 and nearly lost me control of Butlin's.

It all started quite simply. Lying in the sun with a rum punch, swimming in the clear blue water and learning to water-ski was a new experience for me. It appeared to be a new experience for many of my fellow holiday-makers, Americans who were obviously tasting the delights of this Caribbean paradise for the first time. Clearly, also, the Caribbean was a fast-growing holiday area for Americans. Bermuda, for instance, was only about eight hundred miles from New York. Equally clearly, investment in the Caribbean could bring millions of vitally-needed dollars to Britain.

As a result of what I saw and sensed on that holiday, I bought two hotels in the area, the Fort Montagu Beach in Nassau for £445,000 and the Princess in Bermuda for £325,000. Later I spent £100,000 improving the Fort Montagu Beach and another £235,000 on the Princess. Of course I did not have this sort of cash, but once again I had the help of Barclays Bank.

On 2 August 1949 James Cooper described in the *Daily Express* some of the improvements I had made at the Princess:

'He (Butlin) laid an open-air patio on the edge of the Sound, built a huge gold-and-pink oyster-shell dance rostrum—the trade-mark of all Butlin's camps—brought a band from London to play for guests in white dinner suits and off-the-shoulder gowns.

'The lounge was transformed into an Adams Brothers' salon. The way to the terraced dining rooms became a "Quality Street" where, under electric stars twinkling in the ceiling, bull's eye window shops sell English china and Bond Street type of goods to the Americans who can take £100 of gifts home duty-free.

'Concrete was sunk 26 feet on the coral to make a dock so that private yachts and hotels' 50s. an hour speedboat could drop guests right on the terrace . . . '

Laying the foundations of the dock had gone exceedingly slowly, and I was puzzled by this. The diver hired to work on the ocean bed spent a lot of time there but he did not achieve very much. One day, when he had been down for some time, I decided to investigate. I donned a diving suit and sank to the ocean floor, where I solved the mystery. The diver had built an armchair out of the concrete blocks being used for the foundations and was calmly taking his ease!

James Cooper revealed that in the previous two years every major hotel in Bermuda had been transferred to British hands. What he did not reveal, however, was the unpleasant undercover attitude of the Bermudans towards the financial invasion. Among themselves they told a joke that the British were not supposed to hear.

'Have you heard about "The Bermuda Plan"?'

'No.'

'Well, we sell to the British in dollars and buy back in cents.'

It was during this period I first learned the hard way about the toughness of the Bermudans when it came to business. I recall one British manager of the Princess Hotel who was threatened with deportation unless he placed various orders for commodities in the right quarters. I think the Bermudans did not expect the tourist business to be as good as it turned out to be when things settled down after the war, and many of them regretted selling their hotels. One way I helped fill the hotels was to charter four airlines to fly guests from New York. I operated both hotels for a few years and then sold them at a profit.

But the most fateful event during my Caribbean years was meeting Brigadier-General A. C. Critchley, the man who pioneered greyhound racing in Britain. He was staying at my hotel, the Princess, in Bermuda, and one day I told him about an idea that had been simmering in my mind. It was to build a luxury holiday village in the Caribbean catering for middle-income Americans. I was convinced that with the increase in air travel, and with New York being only four hours away, such a project could become a bonanza.

'I know just the island for you,' said Critchley. 'It's an absolutely beautiful spot called Grand Bahama and it's only about eighty miles from Miami. What's more it's very scarcely populated.'

'Well, let's go and see it,' I said, feeling stirrings of excitement. We hired a Goose seaplane and flew there, landing on the clear blue sea. It certainly was an idyllic island, with glorious pink-white beaches. Indeed, it looked like heaven, but little did I know that I would go through hell there during the next few years.

We went ashore and found the place was inhabited by only one white man and a few score natives who felled trees to make props for British pits and spent the rest of their time

187

fishing. We decided this was the perfect site for my American Vacation Village. Immediately on returning to Bermuda I began making inquiries about buying land on Grand Bahama—and here I ran into the first of many difficulties. No one seemed able or willing to help. I inquired in London and Washington, but met a blank wall. Eventually I discovered the reason: part of the island was being used as a hush-hush American experimental guided missile base. No wonder someone wanting to buy land on the island was not exactly welcome. I also discovered, however, that the Americans were about to move to another island—which they did. At last Alfred Critchley and I were able to buy 685 acres at £1 an acre.

We had assumed we would be welcome. After all, what we were planning would undoubtedly bring undreamed-of prosperity to Grand Bahama. But, to our surprise, the local people were most unhelpful at first. Apparently, during the Prohibition years, the island's nearness to Miami had made it a bootlegging headquarters, and this had brought its own rewards; I strongly suspect some people would have liked to see the return of Prohibition, and that this was why they were not keen to have the island put on the map, so to speak. However, when they realized the kind of money they could earn working on and at the Village, resistance melted.

By early 1948 we had formed Butlin's (Bahamas) Ltd., to build the Village at an estimated cost of £1,500,000. I had built Butlin's as a one-man show and had never had a partner in any of my ventures, but as Brigadier-General Critchley had found the site and assured me his group in the City could provide part of the money required I agreed against my better judgement to go fifty/fifty with him. I put £200,000 of my own money into the Company and Brigadier-General Critchley £100,000. The following year we raised the rest of the money by a public issue of £600,000 five per cent £1 Preference shares, half of which were taken up by a financial group headed by City friends of Critchley. In addition, there was an issue of 1s. Ordinary shares and in all we raised £1,100,000. Critchley's City friends also promised they would buy £500,000 of 1s. Odinary Shares when the money was needed.

We could have raised another £500,000 but as we would not be earning anything to pay the interest on it for some time, and we had the promise of this amount from the Preference shareholders when we needed it, we decided that £1,100,000 was enough to start the project. I realized that if the venture failed and we went broke, all the other Ordinary shareholders would get nothing, but I had so much confidence in the scheme I agreed to go ahead.

Our first big problem was to get sufficient workmen. We recruited them from the many small islands that make up the Bahamas, provided them with basic accommodation and an open-air cinema—which amazed many of them who had never seen a film—and eventually built up a labour force of twenty black foremen and some five hundred labourers. They were very slow workers and whenever there was the hint of clouds in the distance they stopped work and gossiped under the trees. It was annoying and expensive. One of the foremen had tremendous authority and influence over the men, and I wondered if he could do anything to speed things up. 'Joe, can't you get your men to work a little harder?' I asked him.

He looked at me and laughed. 'Boss,' he said, 'you'll get like us long before we get like you.'

But our labour difficulties were mild compared with the blow we received soon after we began building when the pound was devalued. Because it was cheaper to buy what we needed in the States rather than bring it from Britain, we shipped or flew all our supplies and materials from Miami, Florida, to Nassau and then ferried them to Grand Bahama. Despite devaluation, it was still cheaper to do that but the cost of everything we bought increased by about 25 per cent over budget. In addition, the men's wages had to be raised because they were paid in dollars.

When the Grand Bahama project was first visualised we had no trouble getting our plans passed by the Nassau Parliament, which controlled Grand Bahama and the other islands in the Bahamas group. Indeed, the Nassau authorities were very helpful. We realized that an airport on the island was essential and we offered to build one if the Bahamas Government would

189

meet half the cost. In return it would own the airport and receive the landing fees and customs dues. This was agreed and, as the only way we could get our customers to the island was by air, we began building the runways first.

It soon became apparent, of course, that we would need more money, but we thought it could be raised more easily if the Village was open and operating successfully. The busy season in the Bahamas is winter, so we planned to open in January 1950 and, when we began advertising in mid-1949, bookings were highly encouraging. They say that nothing breeds success like success, but in this case it did not happen that way. For when it began to look as though the Grand Bahama venture would be successful, the attitude of the Bahamas Government changed dramatically and when we asked for its promised half of the cost of the airport, the money was not forthcoming. I have always felt that the hotel owners and businessmen in Nassau, many of whom were Members of Parliament, thought that the Grand Bahamas project would take business from them and so they put pressure on the Government to back out of the airport deal.

But whatever the cause, it was a serious blow and made the £500,000 promised by the Preference shareholders vital. To show my faith in the project I put another £50,000 of my own money into the project and we got the Village open. It was totally geared to Americans and Canadians, with luxury chalets set in an 'olde worlde' English atmosphere. Each line of chalets, which bore little resemblance to those in the camps back in Britain, was named after an English county. There was a pub called Ye Olde Pig and Whistle and in the main street there were some ancient village stocks. There were no Redcoats—well, we didn't call them Redcoats. They were 'Social Directors'. Their activities were mainly confined to the evening, for during the day the guests mostly spent their time on the magnificent beaches fishing for dolphin, barracuda and tarpan in boats which were provided free. What had been a rich man's sport was now available to people of more modest means.

There was another attraction which proved highly popular.

In addition to the land on Grand Bahama Island, I also bought a small island a few miles away which was inhabited by natives who kept racing pigeons. Every day they came over to Grand Bahama and held races which the guests bet on. More than once a visitor won enough to pay for his holiday.

We opened the Village as planned in January 1950. In six months we had 17,000 customers, a third of the total visitors to the Bahamas. I flew to the States and persuaded several big industrialists to send groups of workers and their families to the Village. We opened with a convention attended by six hundred guests, and a few days later twelve hundred families from the factories of a big combine were due to start arriving.

Labour difficulties, shortages and late arrival of supplies and fittings meant the Village was not completely finished by opening day, despite round-the-clock working. To placate any complaining guests I put a bottle of champagne in every chalet, with a personal note of explanation. The gesture cost me about £5,000—but I made friends and was dubbed 'Champagne Charlie' by the guests. The main point, however, was that we opened on time.

That first night, while laughter and strains of Calypso rhythms filtered from the English Village, I sat in my chalet and totted up the cost of providing two swimming-pools, a golf course, a ballroom, games rooms, a staff of three hundred white and a thousand coloured servants, guides and escorts. Undoubtedly we needed the promised £500,000 to help complete the rest of the Village and tide us over until the dollars started rolling in. For at this stage, having spent £1,150,000 we needed another £800,000 to complete the Village and put the company on a sound financial basis. If we did not raise a substantial portion of that money I knew I would have to face many angry critics and bitter City men who would say I was a fool to take this big gamble.

As I was thinking all this, a servant came into the chalet with a radiogram. I tore open the buff envelope. It was from the American General Electric Company announcing that the first group of GEC workers would start arriving soon. With this kind of support I felt confident of the future—if only we could

191

hold on meanwhile. I immediately began pressing Brigadier-General Critchley to raise the promised money from the City. Over many years I had never experienced any difficulty raising money and I did not expect any now. This time, I was wrong. It was obvious that if anybody was going to raise that £800,000 it would have to be me. Apart from my pride and reputation which would both be badly dented if the project failed—even though it would be the first major business failure in my life—I was concerned about the Ordinary shareholders (of whom I was one!) who risked losing all.

Scouting around for an alternative source of finance, I met an American businessman who had a considerable amount of 'blocked sterling'—money which could not be taken out of the sterling area without government permission in Britain. He agreed to invest £800,000 in the company, provided I could arrange for the amount to be withdrawn from his blocked sterling. Because the venture was such a potential dollar earner I appealed to the Treasury for the necessary permission. In a letter to the Treasury I said that there was little doubt I could raise the additional money required, if blocked sterling could be utilized. I also pointed out that a Jamaican cigar manufacturer had received Treasury permission to use £3 million of blocked sterling to build a new holiday hotel and gambling casino near Kingston, Jamaica so as to provide work in the area—which was precisely what we had done and were still doing in the Bahamas. In addition, I stressed that the Village showed every sign of being a success, and that on its present basis alone I estimated it would earn Britain $5,000,000 a year. To put my case more strongly I went to see Hugh Dalton, who was then Chancellor of the Exchequer. He was sympathetic and I left what seemed a successful meeting, hopeful of government co-operation. But two days later I learned that permission to use blocked sterling would not be granted. Dr Dalton explained to me that huge losses incurred in the failure of a scheme to produce groundnuts in Africa had made the government unwilling to allow sterling to be used for another overseas project.

However, I was still confident that we could raise the cash

from American sources, and with the permission of the board I flew to New York. The day before I was due to meet a group of US businessmen I was strolling around Times Square when I happened to glance up at the moving electric news sign high in one of the buildings. 'War in Korea', I read. Next day Wall Street panicked. It was obvious there would be no American dollars forthcoming in that atmosphere, so I returned home.

Within a few months the crisis deepened. Petitions to wind up the company were filed in London and the Bahamas. There was no alternative but to try and sell the village to the Americans. Back and forth across the Atlantic I flew offering the Village for about £1,500,000.

It was a forlorn task in view of the business climate at the time. And my negotiations were not helped by the fact that without any government backing I had no extra businessman's allowance and I was limited to the £7-a-day doled out to British travellers in those stringent times. Instead of being able to create a good impression with generous hospitality, I was reduced to debating whether I should take a bus or a taxi when I went to a business appointment. For many tortuous months my fight to save the Village dragged on. A New York financier, Lionel Marks, made a bid of £1,450,000, but he wanted to turn the place into a rich man's gambling casino—the Bahamian government rejected the idea.

Another offer came from a Chicago whisky distiller, William Dunn. He offered £805,000 but this was dropped after negotiations lasting eighteen months. Finally, in 1953, Butlin's (Bahamas) Ltd., went into liquidation and was compulsorily wound up.

The collapse of my Grand Bahama dream was a heavy, bitter blow, both financially and personally. When I was making every effort to save the company I was not worried about the money I might lose. I was thinking of Butlin's and my own reputation. As it turned out I lost more than any of the major investors in the company. For they were largely Preference shareholders and had first claim on the company's assets in the event of it going broke. In fact, most of them did not lose money. But the Ordinary shareholders got nothing—and I was the major Ordinary shareholder. For the second time since I had moved into big business—the first time was launching the Skegness camp—I was virtually broke. I had put all my available assets into the project and I had over-extended myself at the bank. My own personal loss was over £200,000. If I had been forced to sell Butlin's then I would not have come out with much.

I have always tried to learn from my mistakes, and so I wrote off the Bahamas episode as experience. What had I learned from it? It was the first time that I had gone into a project without having sole control—and I determined never to make that mistake again. This doesn't mean that I think I am infallible. Far from it. But I have always been guided by my own instincts, and they have served me pretty well.

There was criticism that we had entered into the Grand Bahama project without proper thought and planning. But whether this was true or not—and I do not think so—the fact remains that the venture was sunk by three events we could not have foreseen: devaluation; the Bahamian government's broken pledge to help build the airport; and the failure of the Preference shareholders to put up the money they had promised. Indeed, subsequent events have proved the soundness of the project. After Butlin's (Bahamas) Ltd., went into liquidation the Village was bought by an American company, the Jack Tar Hotel Corporation owned by a Texan, Charlie Sammons, and today it is highly successful.

In 1962, accompanied by Sheila, who later became Lady Butlin, I made a nostalgic visit to Grand Bahama Island. One of the first changes I noticed was that the new owners had scrapped the Village's own currency which we had instituted. We had 6d, 1s and 2s 6d coins with the Queen's head on one side and various animals on the other. Now I was wryly amused to see that the coins had been sunk into the concrete floor of the bar as a decoration. Somehow it seemed symbolic of the burial of all our dreams.

When we left after that visit, an incident happened that neatly summed up another aspect of the venture: the impact it had had on the island and the lives of its inhabitants. On landing at the airport we had been met by a friend, a top executive at the Village who was well known at the airport, and we drove straight out without passing through Immigration or Customs. We thought no more about it, but as we made our way to the plane on our return journey, we were ordered into an office, where an immaculately turned-out black official sat behind a desk. He did not speak but just sat there looking at us, while he tapped his pencil on the desk. Finally, he said severely, 'You did not go through Immigration and Customs on your arrival.'

So that was it. I explained how we had been met by an official from the Village and that we had not consciously avoided going through the normal channels. But once again he sat silent, tapping his pencil. Suddenly he smiled. 'It is perfectly all right. I understand.' And with that he came round from behind his desk and shook my hand. 'You know, Mr Butlin,' he said, 'through what you did on this island, you gave me my first pair of shoes.'

Though the failure of the Bahamas enterprise affected me deeply, another experience arising from it gave me an even greater personal shock. A few weeks before Butlin's Annual General Meeting in July 1950, I was suddenly asked to attend a meeting in the City of representatives of the big shareholders in the company—insurance companies, pension funds and the like. It was held at the offices of one of the big insurance companies. After being kept waiting for half an hour I was shown into a room where some twenty men sat around a long table. There was no chair for me and so I stood like a small boy being carpeted before the headmaster. Their spokesman did not waste words.

'We have a lot of shares in your company,' he said, 'and we are not satisfied with the way you are running it. We propose to put in a new chairman and managing director.' In other words, Ian Anderson, the chairman, and the then managing director—myself—were to be sacked at the forthcoming AGM.

To put it mildly, I was astonished. True, in 1949 Butlin's business was down compared to the boom years immediately after the war and the 1s shares had dropped from a peak of 24s

6d to between 5s and 6s, mainly because there had been several rights issues, but the company was sound. What shocked me, however, was that outsiders could propose such action. Butlin's was my creation; it was my life. Butlin's was me—and I was Butlin's. It never occurred to me that it belonged to other people who could take control of it. I did not think of the shareholders as faceless City men with the power to throw me out, but as millions of small investors. I believed I was working to make profits for myself and them and to give people a good holiday.

But looking back now, I realize that those big shareholders were justified in calling the meeting and proposing the action they did. For the facts made it look as though Butlin's had come unstuck in Britain as well as in the Bahamas—and there were people who had perhaps lost money in both spheres. The City obviously thought I had lost my touch. What had happened, however, was that I had spent a lot of time in the Bahamas immersed in the Vacation Village and I had neglected Butlin's at home. I had not realized that things were going wrong. Since the war the company had been very successful and I thought it could run itself. I was wrong.

Perhaps the main reason for this decline was that I had run the company as a one-man show. I had always made the decisions myself. As a result, while I was away, there was nobody with the experience to take the right decisions. It was my own fault and the episode taught me a lesson. After that I endeavoured to share the load, but I must admit that my nature and the long years of doing things my way made it difficult for me to do this.

As I took a taxi westwards to my Oxford Street office on the eventful day in 1950, I was still dazed. What was I to do? There was little choice. I could meekly accept the edict of the money-men—or I could fight. I decided to fight. Clearly, the vital factor was to get the necessary support at the AGM to defeat the proposals of my critics. I had always had warm and friendly relations with the small shareholders who attended the annual meetings. Would they support me this time against the big City battalions?

My worries were eased in a most heart-warming way. When news of the City moves leaked to some of my senior staff, many of whom had been with me since the beginning of the camps and before, a number of them came to me and pointed out that they were not only long-standing employees but shareholders. They asked if they could attend the AGM and support me.

I thought they could do more good at the meeting than they could at the camps, so I said yes. To increase their numbers I also gave some shares to other members of the staff which entitled them also to attend the meeting. On the fateful day they all turned up at the City's gloomy Winchester House, where the meeting was being held, along with many small shareholders. So, of course, did three or four representatives of the big shareholders. They were spear-headed by a man whom I knew had recently bought two shares in the company so he could speak as a shareholder. I had checked on him and found he specialized in making trouble at company meetings. The large hall was crowded and for some of the five hundred or so shareholders present it was standing room only.

In what proved to be a dramatic and emotional meeting he and his friends asked many questions and demanded that the proceedings be adjourned for more information about the accounts. Before long they were being booed each time they stood up to speak. But there were plenty of speakers who supported me, particularly Jack Trevor Snr, a large shareholder and a well-known estate agent, who made some telling points. As the battle continued the august atmosphere of the Great Hall in Winchester House was shattered by cheers and boos. It was a testing experience for me, but I had nothing to hide and I answered all the questions honestly. As the meeting progressed, and I saw I was winning, I began to enjoy it.

Perhaps some of the City men's questions were valid, but businesses like Butlin's are not built up and run on orthodox lines with every step, every decision being carefully calculated and safe. That is the way to dullness, stagnation and decline. All companies, particularly public ones, must be run

197

professionally and responsibly—but there must be room for instinct, flair and vision that is not always copper-bottomed. That was what I was fighting for in Winchester House. However, I realized that I had been trying to do too much and so I announced I was giving up all my other directorships. These included a seat on the board of the French Hotel Rennie group, owners of such world-famous hotels as the Hotel de France in Monte Carlo, the Carlton at Cannes and the Scribe and the Lottie in Paris. I announced that I would not take my £5,000-a-year managing director's salary until Butlin's paid a 100 per cent dividend again—something we had done for the first few years after the war. I also announced I would concentrate solely on running Butlin's.

After nearly two hours of verbal battle I won the day. The meeting passed the report and accounts with only five of the shareholders present voting against. I was carried shoulder-high out of the Great Hall.

Unhappily, this was not the end of my battle with the City. Later that year it became clear that a financial group was attempting to gain a measure of control of the company. It came to a head at a board meeting in September when there was a vacancy to be filled. Ian Anderson, a stockbroker who was chairman of the company, and his friend Lieutenant-Colonel Sir Edward Stevenson, a director, proposed it should be a City man. I strongly opposed this. I believed the new director should be a practical, full-time man who knew something about running holiday camps. With a business like Butlin's, I argued, the customers and the many small shareholders were more important than the City financiers. If we did not satisfy the customers there would be no business, and I was determined never to be a stooge to any particular section or interest among the shareholders. I believed it was vitally important that the board should not be dominated by financiers. Ian Anderson and Sir Edward did not agree with my attitude and resigned from the board, though they stayed on as chairman and director respectively of a subsidiary company, Butlin's Properties.

A few days later I became chairman of the board in addition

198

to my unpaid duties as managing director. My critics carped that I wanted to be the autocratic and undisputed boss of the company. If they meant I wanted to control my own destiny and the business which I knew more about running than anyone else, they were right. And I make no apology for it.

My battles with the City taught me a lot. Certainly I became very disillusioned. However, I later began to deal with various other financial houses and I built up happier relations with the City. A major role in this transformation was played by Josef Sebag and Co., whose advice and help was—and still is today—of immense help to me and my companies. If they had been advising me during the troubles of the late Forties I believe the situation might have turned out differently.

As it was, my feelings about the City were such that at the start of the Fifties I asked myself: why should annual general meetings always be held in London—thus making it difficult for many small shareholders to attend? I decided to break with precedent and hold the 1951 AGM at one of the camps and invite any shareholders who wanted to attend to be my guest for the weekend. It was such a success that we held the AGMs at the camps for the next nine years, during which time we gradually climbed back to well over the peak we had reached after the war. And in June 1960 Butlin's announced a pre-tax profit of £1,759,000. In 1961, it was £2,698,000 and by 1962, when it was estimated that every pound invested in Butlin's in 1950 was then worth £50, it had reached £3,130,000. In 1967, the year before I retired, the figure was over £4 million.

I was happy to see my business prospering again. Particularly as, unknown to nearly everyone, I had for several years been experiencing difficulties and unhappiness in my private life.

14

'Without her love . . . '

WHEN I was at last free to marry Norah, the woman who had lived with me as my wife for 20 years, it seemed a happy ending to the long years of frustration. We had been unable to marry because my wife Dolly, who was Norah's sister, refused to give me a divorce—though I asked her many times. But in 1958, Dolly died and, though it was not the way I would have wished, the unfortunate situation was resolved.

In the preceding years my relations with Norah had become very tense. To my utter despair she, like her sister, had begun to drink heavily—though she had tried to hide it. We had begun to quarrel frequently and had been on the point of separating several times. Free to marry, we talked it over again. Norah promised to stop drinking and for the sake of our three children Bobby, Cherry and Sandra we decided to make a fresh start in marriage.

All wedding days are memorable, and mine and Norah's proved to be even more memorable than I could possibly have imagined. For as we left Caxton Hall, I was handed a message saying that an emergency meeting of the Crew (Committee) of the Variety Club of Great Britain was being held early that evening. 'What a time to hold a meeting, on my wedding day,' I thought. But we were not going away on honeymoon and as that year I was Chief Barker (President and head fund raiser) of the Club I felt it was important I should attend. So while Norah went home to write thank you letters, I returned to the

200

office and later attended the Variety Club meeting which was being held in the offices of Associated British Pictures. Everybody was very sorry that my wedding day had been interrupted, but they said: 'Never mind, it gives us a chance to have a celebratory drink before the meeting.'

We were having that drink when the door opened, and in walked Eamonn Andrews with his famous red book. 'Billy Butlin,' he said, 'This Is Your Life.'

Quickly, I was whisked away by car to the theatre in Shepherd's Bush, where the show was then put on by the BBC. Knowing my friends in the Variety Club I still thought it was some kind of joke. I kept saying to Eamonn, 'You really do mean this, do you?' But I was finally convinced when we reached the theatre and I found Norah already there. She had been in the secret all along. It was a moving experience meeting old friends—my first girl friend, Joan Coombes, now Mrs Rose, was flown in from Canada—but though I am a showman at heart I found the public display of sentiment a bit embarrassing.

Sadly, however, we had not been married very long before Norah began drinking again, and this time she made no attempt to conceal her addiction. Some nights I left our flat in Grosvenor Square and slept on the couch in my office round the corner in Oxford Street. On these occasions I felt I would like to change places with a happily married lorry driver. Though I had matured considerably since my days with Dolly, I still hated quarrelling and hated even more the cat-and-mouse atmosphere that existed in the home because of Norah's drinking. Eventually, after only a few months of marriage, we finally parted.

So this was my second failed marriage. What had gone wrong? If I am honest, I must take the major share of blame. I deeply regret the way things turned out, for no amount of material success can compensate for this unhappiness and the feeling of failure that a broken marriage brings. To be lucky enough to go through life, living happily with the same partner, is far more important than making money.

I never knowingly made Dolly or Norah miserable, or denied

201

them anything that money could buy, but I undoubtedly neglected them in other ways. Business has always been my biggest interest. It is no coincidence that I met all three of my wives through my business. Dolly I met when she stood for several nights beside my stall at Tiverton Fair, and I only came to know Norah when she and her mother came to live with us at Skegness and she brought my lunch on her bicycle. Sheila I met when she was manageress of the big bar at the Pwllheli camp.

I always put my work first. If I had to choose between taking my wife to the theatre or attending a business meeting, I would attend the meeting. And I have also to face the fact that for many years work frequently took me away from home. Ambition is a great driving force, but it does not always bring happiness. If I had been able to involve my wives in my work and talk to them about it when I *was* at home, things might have been different. But I always found this difficult. One reason for it is that I quickly forget about my business problems and set-backs. But I found that when I told a woman about a particular problem, she worried about it—and worried me about it—long after I had dismissed it from my mind.

And perhaps there is another reason. I have always been a loner, you know. As a child I spent a lot of time on my own, and became used to it. Even the communal Army life did not change me. This characteristic was strengthened still further when I became a travelling showman and spent many hours alone in the cab of a lorry. All this tended to make me a self-reliant person who thought things out for himself and made up his own mind. But despite this, despite the driving force of ambition that made me work all hours, I needed a home and a loving wife.

I finally found the right woman in Sheila Devine. Sheila had been an interior designer with Norman Hartnell, Constance Spry, and at the Bon Marché store in Liverpool before she decided she wanted a change of scene and came to work at the Pwllheli camp. Later she became chief receptionist at the London office. I liked her bright, honest and forthright attitude from the start and our relationship gradually deepened. Once again, however, the pattern of my life repeated itself—only this time it was Norah who refused me a divorce. So Sheila and I were forced to live together for many years, unmarried.

Eventually, with new legislation, I was able to sue Norah successfully for divorce. I had looked after her and the children very well. In 1963, her holdings in Butlin's were worth more than £2,300,000 and at the time of our divorce in December 1975, she had more than £2 million in capital. At first, she intended to fight the case on the grounds of 'grave financial hardship', but in the end her lawyers advised her to withdraw her opposition. Norah died in 1976, only a few months after our divorce was finalized. It was a sad end to a life that had once been full of sparkle and laughter.

Sheila and I were married that summer. 'If it doesn't work this time,' I told myself, 'I'm giving up trying.' But I knew it would be right—and I wasn't wrong. With Sheila I have been happier than at any other time in my life.

One of the greatest compliments I can pay her is to say that without her love, companionship and help I would never have retired.

'Will your building,' demanded the critical town councillor, 'be of the same quality as the Town Hall in which we are now sitting?'

'Yes,' I replied, 'if I can get my money from the same source as you did.'

The little exchange took place at Bognor early in 1959 when I was planning to build my seventh camp just outside the town. As usual, I revealed my plans fully and consulted closely with the council. As usual, there was opposition from some councillors and townspeople. But my plans got the go-ahead and we started work that winter. However, if I had known the difficulties I was to meet building the Bognor camp, I might not have been so keen. I have always enjoyed construction work and as Bognor, like all my other camps, was basically designed by me, I went to live in a cottage near the site. It turned out to be an arduous and unpleasant time. A river ran through the site in a U-bend and we planned to straighten it by diverting one leg of the 'U'. It should have been a simple enough operation, but it was a wet winter and the river overflowed. The site quickly became a quagmire. To make matters worse I developed gout and tramping around the site in Wellington boots became agony. My cousin, Trevor Watts, tells a story about that: 'I could see he was in agony, but when I tried to make him stop walking about he said, "It's only pain"—and plodded on.' I'm not sure I can remember being quite so brave!

You may wonder why we built in the winter when we were more likely to have bad weather, but we always did our construction work then because it provided employment for many men who worked in my amusement parks and camps during the summer. While this sometimes resulted in difficulties due to the weather, it had the important advantage of keeping my men, many of whom had been with me for many years, in full employment all the year round. It also, of course, meant we always had the nucleus of a labour force ready for the summer season.

Eventually, after six long, exhausting months the camp was almost ready for opening. And then, as if we had not had enough trouble with flooding, a water main burst, turning part of the site into a quagmire once more.

This set us back several weeks and created a crisis, for we had already announced the opening date and taken bookings. It was vital, therefore, that we opened on time. We did—but only just. A few of the chalets were unfinished and generally we were in a bit of a turmoil. Most of the campers who arrived that first weekend took the conditions in a good-natured, pioneering spirit and tucked into the champagne we offered them. I well remember the camper who offered me his chalet key with the remark, 'I won't need this. I haven't got a door.'

Some campers demanded their money back—and got it. Others accepted my offer to spend their holiday at the Clacton camp and were taken there by coach. But before the end of the first week, the Bognor camp was running normally, accommodating 5,000 guests who proved to the good burghers of Bognor that a Butlin camp did not lower the tone of the town. Indeed, they soon realized that it brought prosperity. A year later the local Chamber of Trade gave a dinner for me and presented me with a silver cup for being the man who had done most for Bognor since King George V, who liked and visited the town so much that he conferred the title 'Regis' on it.

Flooding again created big problems at the next camp I built in 1962. I was looking for a site in the West Country and I decided the best way to do it was by air. So I hired a helicopter for a couple of days. We whirred over mile after mile of the south coast with no success, so on the second day I told the pilot to fly along the northern, Bristol Channel coast-line. Suddenly, over Minehead, I spotted the kind of site I was looking for. It was perfectly situated on the edge of the sea and near the railway station. The helicopter landed and I had a good look round before continuing my tour. I did not see a site I liked better than the one at Minehead, so I bought about a hundred acres and began planning the camp.

It was strange that I should have picked Minehead, for more than 50 years earlier it had been the first seaside place I had ever visited. I was about eight, so it must have been during the second time my mother brought me to England from South Africa. I remember hearing talk about an excursion to the sea, and one day we got up before it was light and set off. Today I can still recall the excitement of seeing the sands for the first time and digging with a bucket and spade and riding a donkey. When I got home I still had some sand and a tiny crab in my bucket.

Now, in 1961, I planned to spend £2 million building a camp near where I had once built sand castles. I submitted my plans but the council took a long time to approve them, for there was the usual local opposition.

And, while I waited, the very thing I had come to dread happened. The camp site was flooded. When you pick a site because it is convenient for the beach, it is invariably low-lying and therefore vulnerable to flooding. Usually, the reason the area has not been built on is because local house builders have not been prepared to spend the large amount of money necessary to make it flood-proof, because the profit from building a few houses would not warrant the expenditure. Since Skegness I had not had any trouble from the sea. The flooding at Bognor, of course, was due to heavy rain and the alterations we were making to the course of the river. But now, suddenly, the Minehead site was under two feet of water.

One day before I started to build I was standing looking forlornly at the watery expanse when a man out for a walk stopped and stood by me. After a while he said, 'Pity poor old Billy Butlin decided to build a holiday camp on this place.'

'Yes,' I said, 'and I'm poor old Billy Butlin.'

He gave me a pitying look.

Indeed, I did feel a bit sorry for myself when I discovered that the area I had bought tended to be flooded every few years. But then I remembered Skegness, and how I had strengthened the dunes there with earth from the area I had excavated to make a boating lake. Using the same idea I hired two mechanical diggers and dug a moat about thirty feet wide, twelve feet deep and about a mile in length around the perimeter of the site and used the excavated earth to build a dune-like barrier. It cost a few thousand pounds, but since that time the camp has never been flooded.

In the years between Skegness and Minehead, the camps changed and developed in many ways. I had always visualized them as self-contained villages, but not until after the War did I realize that they had everything a normal village had—except a church.

Before the War, local clergymen had visited the camps on Sundays to conduct services in the dining-hall, theatre or the open air. When we re-opened after the War, however, I decided that each camp would have its own church, and also its own resident padre—for I had been impressed by the excellent work the Service padres had done at the 21 Clubs I had set up in Europe towards the end of the war.

With Filey and Skegness being the first camps to open in 1945 and 1946 it was right and proper to ask the then

Archbishop of York, Dr Cyril Garbutt, for his advice on the project, as the first camp chapels would be under his general jurisdiction. Basil Brown, the camps' Director of Entertainments, whose family had lived in York for generations, went to see him. Basil found him enthusiastic about the idea—though the Archbishop admitted, 'I've never been to a holiday camp. What are they like?' Basil began describing the camps, and before long they were both kneeling on the patterned carpet of the Archbishop's study where Basil illustrated the lay-out of the chalets and other main buildings.

Dr Garbutt helped us lay the foundation of the scheme, and in 1947 Canon Tom Pugh became senior chaplain of the camps, a post he held even after becoming chaplain to the Queen in 1962.

I am happy to think that the scheme we worked out was mutually beneficial to the campers and the clergy. What we arranged was that every camp had a resident minister, who—usually accompanied by his wife and family—was changed every month. This meant that the minister got a break from his own parish, and his family got a free holiday. We continued to have distinguished visiting clergy, of course. Dr Garbutt preached many times at Filey, and other camps were regularly visited by three Archbishops of Canterbury: Dr Fisher, Dr Ramsey and Dr Coggan.

I was gratified when, in 1953, Dr Fisher said during one of his visits: 'Many people think that religion, if it has any place at all, is an occasional extra tacked on to a man's life with no real bearing on it. The Butlin camps have become an established feature of our social life, and have brought additional happiness and fellowship in their holidays to many people. I have very deeply appreciated the anxiety shown by Mr Butlin from the start that there should be the proper provision for the encouragement of religious worship in the camps; and it is a splendid thing that in all the camps in Britain and Ireland there are churches and chaplains.'

It was a constant satisfaction to me that our church services were always well-attended. People complain about churches being empty, but they overlook the fact that there are various reasons why people do not attend church: on Sundays, husbands have jobs to do around the house and garden which they cannot do during the week. Wives have young children to look after and lunches to cook. But at the camps, where they were freed from these duties, often more than a thousand people attended the services.

As the individual camps grew in size, some of the Sunday congregations were huge. For by 1958 we were catering for about 48,000 campers a week. Sunday breakfast of bacon and eggs meant that anything up to 96,000 eggs had to be broken and fried. (We never served boiled eggs, for we soon found from experience that from the thousands of eggs we used there were bound to be, on occasions, a few bad ones. When this happened the unfortunate campers concerned usually made such a commotion that everyone nearby left their eggs and had to be served with something else.)

These kind of figures obviously presented big organizational problems. But there were other less obvious aspects of running the camps which called for what could now be called psychology. For instance, 'dinner' was 'evening meal', because most of the campers had what they called 'dinner' at mid-day.

For many years all campers sat at tables for eight. With families and couples this automatically resulted in mixed tables, but seating young people who were sometimes on their own or with friends or their own sex presented difficulties. Did we put four boys and four girls at one table so they could make friends? From experience we learned that the answer was 'No', for sometimes they disliked each other and did not enjoy the enforced company of the opposite sex. We found it was much better to put a table of boys next to a table of girls and let them make their own choice of friends.

Eating with the campers, as I always did, sometimes caused problems. I am not fussy about my food, but there are one or two things I dislike. If that dish was being served when I was there I put up with it. I never allowed the waitress to get me a specially-cooked alternative. I did not want a camper to mutter, 'Oh, what we're having isn't good enough for him.'

But while I was a familiar figure to campers and staff alike, not everybody knew me by sight—as I once found to my amusement. One evening I went to a staff party at one of the camps, and the woman behind the bar, a newcomer, said, 'What will you have, love?'

'A gin and tonic,' I replied.

'Do you want a large one, love?' she inquired.

'No thanks,' I said.

She looked at me and winked. 'Go on,' she said. 'Have a large one—the Guv'nor's paying.'

I always felt it sound sense to involve the campers in the running of the camps as much as possible, and so we set up campers' committees through which criticisms and suggestions could be channelled. The election of these committees was announced on Radio Butlin, the camp's loud-speaker system, as 'one of the most important events of the week'—and I always believed it was. With the campers, too, it was a popular idea. We always had many volunteers and had to limit the committees to about twenty members men and women, for each house, with a Redcoat in charge.

The brilliant satirical columnist Art Buchwald of the *New York Herald Tribune* visited the Clacton camp in 1957, and wrote three witty articles. For such a famous American writer to take the trouble to visit one of the camps was indeed a compliment, but naturally, as a humorous writer, he sometimes stretched the truth—more than a trifle!

As one of the first Americans to visit Butlin's Holiday Camp at Clacton-on-Sea, we insisted on no special privileges. We just wanted to be one of the 6,000 campers who had paid £12 15s for a fun-packed week's vacation.

The Clacton camp is divided into four 'Houses' and we were pledged to do-or-die for Gloucester. It isn't too extreme to say that the battle for Oman and Muscat was won on the playing fields of Butlin's.

In order that Butlin campers may enjoy the most fun for the longest period of time, reveille is at 7.30. Campers

209

awake to a happy jingle set to music which is played on loudspeakers located in every part of the camp.

> *Roll out of bed in the morning*
> *With a great big smile and a good-good morning*
> *Get out with a grin*
> *There's a bright new day to begin*
> *Wake up with the sun and the rooster*
> *Cock-a-doodle like the rooster uster*
> *How can you go wrong*
> *If you roll out of bed with a song?*

We could do nothing else but roll out of bed singing a song, with a big smile on our face. As we washed we could hear other people singing in their chalets also. The camp sounded like the *Anvil Chorus*.

The organizing of the fun at Butlin's is in the hands of 40 Redcoats, attractive young men and women whose main function is to see that everyone has a good time. They are assisted by a Camp Comic, who has to be funny from eight o'clock in the morning until midnight. He, in turn, can call upon the talents of a man known as the Resident Comedian.

A person who is not having a good time at a Butlin's camp is known as a 'knot of resistance'. When a knot of resistance is discovered (in a camp this size it could spread like Asian flu) the Redcoats are called in to cheer him up. If they fail the Camp Comic is sent for. The Redcoats can usually break the knot by throwing the Camp Comic in the swimming-pool. Only in the most serious cases is the Resident Comedian called in for consultation.

At breakfast we were greeted by a smiling Redcoat.

'Are you having a good time?' he said.

'A good time,' we replied, throwing a bowl of porridge at him. 'I'll say I'm having a good time.'

'That's the spirit,' he said, still smiling as he wiped oatmeal out of his eyes.

210

After breakfast we had the choice of entering an electric shaving contest (you shave with a certain make of electric shaver every morning in front of an attendant and the whiskers are put in an envelope. At the end of the week the envelopes are weighed and the one who put in the most whiskers gets a prize) or playing Tombola, a form of Bingo; or going to the Rock'n'Roll Ballroom, or attending a Skiffle Contest, or practising volleyball, or going to a coffee dance in the Viennese Ballroom, or trying our luck at Old Time Dancing, or auditioning for the National Talent Contest. Wanting to be a popular camper, we did everything. The Redcoats in Gloucester started to have us pegged as a 'popular camper'.

After lunch we had to pose for a group photograph, enter a darts competition, see a Butlin Theatre production of Hippo Dancing, attend a bathing beauty contest, look in at a tea dance at the Viennese Ballroom, help judge the Glamorous Grandmother Competition, become part of a whist drive in the Regency Café and row for Gloucester in a regatta on the Butlin lake.

The Regatta is probably one of the highlights of the week at Butlin's. The reason is that it really isn't a regatta but a rowboat race and the lake is only three feet deep and is covered on the bottom with thick mud. The fun of it comes when the campers throw Charlie Fowles, the Chief Redcoat into the water and then pour mud all over him.

Tradition has it that the Camp Comic, Don Cook, also gets thrown in, and the campers shove mud in his face and his eyes and all over him. The best of it is that Charlie and Don have to keep laughing the whole time we do these things to them (except when they're choking in the mud). But it really is fun to see what happens to them and everyone has a good time . . .

Well, this brought us up to five-thirty in the afternoon and we still had three dances to go to that evening, plus a community sing and a thing called 'The Lucky Dip Show' in which the audience participates. We decided to sit down on a bench for a rest before dinner.

A Redcoat came up with a worried expression on his face. 'What's the matter, aren't you having a good time?'

'Sure I'm having a good time,' we said. Jumping to our feet we picked up a brick and threw it through the window.

'That's the spirit,' he said smiling. 'You'll make a good camper yet.'

If that is typical of Art Buchwald's style, I wonder what he would have made of the next chapters.

15

'An elephant parked in Grosvenor Square'

THE motorist searching for a parking place in London's Grosvenor Square could not believe his eyes. There, tied to a parking meter, was an elephant. He stopped his car, got out and looked at the elephant in amazement for a while and then he walked away with a purposeful gait. Billy Smart, the circus owner, and I watched the scene from my flat overlooking the Square. My old friend Billy had brought the elephant along with some other animals to the West End to publicize his circus, which at that time was open at Battersea Park; and as a joke he had hitched it to a meter. Now we were awaiting the results of the stunt.

A little while later the motorist returned with a policeman. As he began to talk vigorously and point to the elephant we left the window and went down to the square, where we sauntered casually up to the motorist and the policeman.

'Is anything wrong, officer?' inquired Billy Smart.

'Is this your elephant?' riposted the policeman.

'Yes,' said Billy. 'The time hasn't run out yet, has it?'

The motorist exploded. 'What are you talking about? You can't park an elephant at a parking meter.'

'Why not?' asked Billy.

'Because it's a parking space for cars, that's why.'

'It doesn't say it's only for cars,' said Billy. 'Wouldn't you agree, Bill?'

'Yes,' I said. 'It doesn't say what you can park here.'

'Don't talk nonsense,' shouted the motorist. 'Officer, I demand you have this elephant removed.'

The policeman looked thoughtful. 'Well, sir,' he said. 'I think the gentlemen are right. As far as I can see there is nothing to stop an elephant being parked at a meter.'

In a flurry of anger, the motorist departed and Billy and I returned to the flat. A little later we saw a traffic warden approaching.

But all she was doing was bringing the elephant a bun. We left the elephant there for about an hour, but very few other people took any notice. I suppose Londoners see so many unusual happenings in the streets, that it takes something pretty extraordinary to make them stop, look and go on to tell their friends that there's an elephant parked in Grosvenor Square.

My favourite elephant story, however, concerns Big Charlie. In 1957, Big Charlie was the largest elephant in Europe, and possibly in the world. He was an Indian male tusker weighing eight and a half tons and standing twelve feet six inches high, thirteen feet long and five feet wide. I first came across him in an airliner high over the Atlantic. Glancing through a newspaper I read a story about a fund that had been started to save an elephant in Scotland. This was Big Charlie, who had been in a circus that had closed down. All the other animals had been sold, but nobody wanted Big Charlie because of the difficulty of moving him. Now his owner had announced that he could not afford to keep Big Charlie any longer, for he was eating two bales of hay a day at a cost of 37 shillings each. Since the circus had closed it had cost £1,800 to feed him. If nobody wanted him, Big Charlie would have to be put down.

Now, I have always had a special affection for elephants, probably because they remind me of my fairground days, when they were always a vital part of the travelling circus. I felt I wanted to do something to save Big Charlie, but I must admit that my feelings were not totally altruistic—he could be a great attraction at the camps, provided he could be safely transported from Craigend Castle, where he was then housed, to the nearest camp at Ayr (a distance of about thirty miles).

It happened that I knew the elephant's owner, Willie Wilson, for his father used to supply animals to my zoos. 'Can you move Big Charlie to Ayr?' I asked Willie on the telephone. 'If you can, I'll buy him from you.'

'Well, it won't be easy,' replied Willie, 'but I think we can do it.' He little realized what he was taking on.

It was Willie's idea to move him on a low-loader. That was easier said than done, for a start. It took Willie and Big Charlie's keeper, or mahout, Shaik Ibrahim (whose real name was Kya Lee), twenty hours to entice him aboard. They had no trouble tethering him down by chaining his four feet to the floor of the low-loader, but they dared not fasten his trunk as an elephant can be driven crazy if he cannot move his trunk. As it turned out it was Willie and the mahout who were almost driven crazy, for Big Charlie's trunk proved a positive menace. He fenced with overhead tramway lines and curled his trunk lovingly around lamp posts and telegraph poles. By the time he reached Ayr he had bent or broken twenty of them and, as no insurance company would insure us for the journey, the bill came to me. But finally they reached Ayr, and Willie thanked the police officer in charge of the escort.

'We made it this time, Mr Wilson,' said he. 'But I'm warning ye, never again.'

However, once arrived at Ayr, Big Charlie repaid us for all the trouble he had caused. He was a great success, and the children loved him and his mahout. Ibrahim had worked with Big Charlie for many years in India. He was totally devoted to him, and had an uncanny sense of what Big Charlie was doing—even when the elephant was out of sight. The relationship between them was tender and touching. Willie Wilson told me that if Ibrahim died I would have to shoot the elephant, and if the elephant died Ibrahim would shoot himself.

Big Charlie was such a success that I dearly wanted him at one of the other larger camps. But there was the problem of moving him, and this time the journey would be much longer than the thirty miles to Ayr. Even to the nearest camp at Filey, it would be some 350 miles. But if the problem could be solved,

215

I knew Big Charlie's trip would make a lot of headlines. Publicity is something I have always believed in, and I make no apologies for it. There is no point in building a better mousetrap if nobody knows it. So I decided to try to move Big Charlie to Filey. For a start I put an advertisement in three national newspapers, declaring:

> Butlin's Limited will pay the sum of £1,000 cash to any person able to arrange immediate safe transport of the largest elephant in captivity from Butlin's, Ayr (Scotland) to Butlin's Filey (Yorkshire). Apply Butlin's Limited, Luxury Holiday Camps, Oxford Street, London W.1.

Within a few days we had over three hundred replies—and what replies. Most of them showed no conception of the problem involved in moving eight and a half tons of a bulky, immensely strong animal that had to be watered and fed on a long journey. I have never seen so many weird, crackpot ideas. Of course, many of them were sent as a joke. An admiral declared that Big Charlie could be transported all the way by canal—overlooking the vital fact that this involved demolishing all the bridges along the route. A London publisher suggested that Big Charlie should be carried in a giant net suspended from two helicopters. Another airlift plan came from the Department of Engineering Science at Oxford. The idea was to suspend him from a barrage balloon. Some 150 members of the Nottingham College of Art planned to move him round the north coast of Scotland on a raft pulled by teams of swimmers. Their alternative plan was one of the craziest of the lot. They suggested that Big Charlie walk round the coast under water with a long snorkel fixed to his trunk. And even that was only slightly more daffy than the one from an hypnotist who claimed he could put Big Charlie into a trance and sleepwalk him to Filey.

Not one of the suggestions was really practical, and so it was back to the man who had already moved Big Charlie once before—Willie Wilson. Willie again proposed moving Big Charlie on a low-loader, but having learned his lesson the first time, he planned to put him in a large crate made of steel girders and nine-inch thick railway sleepers, reinforced with iron bands. I told him to go ahead.

Willie and Ibrahim knew and understood Big Charlie, but to provide further technical advice, I brought in Colonel (Elephant Bill) Williams, one of the world's greatest experts on the animals. Elephant Bill wrote a book about the journey entitled *Big Charlie*, and as I was not able to be on the trip I have based my account on his story and the memories of my chief publicity man, the late Harold Vintner.

Ibrahim was embarrassed because Big Charlie was in 'must' (more or less the male equivalent of 'heat') and his sex was prominently manifest. 'No like go near camp with rude Charlie,' said Ibrahim. 'Plenty nice ladies and children.' Physical appearances apart, however, an elephant in must is difficult to control. He becomes capable of sudden, unpredictable acts of violence. Even with his love for the animal, Ibrahim was forced to admit, 'Charlie no lose temper, but he plenty mischief. Very naughty, Charlie. No listen to Ibrahim.'

But as Big Charlie was not a violent elephant by nature it was decided to attempt the journey. The first problem was to get him into the crate. The low-loader with the formidable crate was backed against a grassy bank flanking some tennis courts, and a ramp of railway sleepers was built for him to cross over into the crate. It seemed simple enough—but Big Charlie was in a bad mood. He declined to co-operate. Elephant Bill was thinking ahead and worrying what might happen if, when they finally got Big Charlie into the crate, he decided to rub himself up against the sleeper walls. Strong as they were, he might possibly burst them or injure himself. To prevent him getting a grip on the walls, Bill decided to coat the inside of the crate with lard. This caused further trouble, not with Big Charlie, but with Ibrahim. For it was against his religion to touch pig fat.

'Pig fat filth,' he shouted when he learned what was proposed. 'Ibrahim no go in box. And if Ibrahim no go in, Charlie no go in, either.'

Ibrahim was assured that margarine would be used instead,

but the problem still remained of getting Big Charlie into his crate. Ibrahim tempted him on to the ramp by scattering apples, his favourite delicacy, before him. Charlie suspiciously explored the crate with his trunk. Inside, he found some bolts, and his trunk neatly unscrewed some of them and flung them like bullets over his shoulder. It began to look as though it was going to take as long to get him aboard as the last time. But Ibrahim persevered. He went inside the crate armed with several hundredweight of apples, buns and bread and tempted Big Charlie with the food. Big Charlie kept eating, but he refused to budge. After about an hour, however, he put his left front foot on the ramp. Two hours later his right foot followed. By lunchtime he was half-way inside the crate. Unfortunately, the crate began to sway and Big Charlie refused to budge any further.

A towing chain was fixed around his front feet and a hastily-assembled tug-of-war team attempted to pull him further into the crate. But Big Charlie took a dislike to this procedure and began to back out. As he did so, the chain around his legs tightened, causing him considerable pain. He seemed to associate the pain with the bridge, which he systematically began wrecking. It was mid-afternoon before the ramp was rebuilt, and Ibrahim once again began tempting Big Charlie with apples and buns. Eventually, about eight o'clock in the evening he deigned to enter fully into the crate.

The journey to Filey took five days for, apart from having to make several detours to miss low bridges, the loader's maximum speed was seven m.p.h. and uphill it fell to a crawl. Big Charlie behaved himself, however, and the main problem was watering him. One night the landlord of an hotel where the party was staying was astonished when he was asked for a round of large Scotches and seventeen gallons of water!

Big Charlie became much loved at Filey and I decided to find him a 'bride'. This proved about as difficult as transporting him about the place. Eventually we found him a mate called Sauce. Unfortunately, she was 62, but Big Charlie and she seemed to get on fine together. Sauce had been in show business since she was five, when she had appeared at the London Palladium in a circus act with four other young female elephants named Vinegar, Pepper and Salt.

Big Charlie and Sauce made a popular pair—but then tragedy struck. Ibrahim fell ill, and the doctor said he must go to hospital for specialist treatment. Apart from the worry of how his absence would affect Big Charlie, there was the practical problem of changing his fetters twice a day. We were warned that Ibrahim was the only person Big Charlie would allow to do this. To solve the problem I brought Willie Wilson from Scotland and arranged for Ibrahim to be treated by a specialist in the camp. Ibrahim acted as go-between, always being present when Willie attended the elephant. Big Charlie seemed to understand that his mahout was ill and that Willie was doing things for him instead. Willie was safe so long as Ibrahim was present.

And when it was time for Ibrahim to change Big Charlie's fetters it was touching to see how the elephant helped him: Ibrahim sat on a stool and Big Charlie gently lifted his feet up to him so that he could transfer the chains from one ankle to the other. As Elephant Bill described it; 'He was like a child holding up his feet for his mother to put his shoes on.' And while this took place, Charlie gently rubbed Ibrahim's back with his trunk.

Despite the best medical attention, however, Ibrahim did not recover from his illness. From the day Ibrahim died, Big Charlie began to fail and we were advised by experts that he should be put down. That was easier said than done, for Charlie was a great favourite with the children. However, it had to be done and so we contacted the London Zoo to ask them the best way to do the job. We were advised that he should be gassed. We contacted the RSPCA, asked them to do it as painlessly as possible, and they came to Filey. They made Charlie's shed, which we had specially built for him when he first arrived, air-tight and then they led a hose from the exhaust pipe of a lorry into the shed—and that was the sad end of Charlie.

Over the years we had several elephants at the camps, and I have memories of them all—particularly the one who fell into the swimming-pool at Skegness and was drowned. But none of them was as popular as Big Charlie.

They say elephants never forget. I will never forget Big Charlie. Nor will I ever forget Fred. I bought him from Hughie Green's father, who told me:

'You know, Bill, that elephant can paint.'

'Pull the other leg,' I said.

'No, I'm not kidding. Let me show you.'

Next day he arrived with a large canvas and several buckets which he filled with different coloured paints. Fred dipped his trunk into them and sloshed around, filling the canvas with a jumble of colours. Of course, there was no rhyme or reason to the daubs—but then, I reflected, there was no rhyme or reason to some modern paintings I had seen and this gave me the idea of playing a hoax.

We cut the canvas into smaller ones and had them framed. Then I called in the press to see the work of a new painter I had discovered, and invited an eminent art expert to give his views. He examined the 'pictures' carefully and then said things like: 'Yes, I can see what the artist is trying to do. Very interesting. Look at the depth in that one. And the colour contrast in that one is impressive.' At last he asked, 'Who is the artist?'

'Fred,' I said.

'Fred who?'

'Just Fred,' I replied.

'But he must have a second name.'

'Elephants don't have second names,' I said.

'I don't think that is very funny, Mr Butlin,' he said, and stomped angrily out.

But I did.

16

'We caused a stir in Iceland . . . '

OF all the many varied and sometimes unpleasant experiences I have had in my life, the time I almost drowned was one of the most frightening. It happened towards the end of the 1958 Butlin's Cross-Channel swim. I had taken over the organization of this annual race in 1953, after the *Daily Mail*, which had started the event a few years earlier, found that the cost of putting it on was not justified in publicity terms because other national newspapers largely ignored it.

I became involved in the race almost accidentally, when the Welsh Swimming Association was holding its national championships in the big pool at Pwllheli camp. During the event several people remarked to me, 'Isn't it a pity that the annual cross-Channel swim has ended?' This, of course, was too much of a temptation for me. I just had to resurrect the race.

That day in 1958 I was regretting my decision. For there I was swimming desperately, and all alone, in a mist-covered sea. All day I had been criss-crossing the Channel in a helicopter, watching the contestants and seeing the Danish-American Gold Medallist, Greta Andersen, move into the lead. For months she had trained on steak and ten hours of sleep a day, and now looked a certain winner for the second year in succession. Landing at Folkestone in the helicopter, I rushed out in a launch to meet her. We had no difficulty in finding her, for she was being followed by a small armada of little boats, most of them containing newspaper reporters and cameramen. It was a scene of great excitement, with hooters blowing, rock'n'roll music blaring from loudspeakers and people shouting encouragement to Greta. Her husband was leaning out of the support boat holding a placard with her swimming time on it, for there was a chance that she could beat the record of 10 hours 50 minutes set up in 1950 by an Egyptian.

As we neared the coast, and I saw the cameramen preparing their equipment, the showman in me came out and I could not resist getting into the picture. I donned some bathing trunks and plunged into the water beside her. My intention was to be photographed walking out of the water with Greta, and for a little while I managed to keep pace with her. But tired and flagging though she was, she soon drew ahead of me—and so did the accompanying boats. Suddenly I found myself all alone and hidden from the beach by the mist. It was also alarmingly obvious that I had misjudged the nearness of the shore and I began to worry that I would not have the strength to reach it. I yelled repeatedly, but nobody heard me.

It is a chilling realization to know that you are alone in the sea, at the mercy of the waves and tides. I knew full well what I was up against. In previous races I had seen swimmers struggling for hours against the tide, sometimes while only a few hundred yards from the shore.

A loud cheer in the distance told me that Greta had landed, but still no one came looking for me. The mist prevented me seeing how far I was from the shore, but it was rapidly becoming obvious that if anyone was going to save me, it would be myself. I struggled on grimly, feeling my strength ebbing away. Finally, gratefully, I felt my feet touch ground and I staggered ashore, helped by a spectator. I was so exhausted that I did not notice until later I had cut myself badly on the rocks. I tottered up the beach, but everybody's attention was focused on Greta and nobody heeded me. However, I finally managed to get into the picture when a photographer snapped me sitting next to Greta.

All in all I had some eventful times in the seven years the race

222

was held. For the first two years, it was organized in conjunction with the Long Distance Swimming Federation, but eventually this led to trouble. At that time the President of the Federation was an Egyptian, General Mohamed Sabry, who led a powerful Egyptian team in the early years of the race. But in 1955 the Egyptians wanted to change the rules. They demanded, for instance, that each country should be allowed to be represented by more than one swimmer. This would have greatly favoured the Egyptians as they had a team of about twelve. Generally, it seemed they were trying to run the show. This aroused anger among many of the other swimmers. For the Egyptians were all Army men, highly professional and disciplined. In 1954, for example, they were the first to arrive at Folkestone, six weeks before the race. They seemed to live mainly on beans which they brought by the sackful and boiled gently all night.

Apart from the Egyptian Hassan Abdel Rehim, who established the Channel record in 1950, another Egyptian came second in 1954, after a dramatic tussle with the little Portuguese carpenter, Baptista Pereira. The Portuguese led all the way, with the Egyptian following him doggedly. Four hundred yards from the shore, Pereira was swept off course by the tide and the Egyptian began gaining rapidly, with his supporters swinging rattles to encourage him. But finally, Pereira broke away from the tide and landed at St Margaret's Bay, near Dover, with a winning time of 12 hours 25 minutes.

In 1955 the race was again won by an Egyptian, Abdel Latif Aby Heif, and the following year General Sabry and his men arrived in force once more. It was then that the simmering situation boiled over, for 1956 was the year Colonel Nasser took over the Suez Canal and Britain and France invaded Egypt to regain control of it. I did not think it right that any one nation should dominate the race. And I have to confess that I did not want them to win that year of all years. After several rows with the Egyptians, I banned them from taking part. 'They've got the Suez Canal,' I was quoted as saying. 'I'm not going to let them have the English Channel.'

In fact, I had been wrongly quoted, but there it was in the

newspapers; and, from the furore that followed, you would have thought that I had personally declared war on Egypt. The Syrians withdrew in protest and I was quickly in trouble with the Foreign Office. I was summoned to Whitehall and told, 'You are interfering with our foreign relations. You must make no more newspaper comments about the Egyptians.'

Not surprisingly, the ban was seen as a nationalistic and political move, and it created a lot of newspaper comment. The Cairo Press declared that: 'Britain is scared of Egypt even in the field of sport.' And at home, journalist Leonard Moseley castigated me in the *Daily Express*.

'I think Butlin made a fool of himself,' he wrote. 'I think his action was wrong in principle. Next thing we know we'll all be back in the mental days of those lunatics during the 1914-18 war who refused to play Beethoven or Wagner or serve the customers who came into their shops with dachshunds.' Looking back, I now think Moseley was right.

He was not alone in castigating me. In the *Daily Mirror* of 3 August, sports columnist Peter Wilson declared: 'I have never heard such poppycock and tomfoolery in all my natural born days.'

But of all the comments, I thought Percy Cudlipp in the *News Chronicle* of 11 August summed up the situation most sanely and wittily in a poem entitled *Butlin Strikes A Blow*.

> When the Middle Eastern ruler
> Seized the Suez for his own
> Some urged war, while others cooler
> Took a diplomatic tone;
> Pineau was for violent action,
> Dulles manifestly loath;
> Butlin, scorning either faction
> Taught a lesson to them both.
>
> Nasser's tactics were tyrannic—
> Of a dictatorial stamp;
> But there were no signs of panic
> In the Billy Butlin camp.

Billy knew the right prescription,
And declared in accents grim,
'No natatory Egyptian
Shall attempt my Channel swim.'

Quite a few expressed dissension
From this shattering decree;
Some suspected its intention
Was to get publicity;
Some with indignation brimming
Said 'These matters do not mix—
What the devil's Channel swimming
Got to do with politics?'

All such hyper-captious asses
With contempt we can pass by;
Drown their carping, lads and lassies,
With a shout of 'Hi-di-hi!'
Worried statesmen, you may rest your
Weary minds and fret no more.
Billy Butlin's made his gesture
And the worst is clearly o'er.

Eventually the storm subsided—only to be followed by another which, if it was more localized, was certainly pretty severe. It began on the eve of the race with a real live storm over the Channel. The sea was so rough that I wanted to postpone the race, due to start from Cap Gris Nez at 2.30 the following morning. But most of the contestants were anxious to get going. This was not unusual. Whenever the race was delayed there were rows and meetings of keyed-up swimmers demanding we start. Sometimes the weather was rougher and more dangerous than the contestants realized and I had to threaten to withdraw from sponsoring the race before the more foolhardy backed down.

On this occasion, however, the forecast was for improved weather, so we eventually decided to set sail for the French coast, setting off as usual in the evening. What a crossing it was. The weather got worse instead of better and most of us were seasick. When we arrived at Cap Gris Nez, a heavy swell made landing dangerous. One woman contestant screamed hysterically, believing she was about to be drowned. I became anxious myself, for water poured into the boat and we were only kept afloat by the efforts of two crewmen bailing frantically.

Many of the boatmen carrying the contestants refused to land, but some of the competitors greased themselves, dived overboard and swam to the shore. When I saw what was happening, I knew I had to land and start the race. My boat was crewed by six young cadets from King Edward VII Nautical College and they courageously ignored the heavy seas to get me ashore. Stripped down to swimming trunks I went over the side. There was no need for me to swim. The waves washed me the last ten or fifteen yards and dumped me unceremoniously on the beach. A team from the 21st SAS Regiment also landed in a dinghy with the communications radio wrapped in a waterproof overcoat. During the row afterwards, some people blamed them for the breakdown in radio communications, but this was unjust. They were only off the air for the hour it took them to land the dinghy in the rough seas.

When I finally got ashore I found only eight of the twenty-two contestants—five men and three women—ready to start. As I fired my Véry pistol and they plunged into the surf I admired their guts. To give them support I rushed into the sea alongside them—and was promptly swept off my feet by the waves. Ignominiously, bedraggled and spluttering for breath, I was washed back to the shore.

None of the swimmers reached the English coast, but there were some heroic performances. A giant American, Tom Park, got within five miles, but was forced to give up after 10 hours 20 minutes. He thought he was the last out of the water, but a beefy Belfast wrestler, Jack McClelland, struggled for 11 hours 2 minutes—though he was still thirteen miles off the English coast when he was hauled into his support boat. But perhaps the most impressive example of guts and stamina came from a 60-year-old Scot, William Barnie, who boasted he trained on whisky and who swam for 9 hours 55 minutes.

Though the race was not completed, I felt that every one of the swimmers who had started deserved a share of the prize money and they collected from £50 to £250 each. The non-starters received £25 each.

Next day a storm of words broke. A number of the contestants held a meeting to protest that the race should never have started, because their boatmen had refused to land them. If none of the contestants had landed in France, I would have been happy to postpone the race. But as some of them did get ashore I felt I had no option but to let it go ahead. Now it looked to me as though some of the non-starters were looking for an excuse—and at the protest meeting I said so bluntly.

'The real cause of this meeting,' I said, 'is that the people who have complained have mostly—though not in every case—been sponsored. They did not like the look of the sea and did not go in, and they have got to think of a very good story to tell their sponsors when they return to their own countries—'

This caused an uproar. Competitors jumped to their feet with cries of 'No', 'No'. One swimmer angrily called it a 'monster insult'. But the fact remained, as I also pointed out, 'If you want an easy swim I don't think you should try to swim the Channel.'

All this unpleasantness, however, was washed away the following year when Greta Andersen became the first woman to win the race. She swam for 13 hours 55 minutes, and it was a particularly fine triumph because off the Goodwins she struggled for three hours, hardly moving, battling against strong tides and big waves. That magnificent and knowledgeable Channel swimmer Sam Rockett, whose expertise as race marshall through all the years we ran the race was invaluable, paid Greta a thoroughly justified tribute:

It was a magnificent performance, especially in view of the fact that she was swimming all the way against a strong head wind which whipped up the waves. Greta

227

was marvellous. To me she is the greatest swimmer I have ever seen. For the first eleven hours she was doing sixty strokes to the minute, while in the last half-hour, when she was obviously tiring, she was only down to fifty-four strokes a minute. Greta's performance was the best ever as far as I'm concerned.

If I had remembered Greta's stroke-a-minute figures the following year, when she won the race in 11 hours, a mere 10 minutes under the record, perhaps I might not have jumped in to swim alongside her. But then, I have always been one to go in off the deep end.

Without doubt I went in off the deep end with my next big contestant. Towards the end of 1959 a new craze began to sweep Britain: marathon walking. It was started by a doughty, if slightly cranky lady, Dr Barbara Moore, who, to prove various scientific and nutritional beliefs, walked from John O'Groats to Lands End in twenty-three days—and in doing so walked herself into the admiring hearts of millions of people. In no time at all, an ever-growing band of would-be marathon walkers were attempting to emulate her—and usually failing miserably.

I have always said that whenever I feel like taking exercise I go and lie down until the feeling wears off. But I could appreciate how Dr Moore's feat—if I may use the word—captured the imagination of so many. Long-distance walking was something that ordinary people felt *they* could do. The wealthy had their horse riding, skiing and motor racing. The more skilled had long-distance swimming and mountain climbing. But any normal, reasonably fit person could walk. Why not, I thought, give them a chance to test their guts and their stamina and feel some sense of achievement? And so I decided to organize a 'Walk to end all walks' from John O'Groats to Lands End, with large cash prizes for the winners, and throw it open to anyone over the age of 18.

We received some 1,500 entries, but unfortunately the weather in Scotland turned nasty a few days before the race.

There were gales and heavy snow and the roads in the far north were lined with deep drifts. Local councils, some newspapers and three MPs instantly began declaring that the race was dangerous and would put an intolerable strain on local services. Sir Myer Calpern, Lord Provost of Glasgow, called for the race to be banned. 'It is outrageous,' he declared, 'that a millionaire showman should be able to turn the unorganized exploit of one woman into the biggest advertising stunt of the century without any regard to the human misery and possible injury and death that may result from this adventure.'

I did not think it was 'the biggest advertising stunt of the century'. Nor did I feel it was dangerous. But like the Cross-Channel Swim it was no picnic—and it was not meant to be. The opposite view was well put, I thought, in an editorial in the Glasgow *Sunday Post* of 28 February. Under the headline *Good Luck to the Blister Brigade*, it said:

> This morning hundreds of men and women are striding down the road from John O'Groats. They all hope to walk a thousand miles to Land's End, across moors, heads bent against gales, drenched by fierce squalls, and slithering over packed ice. It's a tough race all right. But good luck to every single competitor. And to heck with all the kill-joys and doubtful Dicks.
>
> We've had protests from provosts. Criticisms from councillors. A barrage of boos from stay-at-homes. Even a Minister of Her Majesty's Government has had his piece to say.
>
> Yes, it's tough, but the talk of danger is overdone. Hundreds of competitors may not finish the course. OK. But each and every one is an adult, perfectly capable of making up his or her own mind. Nobody need walk unless he wants to. They've decided to give us a most colourful stunt.
>
> A bit of colour like this is always welcome. Folk will turn out in hamlets and towns to cheer them on. Why?
>
> Because a thousand people have dared to pit their wits

and their strength against fantastic odds. Crazy? Daft?

But every big object of this kind is daft at the outset. It was daft to try to climb Everest. Daft to be first at the South Pole. Daft to send a rocket to the moon. Daft to swim the Channel. Dammit, no doubt everybody said it was daft of Columbus to try to sail round the world. Goodness knows, the people on the Butlin walk aren't Everest climbers or Pole discoverers, but they are people bubbling with enthusiasm.

Let them get on with it!

Good luck to them all!

More criticism came during the race when MPs attacked it in the House of Commons. George Thompson called it 'a very irresponsibly organized publicity stunt'. He asked how much had been spent out of public funds to give medical help to competitors. It proved to be about £100 for a few walkers who were kept in hospital for a night, and I paid that. These official figures put all alarmist talk of the knockers into perspective. In an interview in the *Sunday Times*, Susan Cooper quoted me as saying, 'Someone's only got to say a thing can't be done for me to worry myself to death doing it. All my life I've been biting off more than I can chew, and swallowing it.'

That has always been true of me and with the Long Walk I certainly bit off a mouthful. But why had I not postponed the race when the weather turned bad? I explained to Miss Cooper that when it began to snow heavily it was only two days before the walk was due to start and there were nearly a thousand contestants making their way to Scotland.

'I couldn't just call off the race and leave them stranded,' I pointed out, 'so I booked two big halls in Wick and we would have fed them all and looked after them until conditions were OK.'

Fortunately, the weather eased and we were able to start the walk on time—though the conditions were still pretty wintry. In the interview I touched on another little-publicized aspect of the walk. 'I thought the Scots were against it at first, but the help we got was astounding,' I remarked.

230

Indeed it was. People came out of practically every cottage along the rural roads with cups of tea. Towns gave the leading contestants a full civic reception and cheered them on down the road by singing 'Will ye no' come back again?' It was, after all, good publicity for some of these places in Scotland where they wanted to attract visitors. And good business, too. I reckoned the press alone spent over £20,000 in Scotland.

Overall, the race cost Butlin's £30,000-£35,000 not including £5,100 in prize money. Up to the time I spoke to Miss Cooper I estimated that the 80 vehicles we were using during the race had bought 5,000 gallons of petrol and I added, 'Just think what that's brought the State in duty.' In all, we had more than a hundred regular staff from the camps helping to run the race. I summed up my attitude by telling Susan Cooper: 'I could have got as much publicity out of running an Old Crocks' Race. But the ordinary man-in-the-street couldn't have entered for that; whereas the walk is within his means . . . '

The newspapers had been interested in the Long Walk from the moment it was announced. On the eve of the race about forty reporters were at Wick and they swamped the few hotels in the area. They slept on billiard tables, in baths and in the corridors. Perhaps this was why they were not very friendly when I gave a press conference. Naturally, they raised the question of danger to the contestants in view of the rigorous conditions. 'I see no danger in the race,' I said. 'The worst part will be the first fifty miles because of the weather—and to prove it's not dangerous I'll walk that fifty miles myself.' I added, 'Even if it kills me'—not quite the right thing to say in the circumstances!

After the snow storms, the day of the race, 26 February 1960, dawned bright and clear. John O'Groats was more like a fairground. There were big marquees and the local hotel was littered with rucksacks, bags and cases. Long queues stretched outside the tiny souvenir shop selling trinkets and tartan dolls.

The race started at 5 pm with the mass of walkers jostling at the top of the narrow road that led nearly a thousand miles to Land's End. I fired a Véry pistol to start them off and at the same time twelve red and green rockets soared upwards and over the sea—where despite the weather a man had been swimming naked a few hours earlier—and the Wick Girl Pipers played 'Scotland the Brave'.

It the rockets were spectacular, so was the start of the race: to my astonishment, everybody started running off down the road, leaving me behind with the posse of reporters, who were clearly determined to see if I would keep my word about walking the first fifty miles.

We plodded after them, and with a silent resolve to keep my big mouth shut in future, I realized that I had to keep on walking for at least a couple of hours more before I could honorably call a halt for the night and get into my car to see how the race was going. By the time that happened, fortunately, quite a few of the reporters were finding their concern for blistering feet overcoming their desire for a story. Actually, by the time I had walked up and down various stretches of the route throughout the race, I must have covered considerably more than a hundred miles.

But on that first night the reporters and I were not the only ones wilting. In the first few hours about 170 walkers dropped out. We had not walked more than twenty miles from John O'Groats before contestants were asking me how much farther it was.

'Only about another nine hundred miles,' I told them. It was astonishing to discover that some of the walkers had no idea how far it was from John O'Groats to Land's End.

Among the contestants were twenty Old Age Pensioners, one with an artificial leg, two blind men, and a lady from Fiji who walked with bare feet. There were coalminers, nurses, university students and housewives. There were a one-time bullfighter, a chap in a top hat carrying a rolled umbrella, a woman with a feather hat and a shopping basket—and the Duke of Leinster. There was also Miss Florence Lewis, pulling a trolley containing food and clothing: after three hours she had walked only six miles. Slightly ahead of her was 72-year-old William Tully: he was so deaf he could not hear the traffic, so at night he wore a miner's lamp on his head to illuminate him.

I managed to persuade some of the more eccentric contenders to go home, and I paid their fares. Many others were obviously going to fall out early on in the race—indeed on the first three days many did—and so I organized a string of vans along the route to supply hot drinks. These casualties were taken to the nearest railway station and bought a ticket home. For most of the walkers who dropped out were practically penniless—or said they were—and many of them went to police stations and Town Halls to ask for their fares home. When I heard of this I announced that I would refund all sums paid by the authorities for this purpose. In the end, I paid out several thousand pounds.

We had another kind of problem with the cheats who tried to leapfrog their opponents by riding in buses or cars. At the start of the race we had about forty stewards cruising the route in some twenty cars checking on walkers, but I quickly realized we needed more. I sent out an SOS to some of my old fairground friends, and they promptly arrived to help. Soon we had more than fifty vigilant vehicles on the road, stationed about ten miles apart with instructions to note the numbers and times of all contestants. Each night these reports were checked. Any contestant who had not been seen by a steward at any particular point, or who had done more miles than he could reasonably have done on foot was disqualified or watched carefully from then on.

One day I noticed the support car of a national newspaper reporter, who was taking part in the race to write about his experiences. There was no sign of him, however, so I stopped the car and had it searched. Neatly curled up asleep in the boot was our intrepid walker. Catching the cheats was an immense problem, for after a few days the contestants were strung out over two hundred miles. Each night we checked the positions of the first thirty walkers, and became highly suspicious of anyone who had suddenly jumped a large number of places. We also established surprise check-points. At one stage a section of the route was flooded, so we set up a mile or so beyond it. It was obvious that any walker who arrived there with dry shoes had *not* got there on Shanks's pony.

We caught several cheats that way.

But enough of the unpleasant side of the race. There was sufficient heart-warming drama and courage to convince me that I was right to hold it. The earliest leader was the Wakefield cross-country champion John Grundy, who covered the first 39 miles at an average of 8 mph. He stayed the course, and in the end came second. As the lead changed hands the various walkers became national names. For the first ten days the race made the front pages of most of the national newspapers. And then Princess Margaret announced her engagement to Mr Antony Armstrong-Jones! For a couple of days we were pushed off the front pages, but from then on the Walk continued to be well reported and millions of people followed the fate of the leading contestants.

After thirty miles, the bearded David Robinson—a research student from Bermuda—took the lead from Grundy and thereafter the race was dominated by these two and another Yorkshireman, Jimmy Musgrave. David Robinson got as far as Taunton before he collapsed and left the field open to his hard-pressing rivals. But by then he was something of a national hero. In the end it was Musgrave, a 38-year-old Doncaster glass packer, who won.

But it was the first woman home, Liverpool hairdresser Wendy Lewis, whose sheer, courageous determination won the hearts of many. It was a moving, but heartening scene when she arrived at Land's End.

This is how Clifford Luton described it in the *Daily Express*:

A hug, a £1,000 cheque, and the long torture of a race from one end of Britain to the other was over. Wendy Lewis, a 19-year-old Liverpool hairdresser, had done it. And there were 25,000 people to cheer her home, first woman in the mass marathon. The 891 miles from John O'Groats to Land's End took her 17 days, 7 hours, 43 minutes . . . It was 12.45 a.m. when Wendy got to the finishing post. 'There's a long, long trail,' the crowd had been singing to while away the time. Then into the bright lights came Wendy, pale-faced, her eyelids heavy with

234

fatigue. The welcome was fantastic. The crowd went mad. As the tiny worn-out figure in red slacks, green pullover and blue and white shirt stumbled the last 50 yards, hats were flung into the air, car hooters brayed and police gave up the struggle to hold back the swaying crowds. Appeals of 'Don't hurt her—give her room' were shouted from the reception platform.

A flying wedge of broad-shouldered porters surrounded Wendy. Billy Butlin walked forward to meet her with the cheque for £1,000 in his hand. But the attractive, dark-haired girl who was the cause of all the excitement seemed hardly to notice what was happening. She fumbled uncertainly for the steps made of nine beer crates which led up to the platform where she was to be officially greeted.

She had saved the last ounces of her strength to throw off the grinding weariness against which she had fought for the past 24 sleepless hours. 'For she's a jolly good fellow,' sang the crowd. She smiled at them, blinking in the glare of the newsreel lights. Her whispering replies to questions from Billy Butlin were drowned by the constant roar of cheers. Finally they got her down and into the Land's End Hotel. She limped slowly and painfully into the room prepared for her. There she collapsed into an armchair and smiled bravely at me.

'I feel marvellous. Wouldn't you if you had just won £1,000? It's the hardest thing I ever did, but you don't think how hard it is, you just do it.' I asked her how she had felt at Redruth earlier in the evening when fatigue seemed to have transformed her into an automaton, unaware of anything but the need to go trudging westwards.

'I was pretty tired out. I hadn't been in bed for the last two days and nights,' she said. 'All I need is sleep.'

Her face, swollen by wind and rain, broke into a slow smile. She said suddenly: 'This means that I and my sisters Joy and Angela, who is 15, can now have our own hairdressers' business. We shall look around for a nice little shop somewhere in the south. We shall work as a team—we three sisters always do'. As she talked she fingered the backs of her hands. badly swollen and looking bruised. 'It's caused by swinging your arms when you walk for long periods,' she told me simply.

It was at Redruth that Wendy looked worse than she had ever done during the 891-mile walk. As she entered the town—her mouth open, elbows tucked in to her slight, over-taxed body—the crowd was so quiet you could hear the pacemaker counting: 'one, two, three, four; one, two, three, four.' Every step was agony. Every hill a torturing challenge to her unbreakable courage. The swelling of her legs stretched her red slacks. Her head rolled from side to side. Hundreds packed the street outside the Mount Ambrose Inn as Wendy was half led, half carried to an upstairs room.

There she was massaged while outside the crowd roared, 'We want Wendy!' Then Wendy re-appeared, lowering herself painfully step by step down the stairs, clutching the banister. She looked as though she was sleep walking.

At Land's End, the earlier miseries were forgotten. As the tiny figure trudged over the final hill in the glare of the headlights in the procession of motor cars which crawled behind her, the crowd broke into song. Wendy trudged painfully on. The nearer the slight and courageous figure got, the more excited the vast crowd became. At the end of it all I asked her: 'Was it worth it?'

'Yes, it was,' she said with simple conviction.

After it was all over, I was glad I had ignored the moaning Willies and gone ahead with the Walk. You had to be pretty cold hearted not to be impressed by the courage of people like Wendy Lewis and the second woman home, Beryl Randle, along with Jim Musgrave, John Grundy and David Robinson and all the unsung others who finished the race.

For, whether the competitors dropped out after twenty

236

miles or staggered on to the end, they all had one thing in common: guts. And when the aching bones eased and the blisters healed, they all had something else in common: the satisfaction of having a go.

In the summer before The Long Walk I had myself taken part in a vastly different contest: the *Daily Mail* race between London's Marble Arch and the Arc de Triomphe in Paris. Contestants could use any form of transport. I plumped for car, helicopter, Spitfire plane and motor bike.

First of all I had to find a Spitfire; eventually, I found one in a hangar at Eastleigh, near Southampton. Very conveniently it had been converted into a two-seater, but very inconveniently it had no engine. After much searching we located an engine in Brussels.

In the civilian section I was competing in, I had some stiff competition. Other entrants included ten test pilots, British and French racing drivers, an Olympic cyclist, a teenager who had built his own plane in his backyard. Neville Duke, the British test pilot, flew an amphibian loaned by Aristotle Onassis, while racing driver Stirling Moss relied on a hotted-up French car.

My plan was to be driven by Donald Campbell in a Porsche to a spot on the Thames, where a helicopter would whisk me to Biggin Hill and the waiting Spitfire. First we had to find a place for the helicopter to land. After studying the tide-times, we eventually located a stretch by the Chelsea Embankment where the river bed would be uncovered for several hours on the day of the race. I was worried that the helicopter might become stuck in the soft mud, so I put down a couple of loads of gravel to form a firm landing 'pad'.

For me, the race began with a near disaster. When I got the 'Go' signal to make the first of my three runs—you were judged on your fastest time—Donald was so anxious to get away that he had the car moving before I could climb in properly and only by dint of a desperate scramble did I avoid being dragged unceremoniously along the road. To speed our path to Chelsea I stationed Redcoats at every cross-road. When we approached a crossing we sounded our horn and the Redcoats stopped the traffic to allow us to speed through. It worked marvellously the first time, but unfortunately the police put a stop to it on our subsequent trips.

On this first occasion, however, we reached the Embankment in great time. The helicopter was waiting to whisk me to Biggin Hill where I was bundled into the rear cockpit of the Spitfire and we roared off, giving a fair imitation of a Battle of Britain scramble, while I struggled in the confined cockpit to fasten my parachute harness. We landed at a small airfield about ten miles from Paris and there I jumped on the the pillion of a motor bike driven by a French racing ace. He roared off at an alarming speed with me clinging on desperately. I yelled to him to slow down, but he spoke no English and I spoke no French. In fact, he seemed to think I was urging him to go faster. This undoubtedly felt the most dangerous part of the journey.

On the return trip we clipped a few seconds off our time when I transferred from the Spitfire into the helicopter in ten seconds. At Chelsea Embankment I jumped out while the helicopter hovered two or three feet in the air, and tumbled into the waiting Porsche. To reach the finishing post contestants had to run the last two hundred yards and when I finally puffed home—next day the newspapers dubbed me Puffing Billy—I had done the trip in 70 minutes 20 seconds. It was not a winning time, however, for the Frenchman Jean Vinatier beat me by almost thirteen minutes. The overall winner of the race, Squadron Leader Charles Maughan, did the dash in 40 minutes 44 seconds to collect the £5,000 first prize. I came in third, winning a £100 prize. It cost me more than £5,000 to do it.

In 1969, the *Mail* organized a similar race, this time from the top of the Post Office Tower in London to the top of the Empire State Building in New York. Though I had retired from Butlin's by now, I was determined to take part. Wearing a morning suit, complete with crash helmet, and carrying a top hat—so I could look like the American idea of a typical Englishman—I left the Tower on the back of a motor bike driven by an RAF despatch rider. We sped to the Thames near Waterloo and from there a helicopter took me to Hatfield in Hertfordshire, where I boarded a Hawker Siddeley 125 executive jet to fly to New York by way of Iceland, Greenland and Gandar.

That fine journalist Lynda Lee Potter came with me in the plane and wrote an amusing account of the flight in the *Daily Mail* of May 9:

'How would you like to go to New York in a millionaire's jet, drinking champagne and all that?' they said.

'Smashing,' I said and crossed the Atlantic in Sir William Butlin's £400,000 jet which used to belong to a sheik from Saudi Arabia.

Sir William is competitor 222 in the *Daily Mail* Air Race and we've just arrived in New York in his eight-seater white jet—painted with Union Jacks—and which he's renting for £160 an hour.

There are six of us altogether . . . [including] two pilots and me and a rather jolly hostess called Pauline who said that she'd sew on buttons, play cards, feed us whenever we wanted and if there was anything else we wanted that she hadn't got she'd nip out and get it at Iceland. She also said that if we changed our mind in mid-flight and wanted to go somewhere else that would be perfectly all right. 'Anything,' she said, 'to oblige the customers,' which is the sort of service you get when you're paying £160 an hour.

Sir William had to do it the hard way and start from the top of the GPO Tower, but the rest of us went straight out to Hatfield Airport . . . The two pilots were already there, bouncy and bright and saying the wind was on our tail. We all got on board and the plane taxied up the runway to do a rapid take-off as soon as Sir William leapt out of his helicopter. He was coming by helicopter from a Waterloo car park . . . 'I got somebody last night,' said

Sir William, 'to knock a hole in the fence round the car park so we could drive straight in. I saved myself five minutes by not having to go round to the entrance.'

Sir William looked quite something. He was wearing a top hat, pin-striped trousers, morning coat and a large orange bib saying 'Daily Mail Transatlantic Air Race'. He spent most of the trip taking the whole lot off and putting it on again every time we refuelled. It was all quite tricky because he had to be tied into his bib, but it was well worth it and he was a terrific success in Iceland where one Icelandic photographer could hardly bear to let him go. Refuelling was done to split-second timing. One pilot leapt up on to the wings to pour in some more fuel while the other went through the documents with the airport officials. Everybody shouted for everybody else to come and bring their friends to stare at us and there was really rather a festive atmosphere.

We caused a stir in Iceland, but we were a knockout in Greenland. We all had our photographs taken by a lot of rather nice Eskimos. 'I suppose it's walking into that wind all the time,' said Sir William, 'that flattens their faces.' I don't know what the rest of Greenland is like but the airport is grey and cold and horrible. 'Not a fish and chip shop in sight,' said the guv'nor.

There was a rather sad little man who didn't speak very good English who said he was from the BBC and could he have a lift to wherever we were going. We didn't believe he was from the BBC. 'No,' said Sir William, who is the kindest, most generous and gentle of men. 'You do realize,' he told us, 'that you can all sue me if we crash. Well, just think of what it would cost me having an extra passenger suing.'

On the third lap of the trip we had lunch and we were just finishing our brandy with our Camembert when we reached Canada and flew seemingly endlessly over rows of fir trees stuck like pins into a vast and shining pin cushion. Our stop in Canada was quite exciting because we got hemmed in between an Esso van and another from Eastern Provincial Airways and had to be pushed clear by three RAF airmen. Time was all important so we never did find out quite what the RAF was doing there.

The pilots by this time had the scent of blood. We were about an hour ahead of schedule and the wind was still on our tail. 'We've got a radio vector into New York,' said Pauline, 'which means that everybody else has to get out of our way.' Sir William got all dressed up again and we celebrated the good news with brandy and smoked salmon all round. I still don't know how it happened but we all got in and out of New York airport without handing in our immigration forms or showing our passports or going through customs . . .

Sir William leapt into his waiting helicopter to go to the Empire State Building and puffed off into a cloud of blue smoke with his orange iridescent *Daily Mail* bib just gleaming through the haze. We haven't seen him since.

As Miss Potter reported, I leapt into a waiting helicopter and flew off. However, she did not know what happened after that. 'Let's go,' I yelled as I scrambled aboard and we took off immediately. I noticed the pilot giving me an odd look or two, but I assumed it was because of my outfit. He did not say anything until we approached Manhattan and then he shouted: 'Landing conditions are ideal, Mr—. We'll be down in a couple of minutes.'

Without thinking I replied, 'I'm not Mr—'

'Who the hell are you, then?' he yelled.

I told him.

'My God,' he replied. 'I wasn't supposed to pick *you* up. I gotta go back.'

To say I was dismayed would be an under-statement—if we returned to the airport it would add ruinous minutes to my journey. So I tried desperately to persuade the pilot to continue. 'We're almost there now,' I said. 'You're only going to lose a couple more minutes, and I'll see you're well paid for the journey.'

As he hesitated I hastily told him about the race, and that if I

241

won a lot of money would go to charity—for various Variety Club members had promised to top up my £500 prize money to £5,000.

This seemed to clinch the matter and with a muttered 'I sure hope Mr— doesn't blow his top,' he agreed to land me.

At the helicopter port an ambulance and police escort, laid on by the New York Variety Club, was waiting to rush me with sirens wailing to the Empire State Building. We reached it in seven minutes. There, an elevator with open doors was waiting to woosh me to the top of this legendary building.

From the top of the Post Office Tower to the summit of the Empire State Building the journey had taken 11 hours 30 minutes and 41.35 seconds—a winning time for my category. It was a victory that I could not have achieved without the help of the New York Variety Club and my unwitting helicopter pilot. I hope his other passenger was understanding.

After all the planning and effort it was good to win—and it also meant I did not have to keep my promise that if I did not make the first three I would kick my topper off the top of the Empire State Building. So I arrived back at Jersey's St Helier airport still with my top hat. And there, waiting for me, was Sheila with the children, young Bill and little Jacquie, who was then only three. Both of them were wearing tiny top hats.

All the various ways of getting from one place to another as fast as possible were exciting and often uncomfortable. But for sheer discomfort the *Daily Express* Off-Shore Powerboat Race, which I entered in 1961 when it was first started, takes some beating.

With test pilot Peter Twiss I competed in the first race from the Isle of Wight to Torquay, Devon. We crewed a Hunter class boat which I had bought especially for the event. The night before the start, that great marine designer and sailor, Uffa Fox, told me, 'You don't stand a chance of winning. I've got the best boat in the race.' But the next morning the weather was so rough that many of the contestants, including Uffa, failed to start. Peter and I managed to get away, however, though we almost crashed into another boat. As we headed towards the open sea I had high hopes of proving Uffa wrong. My optimism was soon leaking away like water in a colander. The boat bucked and reared on every wave. It was impossible to sit down and each time we slammed into the water it was like hitting concrete. My legs rapidly became swollen with the pounding. The 172 miles from Cowes to the finishing line at Torquay began to look an awful long way away.

So I experienced a mixture of disappointment and blissful relief when we were holed by a floating plank just beyond the Nab Tower Lighthouse. Water poured in and, while Peter struggled with the wallowing craft, I frantically bailed. In this way we managed to beach the boat on the west coast of the Isle of Wight.

Leaving Peter to look after the boat, I hitched a lift to the local airfield and chartered a plane to Torquay. It was a much more comfortable ride—*and* I arrived therefore before any of the competitors. While we waited for the contestants to arrive I talked to one of the race judges, a retired Admiral who commanded the local Sea Scouts. When he mentioned the difficulty of obtaining sea-going boats for his lads, it gave me an idea. I told him he could have my power boat. I felt the youngsters' legs would stand the buffeting better than mine. And, in any case, it would effectively remove the temptation for me to take part in the race again.

Early in 1963, while travelling by train to the Minehead camp, I saw a most unusual sight. Sitting in the corner of the compartment was a distinguished, military-looking figure busily knitting. He appeared to be blind. I introduced myself and discovered that he was Colonel (now Sir) Michael Ansell. He had, in fact, been blinded in the war and he explained to me that he found knitting a relaxing way of passing the time on a long journey.

That meeting resulted in Butlin's becoming involved in another sport: show jumping. For Mike Ansell's absorbing interest turned out to be horse riding and show jumping, and he talked to me with enthusiasm about them. Later I discovered that he had been a great international rider before the war and now he was channelling his enthusiasm into promoting the sport. Today he is a former Chairman and President of the British Show Jumping Association and is regarded as the Father of British show jumping.

It has been mainly through his efforts that show jumping has been transformed from a small-scale county event into an international sport with a following second only to that of football. Television, of course, has helped tremendously in this transformation and millions now share in the thrills and excitement of such events as the Horse of the Year Show. But it is doubtful whether the sport would have developed to such proportions if it were not for Sir Michael.

I had not had much to do with horses since my painful introduction to riding in the Canadian Army, though for six years in the late Fifties I owned four race horses. They ran in the camp colours of blue and yellow and were named Skegness, Clacton, Ayr and Bognor, but they seldom won. As the campers used to back them out of loyalty, and lose their money, I decided race-horse owning was not for me.

On that train journey, though, Sir Michael infected me with his enthusiasm for show jumping and it occurred to me that it could be a popular attraction at the camps. A few weeks later a meeting was held at the London Headquarters of the British Show Jumping Association to look into the possibilities. As a result a Butlin's Championship was conceived, with qualifying heats being held at the camps—the first was held at Pwllheli at Whitsun, 1963—with the finals taking place on the first night of the Horse of the Year Show at the Empire Pool, Wembley. This night is still known as Butlin's Gala Night and the proceeds go to the Army Benevolent Fund. A speed event, with riders racing against the clock, was also begun. This was originally called 'Have a Gamble', but it is now known as the Butlin Top Score Championship. The finals of this are also held at Wembley, along with those of the Pony Club Mounted Games which we sponsor to encourage young riders under the age of fifteen.

Today Butlin's spends many thousands of pounds sponsoring show jumping. Our participation not only helps the sport itself, but it also encourages an interest in show jumping among the campers. Some can even watch a qualifying heat while on holiday and then see the finals on television in October.

It is intriguing to reflect that none of this would have happened if I had not had that accidental meeting on a train. But of all the memorable happenings in those eventful years, undoubtedly my most cherished memory is of the day in 1964 when I went to Buckingham Palace in a topper and morning suit to be knighted by the Queen for my services to the Church. It was a most impressive ceremony. After being ushered forward by a series of imposing-looking officials I finally entered the Ballroom, where the Investiture was held, and knelt before Her Majesty, who touched me on the shoulder with a sword. 'Do you wish to be called Sir William or Sir Billy?' she asked, smiling.

I replied: 'I have always been called Bill or Billy, your Majesty.'

'Very well,' she said. 'Arise, Sir Billy.'

After the ceremony some of my showman friends took me off for a celebration to the fun fair at Battersea Park. At the park entrance the car stopped and I was astonished to see parked in the road a First World War Army lorry like the one I had bought all those years ago soon after I became a travelling showman. Many more of my old showman friends were there, along with a brass band.

Kneeling before the Queen had been an emotional enough experience but now climbing into this old lorry and driving it wheezing and clanking into the Park behind the band, brought the memories tumbling back. What a long and eventful road it had been. And who would have thought that the young man trundling around the West Country with his hoop-la stalls would eventually become 'Sir Billy'?

Certainly not me.

In 1947, I was working at Bon Marché in Liverpool and living at home. But for personal reasons I wanted to get away, and when I saw an advert in the local paper for a manageress for 'the largest bar in the world' at Butlin's Pwllheli camp it seemed an ideal opportunity to leave home, for the job carried accommodation with it. I had no experience of bar work, but with references from a couple of friends who ran nightclubs, and who declared they had employed me, I got the job and bluffed my way along as I learned the business.

But I knew that my inexperience would quickly be spotted by Mr Butlin, so whenever I heard he was going to visit the camp, I took the day off. One day, however, he arrived unexpectedly and I was well and truly caught out. I had my back to the bar, as it was lunch-time and the place was empty, when I turned round he was there. To make matters worse I was smoking, which was against the rules. I was so surprised to see him I nearly swallowed the cigarette.

However, I managed to ask him if he would like a drink and he replied, 'Yes'. I had been told he always drank a large gin and tonic in a tumbler and so I quickly got this. I began pouring the tonic for him, but I was so nervous I spilled some on the bar top. The top was made of aluminium, and it must have been slightly sloping, for with the lubrication of spilled tonic the tumbler started sliding along the bar. I suppose I must have panicked because instead of picking up the glass and wiping the bar I followed the sliding glass with the tonic bottle, still pouring. It was like a scene from a Marx Brothers' comedy. Bill did not say a word–he just stared at me. I expected to be told any second, 'You're sacked.' Instead, after a while he asked, 'What are you doing tonight after the bar's closed?' I told him I was going to a party in one of the chalets. He didn't say any more and shortly went off on his rounds of the camp.

Bill must have inquired about the party for he turned up at the chalet. After a while Frank Bond, the camp controller, came over to me and said. 'Mr Butlin would like to have a word with you. Would you go over?' I thought that was a bit of

246

a cheek as I was off-duty. 'Tell him if he wants to speak to me, he can come over here,' I replied.

To my surprise he did come over. I didn't drink, but I had a glass of warm whisky in my hand which various people had kept topping up until it was full. Bill looked at it and said, 'You don't need that,' and took it away from me. He had a number of guests from Bermuda staying at the camp and in that typical way of his he suddenly decided to have a dinner party in the camp restaurant. He invited me. When I arrived, Stan, the restaurant manager was rushing about organizing things.

'Come on, Sheila, give us a hand,' he said. 'The Guv'nor's coming in a minute.'

I decided to pull his leg. 'I can't,' I said. 'I'm the honoured guest.'

'Don't play silly games,' said Stan. 'I'm too busy.' He ushered me out of the restaurant. At that moment Bill arrived. 'Ah, hello,' he said, and took my arm.

Stan looked astonished. I grinned at him. 'Well, I did tell you,' I said.

A little later Bill asked me to return to London with him, and I lived in a suite of rooms in the Gower Hotel which he then owned. After a while I moved into a flat. Bill visited me regularly and we were very happy.

One day he said in his typical fashion, 'How about you doing some work? Why don't you come and join me in the office. You'll enjoy it.'

I thought, 'My God. I didn't expect this.' But I found I did enjoy it. And if it were not for the experience I gained there I might not have been able to live with him in later years. For as he frankly admitted, his business always came first. He would say: 'Sheil, I'll be home at seven,' and he would arrive at eleven o'clock, explaining, 'I was just leaving the office when a load of press boys arrived for drinks.' That kind of thing did not upset me then because I had seen it happen, and knew he was telling the truth.

We could be going to an evening dress function and I would

think, 'I'll lay out his dress suit, and then we can have a quiet drink before leaving.' What usually happened was that he tore in late, tore off his clothes and changed and then we tore out.

I found you could never plan with Bill. I would think, 'We're doing such-and-such this weekend,' then something unexpected would crop up, like a problem at one of the camps, and he would be off.

Norah was very attractive, and a fantastic hostess for him; but she did not understand the business, nor was she prepared to take a back seat to it. It was no surprise when Bill told me he could not be happy living with her.

So it was an immense shock when he suddenly told me he was marrying her. He was with me on the Friday before the Sunday when the papers carried the news. He had told me, 'I'll stay the weekend with you in the flat.'

On Saturday I went shopping and when I returned the telephone was ringing. It was Bill. He said, 'Sheil don't say anything; don't answer. I'm going to tell you something and I don't want you to learn it from the newspapers. Believe me, there's an explanation. Sheil, I don't want to hurt you, but I'm getting married.'

I was shattered. Only three months earlier he had said: 'We're going to make life for ourselves.' We had decided to have a family.

Later on the Saturday he came to see me and said, 'I can't go through with this wedding without seeing you.' He was crying. He explained that he had decided to try and make a go of marriage with Norah for the sake of the children. It was clear that since he had left me on Friday enormous pressures had been placed on him.

I screamed inside, for I was desperate to tell him that I was pregnant; but I decided to wait.

On the day he got married I went to the office as usual. Halfway through the morning, his secretary Winifred West said, 'Bill wants to see you.' I went into his office and he threw his arms around me.

'I love you,' he said, 'but I'm going to get married.'

I said, 'All right, darling.' We were both very choked.

248

'Wait in the office until I get back,' he said. 'Don't go to lunch.' Half an hour later he returned with the press boys, but he kept them out of his office until he had seen me. He said. 'That's it; it's done.' That was all his wedding meant to him.

In telling the truth here I do not want to put Bill in a bad light. He was very clearly torn, but equally clearly he did what he thought was right at the time, for his children. For myself, I loved him and wanted to be part of him. He was the first man I really loved.

I waited three weeks before telling him I was pregnant. He was thrilled. But just before the baby was due to be born he had to visit Chicago for a trade fair. He said, 'I'm sorry, darling, I must go. I've got to see some new rides.' But Bill was a very romantic man. He flew all the way to Chicago, stayed twenty-four hours, and flew back to be home in time for the birth of our son, William.

While all this was going on Bill's relationship with Norah was most unhappy. Really, I do not wish to be unkind to Norah, because, as I have said, I appreciated her problems, but at this period Bill had no home life. He tried desperately to keep up the appearance of the marriage. He did it for a year—but by then he had had enough. He left Norah and we began looking for a house where we could live together. We eventually found Windlesham Moor, a magnificent country house in Surrey, where the then Princess Elizabeth and Prince Philip had spent part of their honeymoon. There were fifty-nine acres of grounds, and Bill immediately set about creating a lovely garden and a miniature golf course.

When our daughter Jacquie was born Bill was delighted and became more protective than ever. If I carried her from one room to another, he covered her face with a cloth.

'What are you doing that for?' I asked the first time he did it.

'The temperature is very different in the other room,' he explained. 'She might catch cold.'

He also insisted on her cot being in the dining-room when we had dinner. He fetched it himself from the nursery. If Jacquie stirred or moved her arm he asked anxiously, 'Is she all right?'

We could not agree on a name for her, so to spur Bill into choosing one I called her by the first name I could think of—Floss. 'Come on, Floss,' I said, picking her up.

'Don't call her Floss,' said Bill. 'My God! Floss Butlin.'

Finally, when he was reading in the newspaper about the shooting of President Kennedy, he suddenly suggested, 'How about Jackie? Like Jackie Kennedy, but we'll spell it in the French way.' And that's how our daughter Jacquie got her name.

As Bill recalls in his own narrative, he and I were finally married in September 1976. But to be honest it did not worry me whether we were married or not in view of the many years we had been together. However, Bill kept insisting we ought to get married. In fact, on two occasions I set out to put up the banns. Each time I didn't go through with it. I thought, 'We're happy. The kids are old enough to understand. They know he's their father.' Finally, however, we made it, and I am deeply touched by the things Bill says about me in the book. If it was third time lucky for him, it was first time lucky for me. I had to smile, though, when he wrote that 'without her companionship and help I would never have retired'.

BOBBY BUTLIN RECALLS HIS RELATIONSHIP WITH HIS PARENTS:

Billy Butlin's son Bobby throws a different light on his mother's drinking, and recalls his own lonely childhood, devoid of any real family life with its inherent love and attention—a picture that is in stark contrast to Billy Butlin's behaviour in later life towards his third wife, Sheila, and their children, William and Jacquie:

My father, and to a certain extent my mother, were absentee parents. My childhood years and teenage years were unfortunate in some respects. My father says he gave me a good education, and this is true; I think it is also true that when I grew up he was proud of me, but as a child he spent very little time with me. Some of it was not his fault, because when I was five I was packed off to boarding school where I stayed until I

250

was eighteen. During those thirteen years I can certainly count on the fingers of one hand the times he visited me at school.

I can recall many, many occasions when I would come home for the school holidays and my parents were away. I was picked up at school, or the station, by the chauffeur to be looked after by a nanny. And I can remember many, many occasions when I and my two younger sisters, Cherrie and Sandra, were sent back to school a few days earlier because our parents were going off somewhere, or it was not convenient for us to be at home. Even when we were at home and my father wasn't travelling, he usually returned from the office after we had gone to bed. On days when he came home, say, at seven o'clock, my mother would tell us, 'Your father's very tired and all he wants is to have a tray of food in bed, so he doesn't want you kids around.'

Now whether this was so, I don't know. Looking back, it could have been because my mother felt insecure—remember she was not married—and it is possible that she did not want father sharing his affections with us.

We rarely went on a family holiday. And even when we did, he hardly ever came swimming with us, or put his arm around us, or had any close contact.

I have friends with children and there is no way they would send them back to school just because it was a bit inconvenient; there is no way they would not visit their children. There is no way the father would not kick a ball around with a young son, or take him to the zoo or somewhere when he didn't want to go himself. I never felt my father or mother would do anything that would be nice for us children, despite the fact that they didn't really want to do it. So from that point of view we were not a close family. It was very strange, really: that he created the camps for families—and yet never paid much attention to his own. I genuinely believe that the immense amount of charity work he did for underprivileged children, and children without a happy home environment, in his retirement was part of a guilt complex. I feel that deep down he recognized that in the past he had not

251

spent much time with his own kids.

However, I would not like to leave the impression that his apparent lack of interest in me and my two sisters whilst we were children was in any way intentional. I believe that he was so determined to expand the business, which involved long hours and a seven-day week, that it never really crossed his mind that he had a growing family who needed a father around.

My father writes about my mother's heavy drinking, but I believed then and I believe even more so now that most people are driven to drink. He was a very hard taskmaster both in his business and personal life. I think he was unfair to my mother most of the time. He always wanted her to be there, and yet very often he didn't even bother to let her know he wouldn't be home to dinner, when he had said at lunchtime, 'I'll be home at seven. Have a nice meal ready for me.'

I know for a fact that she would sometimes ask, 'What time are you coming home, Bill?' and he would reply, 'I don't know.' But when she said, 'I fancy going to the cinema this afternoon with a girl friend,' he would say, 'No, don't go out. I might be back any time.'

So, although she was a magnificent hostess, when she was not entertaining my mother never went out without him. She never had a life of her own. She lived like a trapped butterfly. So she became desperately lonely and bored, and what do you do when you're bored?—reach for the bottle. And, of course, once that starts, things go from bad to worse.

BILLY BUTLIN'S 20-YEAR-OLD SON, WILLIAM, HAS HAPPIER MEMORIES OF HIS FATHER:

I think Dad realized he had made a mistake with his other children and told himself, 'I mustn't let that happen again.' Certainly neither Jack nor I can complain about the way he treated us. He was a wonderful father who took an active interest in us. He taught us to swim in the indoor pool at Windlesham Lodge, and took us to London to see the sights and visit museums. He once arranged for me to have a conducted tour of Scotland Yard, and spend a couple of hours cruising in a Panda car. As a boy, I particularly enjoyed fishing with him.

He spoiled us, but he did not overdo it, and he could be strict with us. When we were young, so many Christmas presents were sent to Jack and me by people with whom Dad did business that they filled a whole room. We were overwhelmed by them, and early one Christmas morning we went into the room where the presents were stacked and tore them all open, with the result that Mum and Dad had great difficulty finding who had sent them. In some cases we had even destroyed the operating instructions for the toys. So Dad decreed that for the next few years, whilst we were still very young, we would only be allowed one toy each on Christmas morning. We were to play with those for a week or two, he told us, and then, if we wanted to change, we should put them outside his bedroom door in the morning, and he would give us two more.

One year Jack returned a toy dog with one leg missing. 'What happened to this?' Dad asked.

Like a lot of little girls, Jack could be quite imperious with her father. 'Now listen, Daddy,' she said, waving a finger at him. 'It was like that when I got it.'

'I don't think so,' said Dad.

'Yes it was, Daddy,' she insisted.

'Well, we'll take a more careful look at the next one,' replied Dad, firmly ending the discussion.

He often bought us magnificent toys. When we became fans of Doctor Who, he gave us a huge Dalek—twice the size of the ones on television—which we propelled around by means of a tricycle inside. Then there were the scaled-down toy cars, some of which had little engines. Whenever Dad attended a trade fair, he would come back with all kinds of toys and gadgets. And at social functions he collected autographs for us.

I have alway been grateful to my father for sending me to Gordonstoun School. The distance from London to Scotland naturally prevented him making frequent visits to see

253

me—though I well remember one occasion when he fought his way through a snowstorm to get there—nevertheless, he often telephoned and wrote long letters to me.

After we moved to Jersey, Dad held regular business meetings at home, and I shudder now, remembering the times I interrupted them.

'Look at this, Dad,' I would say, presenting him with a model plane or something I had just made. Instead of saying, as most fathers understandably would in the circumstances, 'I'm busy, go away,' he would break off the meeting to talk to me.

Perhaps that remarkable kind of indulgence best serves to illustrate how Dad's attitude and behaviour towards his children changed, and that in later life, he put his family before business.

PART **4**

A Showman to the End

17

'A terrible decision to make'

THE most poignant scene in London last night was an elderly face sitting alone in an empty office. No telephone rang. Nothing on his desk but his hat. All his cupboards and safes empty.

It was Billy Butlin, who tried to smile as I put my head round the door, but he was clearly near to tears. He looked utterly bereft.

That was how, in the *Sun* newspaper of 3 April 1968, Noel Whitcomb described me after I had announced my retirement as chairman and managing director of Butlin's.

It was a pretty accurate description. For although I was to become a consultant to the company, I was cutting myself off from the active running of a holiday business that I had created and built up to a position where, at one time, it was catering for more than one million people every summer—roughly one in fifty of the population. It was an immense wrench and it proved to me there is nothing like the aching emptiness of losing a way of life.

My decision to retire was taken suddenly, but far from lightly. I remember vividly how it all happened. It was Thursday 28 March 1968 and I was meeting with my good friend and accountant Peter Hetherington when he dropped the bombshell that in the tax year 1967/8 I would have to pay a 'one off' special charge of 9s in the pound tax on my income on top of my ordinary tax.

257

'What will it cost me?' I asked.

'Including income tax and surtax it will mean you will be paying 27s 3d on every pound of your income,' he replied. To put it mildly, I was stunned. In the year 1965/66, for instance, my total income was £232,000 and on that I had paid more than £200,000 in tax. Peter Hetherington explained that this 'special charge' would mean paying about £30,000 more than my total income. The only way I could pay this huge bill was to sell a large chunk of Butlin shares.

This was bad enough, for my shares in Butlin's were my only liquid assets. But what worried me more was if this special charge was not a 'one off' or an isolated tax? What if it were repeated in future years?

To judge from the newspapers and television this could well happen. For there was talk in some quarters of still more punitive taxes on the wealthy—ignoring the fact that many of those to be hit had worked damned hard for their money as well as producing work for thousands of people. As I thought about this I was reluctantly forced to ask myself if I should leave Britain.

It was a terrible decision to make. I hated the thought of leaving the country that had been my home for most of my life, where I had created a major business and where most of my friends lived. But the consequences of staying could be enormous. If these huge taxes continued everything I had could be swallowed up. I would have nothing for my old age. It would be difficult to leave my children anything. And I had to consider the long list of retired employees who received pensions from me. What also concerned me was talk of taxing donations to charity. If *that* happened it would make it impossible for me to continue to help the many charities I was interested in, and some that depended on me.

I want to help the people and charities of my choice, I thought. Not give the money to the government.

All these thoughts passed through my mind after my accountant had left me. It was an undeniable fact that as far as paying tax was concerned I had more than done my bit over the years. My company and I had paid more than £50 million in

258

taxes. Why should I go on working and then pay all I earned to the government?

By Saturday I had reluctantly reached the conclusion that the case for leaving Britain for some less harsh tax climate was overwhelming. But where should I go? I considered Bermuda, where I had lived for a while, or the Bahamas. I even thought about returning to South Africa or Canada. Finally, on the recommendation of my old friend Charlie Lytle, who lived there, I chose a haven much nearer home. It was Jersey in the Channel Islands.

Later that day, Saturday, I contacted Peter Hetherington. He was attending a wedding in Norwich, but a message was got to him and he came to see me on the Sunday. I told him my decision.

'Well,' he said, 'if you're going you ought to go before the end of the financial year on April 5th. Otherwise you could find yourself liable for tax next year.'

And who knows what that might be? I said to myself. Aloud, I said to Peter, 'But that only leaves five days. What does it involve?'

He explained. 'You'll have to resign your position with Butlin's and relinquish any other directorships and business interests in Britain. Every single one of your assets, share certificates, the lot, will have to be transferred to Jersey before April 5th. You'll have to put your house, Windlesham Moor, and any other property, on the market and not set foot in them until they are sold. And, of course, all your personal possessions will have to be removed.'

I looked at him. It was an immense task to be done in five days. 'Can we do it in time?'

'We'll have a damned good try.'

The next day, Monday 1 April, I told my son Bobby: 'I'm handing over the business to you.'

I telephoned some of my closest friends with the news. They expressed shock and sadness, but they all agreed I had done the right thing. I had hoped that they would understand my position—and they did.

On Tuesday I held a press conference at my Oxford Street

259

office to announce my retirement, and explained that I was reluctantly going to live in Jersey for tax reasons. Most of the reporters were sympathetic and their attitude was reflected next day by the 'Opinion' column of the *Daily Express* which said:

> Sir Billy Butlin's decision to quit Britain for Jersey because of tax burden is a most unhappy one. Few countries—least of all Britain which relies so heavily on the talents of her people—can spare men of outstanding ability. Yet, as Sir Billy says, why, after giving £2,000,000 to charity, should he hand over the rest of his fortune to the Exchequer?

LADY BUTLIN RECALLS THAT TIME:

Perhaps because he did not want to tell her until the complex financial and legal moves were completed, Billy Butlin did not reveal his plans to retire and live abroad until he arrived home after the press conference.

I was the last to know. He came home as though nothing had happened and we sat and had a drink. Then, in the middle of dinner, he suddenly said, 'Sheil, I want you to sell all the property I own, including the flats and this house, and all the silver'—he was a keen collector and had some fine pieces.

I looked at him in astonishment. 'Why? What's happening? Where are we going?' I asked.

His reply was: 'I'm leaving the country, and I'm never coming back.'

'But Bill,' I protested, 'you can't do that. We've got this lovely house—and you said this is where our roots were going to be.'

He looked at me across the table with that bland, poker-faced expression he sometimes had and said, 'Sheil, don't tell me I can't. I've decided to retire and I'm leaving in the morning. I have to do it quickly for tax reasons.'

I lay awake all night, stunned by the news. Where on earth

260

were we going? Next morning Bill still didn't enlighten me. It was his never-broken custom before he left for the office to walk round the grounds hand-in-hand with young Bill and Jack. That morning he walked with them as usual and then got into the car as usual. It was just as though he was going to the office—except that he had half a dozen shirts and some clean underwear stuffed into a little leather bag. He kissed me goodbye and said, 'I'll ring you in the next forty-eight hours, Sheil.' I still had not the slightest idea where he was going.

When he rang he said, 'I'm in Jersey.'

I replied, 'Lovely. Where's that?' I honestly didn't know.

'In the Channel Islands,' he explained. 'It's a fabulous place and the weather's beautiful.'

When I arrived he told me, 'I've some houses I want you to look at.' He needed to buy a house quickly to establish residence qualifications, and we looked at quite a few.

One of them I particularly remember was in such bad condition that the estate agent said defensively, 'Don't look at the house. Look at what can be done with the barn.' I soon saw what he meant. The first room we entered had a dirt floor. Two women sat by the fireplace, one of them peeling potatoes. 'You look very cosy,' I remarked, for something to say. 'It's the cosiest room in the house,' one of them replied. Barn or no barn, I did not bother to look further.

As night fell we had not found anything suitable, and I told Bill, 'Jersey isn't for us.'

'It is, Sheil,' he replied. 'I like it.' Though the island did not appeal to me then, I love it now. I am so happy we stayed.

On 4 April 1968 I arrived at St Helier airport, Jersey, with my two suitcases, to look around the island, which I had never visited before. As I waited for my luggage in the high-ceilinged, oblong arrivals hall, I scanned the hotel advertisements on the walls. I chose one and telephoned for a room.

'What name, sir?' asked the receptionist.

I hesitated momentarily, and decided to remain incognito for the time being. 'Burgess,' I said, giving the first name that occurred to me. Only afterwards did I realize it was the name of an old Army pal from the First World War. What strange tricks memory can play. However, my deception was of no avail. When I arrived at the hotel the receptionist took one look at me, then said, 'You're not Mr Burgess, you're Billy Butlin.'

It was, I felt, an inauspicious start to what proved to be a most happy stay on the island. Originally, I had wondered if I would like Jersey, but I soon found that I did—for it is a beautiful island with nice people. It is also highly convenient for both the Continent and London. When I wish to go to London, which is not very often, I can reach it almost as quickly as when I lived at Windlesham Moor, near Sunningdale, a mere twenty miles from the capital. In 1968, of course, Windlesham Moor had to be sold and, while I looked for a house in Jersey, Sheila stayed behind in England to wind up all my personal affairs. Windlesham was sold, with all its contents, to one of the world's richest men, Sheik Mahda Al-Tajir, later the Dubhai Ambassador to London.

By then, I had bought my present house, and was settling down to a new way of life. But, gradually, the full impact of my retirement hit me, and after a lifetime of seven-days-a-week activity, the days began to drag. I had more time to study and 'play' the stock market, with some gratifying results. I was able to step up still further my charity work. And I spent many happy hours landscaping the garden and grounds around my new home. When I bought the house it had a field with one tree adjoining it. Now it has a hundred apple trees, forty flowering cherry trees, seven thousand rose bushes, more than a thousand rhododendrons and five hundred camellias. There is a stream with three little waterfalls and a pond. Seventeen peacocks strut about the lawns and in a large aviary live about twelve hundred budgerigars, which fly freely all over the island. Many of them stay out all day. I have no idea where they go—but since I started with six hundred, and have not bought any more, they must enjoy life.

Still, this kind of life was not sufficient for me. I realized I was incapable of retiring. I missed being involved in business. What it amounted to, of course, was that I missed being involved in Butlin's.

On my retirement I had become a consultant to the company—but nobody consulted me.

Bobby was 34 when he took over the business. He had been in it for fourteen years and obviously had different ideas from me on how it should be run and developed. I had always been proud of him. I gave him a good education at Stowe and I was pleased when he took my advice and, instead of following his friends into the Guards or the RAF, did his National Service in the Army Catering Corps. He became a Second Lieutenant, and was awarded the Sword of Honour for the best soldier at Aldershot.

But I must admit I was angry when he did not consult me about company affairs—particularly when he began to make changes. For with the great bulk of Butlin shares being held by small investors—in 1968, for example, about 80 million shares were held by 700,000 people—I was the largest individual shareholder. Looking back now, however, I realize it was natural for Bobby to want to go his own way without any interference from me. I doubted whether I would have been willing to take my father's advice. And it must be said that Bobby has proved himself a fine businessman who has moved the company along to meet changing times and tastes.

As often happens when there is division in a family, it took a threat from outside to heal the rift. That threat came when Phonographic Equipment, a firm supplying gambling and other slot machines, and which had acquired about ten per cent of Butlin shares, made a takeover bid for the company. I strongly opposed the merger and wrote to Butlin shareholders advising them to reject the bid. I believed that any organization connected with gambling was not suited to run Butlin's which has always been—and always will be—a business catering for families. If I had wanted to put gambling machines into the camps I could have done so years previously. I did not do so because I felt it was wrong. We had Bingo, filmed horse-racing and penny fun machines, but there was a big difference between those and gambling machines. With the latter in the camps some people would be broke after the first few days of their holidays.

Bobby totally agreed with me. He said at the time, 'I hate to think what would happen if our camps were full of gambling machines.' He made a further point: 'Phonographic say that they could improve the profitability of Butlin's. So could we. But what it would do to the business in the long term I shudder to think. We *could* easily increase our profits by charging children for the rides they now get free at all our camps—but we would not dream of doing that. We *could* charge customers for the shows that we put on, but I doubt if they would come back to us again and again as they do now.'

Happily, the bid failed. Happily, also, I began to be more active as consultant to the company. It was not that I wanted to poke my nose in again—it was simply that I was worried by the problems facing the company. The results for 1970-71 were poor, with profits dropping to £2,804,000. The cost of modernizing the camps had proved to be hefty and a postal strike hit bookings at a crucial time. Meanwhile, faced with strong competition from package tour holidays abroad, we were not in a position to increase our prices. But by 1972 the sun was shining again. At the nine camps and three hotels, bookings were at a record level and a big campaign to obtain off-season business had begun. Profits rose to £4,200,000.

Though Butlin's had undoubtedly moved into better times, there was still the threat of other undesirable take-over bids. To be able to ward off these, and to provide the necessary capital for expansion, it seemed to me that the company needed the protection of a large concern with ample financial stability and resources. So when, in September 1972, the Rank Organization made a bid of £43,000,000 for the company, offering one Rank A share plus £9.50 in loan stock for every 50 Butlin shares valued at 40p a share, I supported it.

BOBBY BUTLIN RECALLS HIS FATHER'S RETIREMENT, AND SUBSEQUENT EVENTS:
My father was never a man for formal meetings. In fact, I don't recall attending a proper board meeting as such. His method

was to call into his office those directors who were in the building—which is what he did on Monday 1 April 1968. Those present, as far as I can recall, were Norman Maclaren, Basil Brown, George Ogg and myself. In his laconic, to-the-point manner, he told us, 'I'm leaving the country because of tax reasons and I must be out by 5 April. I'm appointing Bobby as the new chairman.' So I became chairman of Butlin's on All Fools' Day—and, as a City journalist once put it, I've been trying to see the joke ever since.

But on the day I felt a surge of excitement, though I was somewhat apprehensive. I was just coming up to 34, and many of the senior people in the company were of my father's generation. Obviously I was now about to get involved in what the Americans call 'an entirely new ball game'. As chairman of a publicly quoted company you have the stock market and merchant bankers to worry about. I had no formal training in, or experience of, such matters. But, because of the way the business had deteriorated over the previous two years, I felt relief in one respect: I could now get to grips with the problems as I saw them. It was not a challenge I was frightened of at all.

One worry, however, was that nobody, including myself, had much experience of making decisions. The 'Old Man' was the autocratic type of boss, giving us responsibility without authority. Unfortunately, from about 1965, the company had been growing so big it was almost impossible for a man getting older to make every single decision. For example, he would regularly phone the department heads at every camp and give them instructions—without advising the general managers. If there was a building programme going on, the chalet doors could not be painted until he had decided the colour. When his staff pointed out that the camp was scheduled to open on a certain date, he would reply: 'I'll be there in a couple of weeks, I'll tell you then.' Inevitably, because he was slowing down a lot and did not get through the work like he used to, he failed to get there in two weeks. As a result the doors were not painted, and opening day came nearer and nearer. Finally, I would say, 'Paint the damn things whatever colour you like.'

This sort of thing was happening around the mid-Sixties, and in my view the business was suffering. Bookings fell dramatically in 1966-67, by 160,000 from the previous year's total of 900,000, and profits were under terrible pressure. I felt it was time we began making some fundamental changes. In 1966, I was appointed joint managing director, but all the senior management in the company knew the appointment did not mean anything, beyond, perhaps, being a compliment. Soon my father and I began to disagree over the changes I suggested.

He would argue, 'I built up this business. You've only been in it for five minutes. What makes you think you know what should be done? Don't you think I know what should be done?' His argument was probably valid. He knew the British public and our type of customer better than I did. He had been successful for thirty years—and he was determined he would decide when any changes were made.

But I sensed the leisure industry was changing—and it can change very rapidly. We were going to run into competition from package holidays abroad. Fred Pontin had started self-catering in his camps, which greatly cut down his labour costs and broadened the base of his market. At that time we had terrible labour problems. We were employing 20 to 25 per cent more staff than we do now, when the business turnover is much bigger. Now we have fifty-one sites, big and small, while in those days we had twelve. But my father did not want to go into self-catering or any other kind of diversification.

He says he was angry after he retired at not being consulted on the running of the business. I knew he was hurt, but I had to do things the way I felt was right and that meant cutting myself off from him. I could not go through with the charade of consulting him and then totally ignoring his views. That would have upset him even more.

When the Phonographic Equipment bid was made in October 1968, I needed his support and he very readily gave it, which obviously pleased me very much. He immediately checked with his accountant, Peter Hetherington, to see if his affairs were in order so he could return to Britain. But he told

266

me that even if they were not, he would still come to London to help fight off the bid. This was generous of him because he could have been taking a considerable financial risk. As he says, we defeated the bid, but he still obviously felt he should have been consulted more. He could see, however, that we were gradually getting the company right. In 1972 we had a very good year, topping a million bookings for the first time.

But it was in that year that my father set out to try and oust me as chairman and managing director of Butlins. Whether it was because I had not consulted him sufficiently, or because I had upset him over some matter, or because he had simply become bored in Jersey, I do not know. What I do know is that he approached the old Phonographic Equipment company, now Associated Leisure, which had a 12½ per cent holding in Butlin's as a result of their unsuccessful bid, and suggested it link up with his own personal holding of some 7 per cent to form the basis of a consortium he would set up—Butlin shares were very cheap at the time.

I believe he got very close to a position where he could have either forced me to consult him more, or called an Extraordinary General Meeting for the purpose of removing me as chairman of Butlin's. If he had got that far he would undoubtedly have been in an exceedingly powerful position. For he still had a terrific following among the small shareholders—in any clash between him and me they would have sided with him every time. It was a most unhappy situation; had it reached the stage of an EGM, I would have dug in my heels and would probably have been forced to tell the shareholders how bad things were before he retired— which was the last thing I wanted to do. It looked as though we were heading for a major public row.

Then, at the last minute, a head-on clash was averted when the Rank Organization made its bid. I suspect, in fact, that the 'Old Man' had been working behind the scenes to bring about a bid from one quarter or another in order to avoid a damaging clash between us. Whatever the facts, the Rank bid came along just at the right time. It was a very good offer which I and my directors were able to recommend to our

267

shareholders to accept. That decision has been fully justified in that we have been able to improve, expand and diversify the company much more rapidly than we ever could have done as an independent.

After Rank's successful take-over, which left me as managing director, the situation between my father and me eased considerably, and in the last few years of his life we became good friends.

Today I have no financial interest in Butlin's, though I am still a consultant to the company. However, I have acquired new business interests in Jersey, where I have built up a family concern which owns and operates Portlet Holiday Village and several hotels among other property. I have also joined Sir Fred Pontin as a director of his Jersey holiday camp. Through these interests I have the satisfaction of knowing that I have ensured the future of my family. I do not believe in leaving large amounts of money, particularly to children. If I had had money when I was young I probably would not have worked so hard and enjoyed life so much. I believe it is much better to leave your children a business and let them have the pleasure of building it up—like I did.

Having achieved this aim, my main interest now is undoubtedly charity work. I have been fortunate enough to make a lot of money and through various trust funds I have, I hope, been able to help many deserving causes, particularly those which help young people. People ask me why I work so hard for charity. The answer is simple. When I was young I had a tough time and I can remember what it was like to be what we now call 'underprivileged'. It gives me great satisfaction and pleasure to help others worse off than myself. In any case, you can't take your money with you.

Several charities have benefited in recent years as a result of an annual convention Sheila and I organized in Jersey. In 1977 Princess Margaret was Guest of Honour and attended a mini 'Royal Variety Performance' at the Odeon Theatre in St Helier, with such stars as Vera Lynn, Arthur Askey and Eric

Morecambe and Ernie Wise. Next year, Prince and Princess Michael of Kent graced the Convention and in October 1979, we were greatly honoured by the presence of the Duke of Edinburgh. To our immense pleasure he accepted our invitation to spend the weekend at our Blair Adam House, and proved to be a charming and friendly guest who would pop into the kitchen for a cup of tea and a chat.

One of the spheres I have been most active in is the Variety Club, an international organization which has a red heart as its emblem and does an immense amount of work for under-privileged children. What happy memories I have of good friends in Variety. There were the golf tournaments organized by Johnny Riscoe, for instance. During them I sometimes followed the players in a helicopter, hovering over the greens to offer them a glass of champagne. Most appreciated the champagne, but not everyone appreciated the style of delivery because the draught caused by the helicopter's blades blew the balls all over the place!

One particularly fond memory I have is of a visit to New Orleans to attend a Variety Club Convention. We were a group of ten, including the late Tom O'Brien, Secretary of the National Association of Theatrical and Kine Employees, who was a genial extrovert. Some years earlier, Frances Parkinson Keyes had written a novel called *Dinner at Antoine's*; Antoine's is a New Orleans restaurant, and the book had transformed the place into a tourists' Mecca. We decided to go there, but when we rang up we could not get a table. We were disappointed, but then I had an idea. 'Tom,' I said, 'why don't you telephone and say you're the British Ambassador visiting the city to make plans for a future visit of the Queen, and you would like your party to dine at Antoine's?'

Tom thought this was a great idea and promptly telephoned the restaurant. We got a table for ten without any trouble. All of us, except Tom, went ahead, and when he arrived we formed a guard of honour for him inside the entrance to the restaurant. The staff and customers all appeared very impressed. We were ushered to our table and given VIP treatment.

Unfortunately, we were all nicely merry and this led to our downfall. We started telling funny stories and every time Tom told one, we stood up respectfully. Before long Tom began acting as though he were the British Ambassador. Then, halfway through one of his stories, someone said loudly. 'Oh, shut up, you silly bugger!' There were looks of astonishment from the waiters, and from that moment the attentive service stopped.

FILM PRODUCER SIR JAMES CARRERAS REMEMBERS THE INCIDENT WELL: *Originally, Bill was not going on the trip to New Orleans, but as our party was gathering at London Airport he suddenly arrived.*

'Hello, Bill,' we said. 'What are you doing here?'

'I'm coming with you,' he said.

'Have you a ticket?' we asked.

'No,' he replied.

Luckily, getting a ticket was no problem, but, like Royalty, Bill never carried any money. On this occasion all he had on him was about £30 in travellers cheques—five years out of date. So we had a whip-round for his fare.

The Antoine's incident was typical of his impish sense of humour—I always thought of him as a little pixie. It was a great pity the joke misfired. In fact, some of us in the party, including myself, have a different recollection from Bill of why we suddenly became unpopular at the restaurant. We understood that the manager of Antoine's knew the British Ambassador, but at the time of our visit he was off-duty. However, his deputy telephoned to tell him of the visit and, unfortunately for us, he decided to pay his respects to the distinguished customers. Of course, when he arrived he realized at once that Tom and the rest of us were impostors. Whatever the reason was for our cover being blown, we had fun while it lasted.

The countless good deeds the Variety Club has done are far too numerous for me to mention here. So many of its members work so hard and donate so much to provide an amazing range of things from Sunshine Coaches, which take children on outings they would otherwise never have, to the latest and costliest medical equipment and facilities. I have been happy and grateful to be among them. Indeed, one of the honours I am most proud of is the Variety Club's annual Humanitarian Award, which I received in 1972.

It is the Club's highest individual honour and its distinguished recipients range from Dr Albert Schweitzer, Dr Jonas Salk and Helen Keller to Danny Kaye, J. Edgar Hoover and Henry Ford II. In Britain, only six people apart from myself have received it since its inception in 1938—the Duke of Edinburgh, Lord Mountbatten, Sir Winston Churchill, Sir Alexander Fleming and Leonard Cheshire and his wife Sue Ryder.

I have also gained much pleasure and many friends through being a member of the Grand Order of Water Rats, a brotherhood of show-business artistes which promotes philanthropy and good fellowship. I am a Companion of the Order, a kind of Associate Member, whose ranks include the Duke of Edinburgh and Prince Charles, and I am particularly pleased to be only the seventh member and the first Companion to receive the Order's Badge of Merit.

Today all these activities keep me occupied and—touch wood—keep me well, for there is nothing like having plenty of interests to hold at bay the impact of advancing years. And not only in old age. For I am sure that having been constantly busy and involved through the years, is one of the main reasons why I am still here and enjoying life as much as ever.

18

'I Enjoyed Every Moment'

A MILLIONAIRE, once asked to give twelve rules for making a million, replied, 'Repeat "Hard Work" twelve times'. I appreciate this philosophy. Hard work is essential for success in life, but I differ from him in one vital respect. I believe you should not regard it as hard work. Indeed, if you do, you will need to be an exceedingly dedicated individual. The secret of success in life, and consequently of making money, is to *enjoy* your work. If you do, nothing is hard work—no matter how many hours you put in.

So to young people who are starting out on their careers my advice is: don't take a job just because it pays the most. Take the one you think you will enjoy doing. And if you can find one which may lead to you becoming your own boss some day, all the better. What my philosophy amounts to is this: Whether you make a million or not, you will never get anything more out of life than doing a job you enjoy. I know what I am talking about—for most of my life I have enjoyed my work, and I am grateful for that. I enjoyed *every* moment as a fairground showman, and I enjoyed *every* moment running my holiday camps.

Of course, finding a job you think you will enjoy is not always easy. When I returned to Toronto after the First World War, I knew I did not want to spend my life in an office. True, I enjoyed drawing and I would probably have been reasonably happy as a commercial artist. But I also knew that this was not what I really wanted. What I was looking for was a job that took me into the open air and gave me an opportunity to meet people. This is an urge basic to my nature. I like people. I like being with them and I enjoy seeing them enjoying themselves. When I ran my camps I was always happiest being out and about mixing with the campers.

In Toronto, after I left the Army, the problem was: what kind of job *could* I do? For apart from my limited training as an artist, I was uneducated and unskilled. I thought about it a great deal, and found myself becoming increasingly attracted to the idea of joining my relations on the fairgrounds in England. Actually it was a decision that went deeper than mere practical considerations. I had a showman's instincts in my blood. Looking back now, it is clear that I was a born showman. And I have been a showman all my life. It has been the mainspring, not so much of everything I have done, but certainly of the way I have done everything.

Because I was a born showman I enjoyed working on the fairgrounds, despite the hard times. But then, I have learned that hard times never hurt anyone. Until I was 25 I had a tough life. My years in the Army were grimly horrifying, but they gave me a sense of proportion. Later in life, no matter how bad things were, I was able to tell myself, 'Anything that happens can't be as bad as what you've been through already. So you must be winning.' For when you have never had much, you do not expect much, and if times are hard you can adjust to them much more easily.

Of course, while working at a job you enjoy invariably brings happiness, it does not necessarily bring material success. Many people undoubtedly think that my success has been largely due to a series of lucky gambles. How true is this? I am not a gambler by nature. I ran a 'crown and anchor' board in the Army—but from my point of view that was not a gamble. I knew the owner of the board always won in the end. Later in life I was guided by the same principle. Moves I made might have appeared to be gambles, but they were not gambles to me because I never seriously thought I would fail.

Lucky? I have never been aware of being lucky in the normal

sense. In fact, I have been very unlucky in my private life. What people tend to call luck is often doing the right thing at the right time. On this basis, I admit to being lucky. For I took two major, far-reaching steps at the right time. Firstly, I stopped being a travelling showman and opened seaside amusement parks just as the charabanc and the motor car began bringing more people than ever before to coastal resorts. Secondly, I started and developed my holiday camps in a period when large numbers of people were getting holidays with pay for the first time.

Doing the right thing at the right time is certainly important, but you must also do what you believe in. I have always been an individualist, thinking things out for myself and following my own instincts. Both on the fairgrounds and in my holiday camps I gave people what I liked myself, and because I am an ordinary person with ordinary tastes, I gave millions what they wanted.

Not that I am suggesting I never made a mistake. Until 1939, there was a field on the outskirts of Skegness belonging to an old friend of mine, a farmer called Freddie Rye, which was full of the mistakes I made as a fairground operator. They were the rusting remains of amusement park rides which had flopped with the public. When this happened I always found it best to dump them—though I always tried to discover why they had failed.

When buying new rides—today they come mainly from the US, Germany and Italy—a showman must consider the psychology of his customers. For instance, a ride that people can control themselves, by using a little skill, is almost certain to be successful. The Dodgems are a classic example of this.

But whether it was buying a dud fairground ride or losing £250,000 in the Bahamas project, I tried to forget my mistakes as quickly as possible. I certainly learned from my mistakes, but I never lost any sleep over them. I never lay awake at night worrying—even when everything I had was tied up in a project. I have always preferred to dwell on the future rather the past. I learned that a problem I worried about one day was something I could not remember three months later.

274

What else would I advise? 'Have the confidence to strike out on your own, and start working for yourself as soon as you can.'

When I left Toronto I decided I would never work for an employer again. I have never regretted that decision—though sometimes I would have eaten better if I had been merely a hired hand. But if you do strike out on your own, you must have determination. When anyone said to me, 'It can't be done', I had to prove it could be done. Certainly I have surmounted plenty of opposition over the years. Whenever I planned to open an amusement park or a holiday camp, there were always people who tried to stop me. Usually it was because they thought the project would spoil the area. Often it was only the opposition I met that made me press ahead with my plans. Without any opposition I would have thought there was something wrong with the place!

Opposition, mistakes and downright bad luck can often be a spur. That is why I believe an ambitious youngster can be handicapped by having something to fall back on when things go wrong— like another job, or a family to take him back into the fold. For when your business plans falter or fail you can either give up, or you can press on. If you have nothing or nobody to fall back on, you have no choice—you must keep going.

Always ambitious to improve myself, I never thought of stopping. My mother constantly asked me: 'When are you going to quit?' But everything I did was a step forward to something else. When I retired to Jersey it never occurred to me to stop working completely. If I had been made otherwise, I would probably have eased up when I had my first £1,000 in the bank. For in those days that was a lot of money, especially for someone who had started with nothing.

For years I never knew the size of my bank balance. There were two reasons for this. Firstly, during my early years as a showman, my mother held the purse strings—and no accountant could have been more cautious. She took a lot of convincing before she agreed to me spending money on a new venture. She was constantly worried I would over-reach myself. Secondly, I was never *concerned* about how much money I had—providing I was not overdrawn. Normally, the only time I was interested in my bank balance was when I needed capital to develop my business. Many people may not agree with this attitude, but to me it makes sound sense. For if you are concerned about your money, you may be loath to risk it—and that can be bad for your business.

To succeed in business you must be prepared and able to take chances. And that is why I would advise a man not to marry too young. The responsibilities of a wife and family *can* spur on a man, but all too often they inhibit him from going out on a limb. A man is lucky if he finds a woman who thinks like him when it comes to matters of business or career. By their very nature, women tend to play safe. In fact, it is my experience that women and business do not mix. Very few of them are happy or even prepared to take second place.

For some strange psychological reason some wives resent their husbands becoming successful. They refuse to take an interest in his work. Some even go as far a to belittle it. A man thinks he is doing well, but his wife pretends his success does not amount to much—a wounding and discouraging attitude. Such a wife gives no help or sympathy when her husband's business or career is not going too well—the very time when he needs sympathy. Of course, the right wife does not need to be told her man's career is in difficulties, she knows it instinctively and gives him the support he needs. But when all a man gets is 'I told you so', it is disastrous to his morale. I speak from the heart here, for both Dolly and Norah did this to me.

Running a business, of course, involves working with other people, and a man's attitude towards his employees is important. I have always believed you should be able to do any job you ask them to do—particularly if it is a dirty one. Many of my staff worked with me for years and I had good relations with all of them. My top executives usually referred to me as Mr Butlin and later Sir William. To the managers of the camps and amusement parks I was the Guv'nor, while the lower grades of staff, like kitchen porters and cleaners, called me Bill. I was happy with all three of these forms of address.

One business philosophy I have always practised is, after deciding general policy, to personally look after the little things. You can pay people to attend to major matters, but the little things which make all the differences can so easily be overlooked or ignored. That is why I spent almost every weekend visiting the camps and walking round them. That way I not only got to know the campers and hear their comments, but I satisfied myself they were getting what they had paid for. I also knew exactly how the camp was being run, for I looked at everything down to the conditions of the dustbins.

This latter practice was not purely for hygienic reasons. You can learn a lot from dustbins. For instance if I found large quantities of a certain dish being thrown away, it meant it was not popular and I had it taken off the menu.

BILL MARTIN, PAST SCRIBE, COUNCILLOR, OF THE GRAND ORDER OF WATER RATS:
This is a story about Billy Butlin's habit of inspecting the dustbins which aptly reflects his sharp eye for his quiet sense of humour. One day, while poking about in the dustbins, Bill spotted a dead goldfish. Later, while walking around the camp with the manager, he stopped beside the goldfish pond. For several long moments he stared intently at the fish, and then he turned to the manager and said, 'There's one missing.'

There is one question I am asked more often than any other. 'Is it possible, today, to build up a successful business as you did, from nothing, and make a fortune?'

My answer is: 'Yes—but generally speaking it will be much more difficult.' What Britain needs today are lower taxes and less bureaucracy, to provide more incentive and opportunities for people with ideas, initiative and energy. But even allowing for such changes—and they will need to be far-reaching— the odds are against the founding and building up of a really big business.

I hope this does not appear to be the pessimism of old age, but as the song says, 'Fings Ain't What They Used To Be'.

Luckily, however, there is still much to be got from life. There is still the satisfaction and pleasure of doing a job you enjoy—and who knows where that can lead? Look where it led me.

Afterword by Lady Butlin

WHEN Bill said that being so active kept him young, he was certainly right. You can tell this yourself from reading his book. But, typically, Bill has only revealed the half of it. For he was always doing something; going somewhere. Business decisions apart, he could be very much a man of sudden impulses. In his hey-day he would throw a party or a dinner for a score of people on the spur of the moment. He travelled the world on business or to attend Variety Club functions—and often, as in New Orleans, something out-of-the-ordinary happened to him.

In an attempt to convey another facet of his elusive personality I have collated here a random selection of stories about his travels:

We were visiting the World Fair in Seattle, and on the day we were returning home, Bill suddenly said, 'Why don't we check in early at the airport and fly to Vancouver for lunch? There are some excellent restaurants in Chinatown.'

I thought it was a wonderful idea, and so it was arranged. At the airport he said, 'We don't need to take anything with us. We can leave our hand luggage and coats in a locker.' All went smoothly until we were about to land in Vancouver when he asked me: 'Have you got your passport?'

'Yes, it's in my handbag,' I replied.

'Mine's in my overcoat in the locker,' he said.

As there was nothing we could do about it, we just had to

hope we would not be turned back. Luckily, as we reached the immigration desks, one of the officers shouted, 'Hi, Bill, how long you here for?'

'Until five o'clock,' said Bill.

'Why so short?'

'We're only here for lunch, and what do you know? I've come without my passport.'

'No trouble, Bill,' said the officer, 'I'll let you through now, and I'm on duty till six.'

So, with his help we went in and out of Canada without any difficulty. But it was a different matter when we landed back in Seattle. The US immigration official was decidedly suspicious when Bill explained he had no passport, and promptly called the police. They cross-examined him still further. Finally with a burly policeman on each side of him, Bill was marched off at gun-point, his feet hardly touching the ground, to prove he really had left his passport in a locker.

Where hats and coats were concerned Bill was very forgetful— with surprising results sometimes: like the time we took the children to Disney World, near Orlando, Florida. We flew to Miami, where we changed planes for Orlando. As we had a little time to wait we went into the coffee shop, where Bill hung his hat on a rack. On the plane we discovered he had left it behind.

Two weeks later we arrived back in Miami and once again went into the coffee shop. To my astonishment, the hat was still hanging there. When we left, Bill took it from the rack, stuck it on his head—and walked out without saying a word.

This was not an isolated instance. Another time he left his coat on a plane. Returning a few days later, he happened to catch precisely the same plane and in a further coincidence, sat in the same seat. When he opened the compartment above his head—guess what? There was his coat!

For someone who gave away millions, Bill was often thrifty in personal matters. Once, when the children were young, we stayed in a Nassau hotel with them. They usually took their meals in our suite, and one day they had chicken for lunch. They did not eat it all, so I put what was left in the fridge.

That evening Bill was nursing Jacquie, who was then about three years old.

'What would my little princess like for supper?' he asked.

'Chicken Daddy,' said Jacquie.

Bill was clearly delighted by the prospect of not having to order something from room service. He took the chicken out of the fridge, put it on a plate and gave it to Jack. She looked at it.'I want it hot, Daddy,' she said.

'Yes, darling,' said Bill. But he was not ordering any more chicken. He found a plastic bag, put the chicken inside and hung it from the hot tap of the bath. Then he turned on the water and let it pour over the bag. 'Daddy's making it hot for you, darling,' he said.

When Bill and his friend Charlie Lytle made a business trip to Copenhagen he took young William with him. They had an enjoyable time, with Bill taking great delight in showing his son the famous Tivoli Gardens.

Came the time to leave, however, Bill found he had not enough traveller's cheques to pay the hotel. He knew he could borrow the remainder from Charlie, but Charlie had gone to an appointment in another part of the city. As he had no idea when he would return Bill decided to go and find him. But the manager was reluctant to let him leave the hotel without any collateral.

'I tell you what,' said Bill. 'I'll leave my son here. You can't have better collateral than that.' And off he went.

William, who was only about seven years old, sat on a chair in the manager's office, as he carried on with his work. After they had been waiting an hour or so, the manager looked at William and asked, 'Does he do this often?'

Another trip Bill made with Charlie Lytle was to Hong Kong, where Charlie had some suits made. Not being greatly interested in clothes, Bill contented himself with having the suits he had with him cleaned and pressed. Some months later, we were in Bermuda, and Bill chartered a large motor yacht for a day's fishing. For the trip he wore the trousers of one of the suits he had taken to Hong Kong.

We had an enjoyable day and were cruising home when Bill decided to look at the radar installation on the boat's super-structure. To reach it he had to climb a ladder, and as he did so I saw to my horror that the entire seat of his trousers was missing, revealing him in all his glory in his underpants.

'Bill,' I shrieked 'for God's sake come down! You're indecent!' What on earth could have happened?

The only explanation we could think of was that when the suit had been cleaned in Hong Kong it had been treated with some chemical which—in the heat, and with Bill sitting down for so long—had destroyed the cloth.

But what concerned us was how we were going to get Bill back to the decidedly swish Fontainbleu Hotel. It was not possible for Bill to stay on the boat until I fetched him a new pair of trousers, so there was nothing we could do but to sneak back the best way we could.

Oh, I wish you could have witnessed the scene when our car returned us to the Fontainbleu. As soon as we alighted, I took up station right behind Bill, and in that fashion, with my arms around him, we shuffled through the foyer to the elevator—to the astonished amusement of a throng of hotel guests, all dressed to the nines for dinner.

What a relief it was when we finally made it to our suite, where we collapsed in hysterical laughter.

Epitaph

by Sir James Carreras, KCVO, MBE, Past President Variety International, and Chief Barker, Variety Club of Great Britain, 1954-1955.

BILLY Butlin was one of the most human beings I have ever met. He was pleasant and nice whether things were going well or badly. He was a man concerned about people. He cared about them. There are very few who cared as much as he did. You cannot talk about Billy Butlin the man or Billy Butlin the benefactor. There was no difference between them.

Let me quote just one example. We, in the Variety Club, had brought to our attention the case of a young girl who was blind, deaf and dumb. Bill started a trust fund for life for that girl and she is still living in hospital with wonderful medical care in a special wing he financed.

Bill was one of the great supporters of the Variety Club's Sunshine Coaches project, which originated from a visit the late Leslie MacDonnell, former managing director of Moss Empires and the Palladium, and I made to Carshalton Hospital to see a special therapy swimming pool for handicapped children donated by the Variety Club. While we were there the Matron took us into a room where a number of severely handicapped children were strapped into wheelchairs.

'These children,' she said, 'have a life expectancy of ten years, and none of them have been outside this hospital.'

'Why is that?' we asked.

'Because we have no vehicle that can accommodate their wheelchairs,' she replied.

Leslie and I thought this was a great shame and we went away and conferred with Trevor Chinn, now chairman of the Lex Group, who owned a coach-building firm. We devised a specially fitted mini-bus with a ramp up which the children's wheelchairs could be pushed. Unfortunately, many of the nurses did not have the strength to manage this. However, we solved the problem by providing a small hydraulic lift which raised the children's chairs to the level of the coach floor.

Bill bought the first Sunshine Coach and eventually provided another 47 costing in all more than £200,000—the largest number bought by anyone in the world.

The Variety Club was founded in Pittsburg in 1928 and the British branch—we call them 'Tents'—was started in 1949 by a group of London-based American film distributors. It is no exaggeration, however, to say that the British Variety Club did not start raising really big money for charity until Billy Butlin joined in 1952. He created Variety Club history by becoming Chief Barker (chief fund-raiser) of the British Tent three times, was Chief Barker of Ireland twice, and also Chief Barker of Guernsey.

He was the instigator of what I call the 'Big Givers'. It was he who inspired the Michael Sobells of this world, who inspired the Charlie Clores of this world and all the other generous benefactors who somehow made it the right thing to support Variety Club charity projects.

For three years he put up $50,000 to finance a Variety International membership drive and an incentive scheme to reward the Tent which made the greatest percentage increase in its fund-raising. It is not surprising that Billy Butlin is as well known in the United States as he is in Britain. And loved as much as we loved him here.

Billy rapidly became part of the international Variety scene. He founded the Jersey and Guernsey Tents—without Billy there would not be a Variety Club in Ireland—and he was a tremendous help to the Israel Tent. In fact, there is not a

284

Variety Club anywhere in the world that he was not a part of.

Without Billy Butlin I am sure that Variety International would not be the size it is today; nor would it enjoy the prestige it enjoys today. These are the facts. Other Founder Members, like Nat Cohen, David Jones, Nat Rosenfeld and Jack Goodlatte, would tell you the same. In the formative years of the Club he was always in the background—and yet he was the biggest influence of all. He gave more than £2,000,000 to various Variety Club charities, including £250,000 for an EMI brain-scanner for the Great Ormond Street Hospital, which does so much for children in great peril.

But I am only talking about the Variety Club. The Adminstrators of the Duke of Edinburgh's Award scheme, the National Playing Fields Association, the Outward Bound Scheme, the Lords' Taverners, the London Federation of Boys' Clubs, the Police Dependents' Trust, the Saints and Sinners Club and many other charities, will tell you the same.

Bill was last in London just before Christmas 1979, when the Variety Club gave a lunch in his honour. In my speech on this occasion, I said: 'Billy is well known to all of us as a great benefactor, but I doubt if any of us realize the full extent of his generosity.'

To prove my point I gave a list of *some* of his benefactions: £100,000 for the establishment of the Police Dependents' Trust; £30,000 for a remedial pool at Harman's School for Handicapped Children; £100,000 to the Duke of Edinburgh's Award Scheme to help prepare young people for the future; £15,000 to the Outsider's Trust, to pioneer new types of youth work; £50,000 to the Printers' Charitable Corporation to benefit orphans and deprived children; £15,000 *each* to the Save the Children Fund, the National Playing Fields Association and the Children's sections of the Army Benevolent Fund and the King George the Fifth Fund for Sailors; £15,000 for the building of a new headquarters for a boys' club in East London; £10,000 and 12 new vehicles to the Young Volunteer Force Foundation; £20,000 towards a research wing specializing in children's diseases at St Mary's

Hospital; £40,000 for swimming pools for handicapped children in Britain.

I continued: 'He takes a tremendout interest in the blind and handicapped children of Ireland. Some time ago he was told about the problems facing a children's hospital in which the Variety Club of Ireland were deeply involved. From that time on, that hospital became one of the prime objects of his wonderful generosity and an entirely new building has emerged costing over £300,000.

'The full extent of his charity commitments no one will ever know. When the administrators of his Trust have questioned the genuineness of some of the appeals, Bill has insisted on donations being sent with the comments: "If it's a phoney, then it's on their conscience, not mine." What is certain, however, is that his kindness has made life happier and given health and hope to untold thousands of children all over the world.

'Despite (or perhaps because of) his humble beginnings and the building of a mammoth holiday empire which made him an international celebrity, Bill has remained a man of much humility, charm and friendliness. He is always sensitive to the feelings of others, to whom he unfailingly shows respect and consideration.

'Completely without humbug or pretension, he has a quiet sense of humour as displayed when he says "For public addresses I have only two speeches—one short and one long. The short one is 'thank you', and the long one is 'thank you very much."

'Bill has demonstrated, time and time again, through the years that he is utterly devoted to Variety's cause—he is a true humanitarian concerned deeply with the welfare of the sick, the disabled and the less fortunate, regardless of nationality, colour, religion, background or any other factor.

'He has earned the admiration, esteem and affection—even love would not be an exaggeration—of all who care about their fellow humans.'

Perhaps that is the right note on which to end this tribute to Billy Butlin, a most remarkable gentleman.

Extract from the Address by Basil Brown, at the Memorial Service for Billy Butlin at St Martin's-in-the-Field, London, October 2, 1980:

It gives me comfort to dwell upon
Remembered friends who are dead and gone,
And the jokes we had and the fun.
How happy they are I cannot know
But happy am I who loved them so.

Noel Coward